GEORGE BEST

FIFTY DEFINING FIXTURES

Iain McCartney

AMBERLEY

First published 2015

Amberley Publishing
The Hill, Stroud
Gloucestershire, GL5 4EP

www.amberley-books.com

British Library Cataloguing in Publication Data.
A catalogue record for this book is available from the British Library.

ISBN 978 1 4456 4024 2 (print)
ISBN 978 1 4456 4033 4 (ebook)

Typesetting and Origination by Amberley Publishing.
Printed in the UK.

Contents

Introduction

George Best. A name that epitomises the swinging sixties. A face that everyone recognised, from football supporters to bingo-loving grandmothers. A player who could do things with a ball that most could only dream off. Long flowing locks, cheeky grin and dimpled chin. Just realised, that rhymes. Quite apt really as, on the pitch, George was poetry in motion.

Once George crossed that white-painted touchline, he made lesser mortals look inferior and, in reality, they were. No one could match the sublime skills of the Belfast Boy. His talents were numerous, blessed with a brilliance that left defenders a quivering wreck and the crowds who flocked to see him singing his name in unison.

The scrawny youngster arrived on the scene as Manchester United regained a foothold on the game's honours list by winning the FA Cup in 1963. He took those first few tentative steps in leaps and bounds and once Matt Busby realised what he had within his grasp, he introduced him to the English First Division, a League where youngsters had to fight for survival against seasoned professionals. They held little fear for George, and throughout the sixties he teased and tormented, playing his part in taking the Old Trafford club to the pinnacle of both domestic and European football.

Few, if any, who have pulled on the red jersey of Manchester United can have made a greater impact on the club's glorious history than the boy from the Cregagh Estate in East Belfast. He brought joy and tears, often in equal measures during the final days of his Old Trafford career, to those who sang his praises from the sprawling terraces, or who worshiped from afar. As the sixties evolved into the seventies, his image became tarnished, eventually turning into something far removed from its original beauty.

There have been many books on the 'Belfast Boy', too many some might say, but while telling the story of the player whom many believe to have been the 'best ever', they have merely skirted round many of the games when he laced up his boots, pulled on the jersey and went out and caused havoc in opposition defences and brought delight to the thousands who stood in awe. Here, however, within the pages of this volume, those games and his career come to life. His bewitching skills and his off-field life of turmoil come under the microscope in *Fifty Defining Fixtures*.

The sources used include: *Daily Express*, *Sunday Express*, *Daily Mail*, *Daily Mirror*, *Sunday Mirror*, *The Daily Telegraph*, *The Sunday Telegraph*, *The Times*, *The Sunday Times*, *Observer*, *The Guardian*, *The Sun*, *Manchester Evening News*, *The Sunday Post*, *London Evening Standard* and the *Sunday People*.

Thanks to the journalists of the above for painting the pictures for those who were not present at all the fixtures and incidents with these pages.

United 'B' vs Bury 'B'

30 September 1961

'The 'A' and 'B' teams continue in the Lancashire League and although we are likely to field younger sides than previously it is hoped that quality will off-set any lack of experience, particularly in the early games' was a statement found in the first issue of Manchester United's official match programme the *United Review* for season 1961/62. The small article, under the heading 'With the Reserve and Juniors', went on to add, 'The customary additional Irish flavour in the younger teams is still undetermined at the time of going to press. A number of boys "from across the water" are showing their paces in trials and any that measure up to the high United standard will be retained and no doubt be catching the eye in these notes as the season progresses.

There was no mention by name of any of those Irish lads, perhaps due to the fact that a certain youngster from the Cregagh estate in east Belfast had come over for a trial in the summer of 1961, along with another Northern Ireland youngster, but had been so homesick that twenty-four hours later they were both heading back over the Irish Sea. United were content to allow Eric McMordie to remain in his more familiar Belfast habitat, but for the other fifteen year old, of whom Northern Ireland scout Bob Bishop had described to Matt Busby as being 'a genius' even at this early age, they were not going to let him remain in Ireland without attempting some gentle persuasion in the attempt to coax him back across the water. The prospect of George Best making the grade as a footballer were too high to ignore.

Matt Busby, with Bob Bishop's 'I have found a genius' telegram clutched in his hand, was soon on the telephone to George's father Dickie and within a couple of weeks the talented young footballer was heading back to Manchester, with the promise of regular return journey's back home if he lived up to expectations and joined United.

With Manchester United still in the process of re-building, following the Munich air disaster in 1958, the junior sides received only limited coverage within the *United Review* and there is certainly no mention of the United Youth team's fixture against a 'Selected XI' at Pwllheli on Tuesday 5 September 1961, the match regarded as George's first in a red shirt. Neither, unfortunately, is there anything other than the United team for the 'A' team fixture against Stockport County four days later, his first appearance at this level, playing at inside right in the 2-1 victory.

The United 'A' team was a level above where George was to play his trade in those now distant early days and his name was to be found on a regular basis among the Lancashire League Division Two fixtures during the 1961/62 campaign following his initial appearance in this competition against Oldham Athletic, (whose 'A' team played at this level), on 23 September.

For those die-hard enthusiasts who watched games at this particular level, they did not have to wait long before making their assessment of this new arrival to the ranks, with the 5-1 victory over Bury 'B' on 30 September convincing them then and there, that he was a youngster to watch closely.

It was a game, according to the reporter who had observed the ninety minutes for the *United Review*, that saw the United 'B' team as being 'good value for this win, but it took them a long time to gain command.' It was, however, George Best who not simply made the initial breakthrough with a 'well-taken' goal on the half hour mark, but became instrumental in United's ultimate victory.

Taylor made it 2-0 and midway through the second half George picked out Gorman who scored the third. A handball prevented George from making it 4-0, but from the resulting penalty Keogh did score the fourth. Bury were seldom in the game, finding young master Best and his teammates a little too hot to handle, but a poor clearance by Wright saw them pull a goal back through Adamson. It was to be little more than a consolation, as Gorman made it 5-1.

Manchester United: Wright, Keogh, Box, Noble, Wardle, Hampson, Taylor, Best, Gorman, Grayson, Kinsey.

Scorers: Gorman (2), Best, Keogh, Taylor.

Manchester City 'B' vs United 'B'

9 March 1963

In order to follow the early games in George's career we have to rely more or less on the Manchester United programme, the *United Review*. A commendable publication for the period it included well-written and informative articles as well as also providing good statistical coverage of not only the reserve eleven in the Central League, but also the 'A' and 'B' teams in the Lancashire League Divisions One and Two and of course in the prestigious FA Youth Cup competition.

For George, there was no whirlwind progress from the 'B' team through to first eleven, only the same plotted course that many others had taken in previous years, perhaps with the exception of a youngster named Duncan Edwards. But the boy from Dudley was built of sterner stuff than the slim waiflike teenager from Belfast and was practically ready for first team duty on the day that he first arrived in Manchester.

Eighteen months on from our first featured match, George could still be found in the United 'B' team, with occasional 'A' team outings alongside other hopefuls such as John Fitzpatrick, Barry Fry, Wilf Tranter, David Sadler, Jimmy Ryan and Eamon Dunphy. His performances doing enough to merit mentions within those *United Review* match summaries.

'A goal from Best forty seconds after the interval gave us a win' stands out in the report for the match against Blackburn Rovers in December 1962. 'The "B" team extended their unbeaten run but it was only in the closing minutes that a header from Best saved the day at Rochdale' had appeared a couple of months previously. Then from a 3-0 victory over Bolton in March 1963 we had 'the first goal came in fourteen minutes when Miller in attempting to collect a low centre from Best turned the ball into his own net. Dunphy engineered the second goal, his neat through ball finding Best well placed to glide the ball past the advancing Miller.' A run out in the 'A' team on 18 April produced a 4-2 victory over Tranmere Rovers and saw George score twice in five minutes, but perhaps George's most telling ninety minutes in those Lancashire League fixtures came on 9 March against Manchester City, when the United youngsters didn't simply defeat their across town neighbours, but gave them a severe hiding to the tune of 7-0.

The ninety minutes certainly did not get off to the ideal start for George as he missed something of an easy goal-scoring opportunity within the first sixty seconds, a chance that he would have normally put away without any problem and then, a couple of minutes later, he blasted the ball against the crossbar with the 'keeper beaten'. Such missed opportunities would have been enough to knock the confidence of any aspiring youngster, but in this instance, it only made George even more determined to get his name on the score sheet.

It took the United youngsters fifteen minutes to finally get the ball past Downes, Latham scoring from an acute angle, but it should have been all square soon afterwards when Burrows through on goal, with the United defence nowhere to be seen, blasted the ball wide. It an opportunity that the home side were to rue, as they were soon to find themselves really up against it as United pilled on the pressure, but for all their possession, they were only to score once more before the interval. A half-hit clearance out of the City defence dropped kindly for George; he accepted the gift and calmly fired past Downes for United's second.

After the interval, it was little more than one-way traffic, but those opening second-half minutes were little more than a mirror image of the first with United squandering the opportunities that came their way. Undeterred, they continued to lay siege on their opponents goal and a third goal materialised when Mitten evaded two tackles before beating Downes.

George was perhaps a little fortunate when he scored United's fourth, his initial shot rebounding off a City defender, giving him a second opportunity and on this occasion he gave Downes little chance. Neither did the City goalkeeper have any chance in saving United's fifth goal, George claiming his first hat-trick for the club, converting a centre from left-back Box.

Latham claimed his second of the match and United's sixth following a mix up in the City defence and, to really rub it in, George made it seven when he accepted a fine through ball from Fitzpatrick before once again beating Downes.

City did have the odd opportunity to reduce the leeway through Lenthall and McAlinden, but both were denied by fine saves from Maneely in the United goal.

It would be some seven years before George would equal, and better, scoring this number of goals.

City 'B': Downes, Harold, Green, Goddard, Darlington, Howard, Jones, Bates, Lenthall, Mcalinden, Burrows.

United 'B': Maneely, Hampson, Box, McBride, Farrar, Marshall, Latham, Best, Mitten, Fitzpatrick, Morton.

Scorers: Best (4), Latham (4), Mitten.

Attendance: Unknown.

United Youth vs Newcastle United Youth

24 April 1963

In the formative years of the FA Youth Cup, Manchester United enjoyed considerable success, winning the inaugural competition in season 1952/53 with an emphatic 9-3 aggregate victory over Wolverhampton Wanderers. Twelve months later, it was the Molineux lads who were once again to stand between United and victory and on this particular occasion they fared reasonably better, holding United to 4-4 draw before losing to a solitary goal on their home ground.

Season 1954/55 saw West Bromwich Albion beaten 7-1 on aggregate in the final, while the name of Manchester United was once again etched upon the trophy following their victory over Chesterfield by the odd goal in seven in the final of the 1955/56 competition. West Ham United were unable to prevent the next batch of United youngsters from making it five in a row in 1957, losing 8-2 over the course of the two legs.

Then, for some unknown reason, the finely tuned conveyor belt ground to a halt. Wolverhampton Wanderers gained some form of revenge with a 1-1 draw at Old Trafford followed by a 3-1 victory on home soil in the 1957/58 semi-final then, twelve months on, Blackburn Rovers claimed United's scalp, again in the semi-final stage. Preston North End doing likewise in 1959/60.

Stoke City ended any hopes of re-claiming the trophy in season 1960/61 with a 2-0 fifth round victory, but those hopes were certainly rekindled in 1961/62 with a 10-1 victory over Wigan Athletic and a 9-0 triumph against Bradford City, alongside 3-2 and 3-0 victories against Everton and Manchester City respectively. Newcastle United in round four, proved to be a different proposition altogether, leaving Old Trafford for the return journey to the north-east having recorded a 2-1 win.

There were groans of disapproval in Yorkshire when Bradford City once again followed Manchester United out of the hat in the draw for the second round of the 1962/63 competition. They were to be well founded as the United youngsters went six better, scoring fifteen without reply to progress into the next round, where Sunderland were to provide a much sterner opposition. At Old Trafford, the Roker Park juniors managed to hold United to a 1-1 draw, but back on home territory, they were to lose by the odd goal in five, a victory for United that handed them the chance to gain revenge for last season's fourth-round defeat by Newcastle United.

Having knocked United out of the competition a year ago, Newcastle United went on to win the FA Youth Cup, so revenge and the opportunity to knock the current holders out of the tournament gave the Old Trafford youngsters a double goal to aim for, while the journey from the north-east to Manchester held no fear for the St James' Park youngsters.

In the previous three Youth Cup fixtures of this season, there had been only two changes in personnel and both had been for the Sunderland replay, with John Pearson taking over from Mervyn Maneely in goal and Alan Duff replacing Ken Morton at outside-left. But for the visit of Newcastle, there were to be three chances to the United side. In goal came David Ikin, with David Sadler taking over the Number Nine shirt in place of Albert Kinsey, who had moved to inside right in place of Barry Grayson and at outside-left, replacing Alan Duff came George for what was his first FA Youth Cup tie.

There was a good crowd at Old Trafford to cast their eyes over the latest crop of red-shirted youngsters making their own personal opinions as to who, if any, would be making regular appearances on that same pitch for the United first team in years to come. The 12,000 who turned up were certainly not to be disappointed, with two or three of the youngsters catching the eye.

There was never likely to be a repeat of last season's defeat at the hands of the Geordies, but neither was it an overwhelming victory as it was not until the later stages of the game that the outcome was actually decided.

United began well, taking the game to Newcastle, but for all their possession their finishing was at times somewhat erratic. But mid-way through the first half, they did manage to take the lead through Fry, a goal that was to take some of the urgency out of the play, allowing the home side to settle and play some attractive football.

George began to make a telling contribution to the game, but still United struggled to make their superiority count and it wasn't until six minutes from time that they were to score a second when Kinsey side footed a Walker free-kick from the edge of the area, that looked to be going well wide of the mark, past Imrie in the Newcastle goal.

Three minutes later, the result was put beyond all doubt when United scored a third. A long ball down the middle from George caught the Newcastle defence flatfooted and Kinsey ran through to beat centre-half Pickering and the advancing Imrie to give United a well-deserved victory.

United: Ikin, Harrop, Noble, Walker, Tranter, Dunphy, Anderson, Kinsey, Sadler, Fry, Best.

Scorer: Kinsey (2), Fry.

Newcastle United: Imrie, Markie, Watson, Smith, Pickering, Moncur, Robson, Caldwell King, Allen, Webster.

Attendance: 12,000.

England Youth vs Northern Ireland Youth

11 May 1963

It is difficult to believe that a player who was to go on to become one of the greatest that the game has ever seen – the greatest, full stop, if you listen to many observers – failed to make his country's schoolboy international side. But that is indeed something that George Best actually failed to do.

The snub by the selectors at schoolboy level was soon to be rectified, however, as those who selected the players to represent Northern Ireland at Youth level knew a talented young player when they saw one and selected George for his first representative honour against England at Boundary Park Oldham in May 1962. A local Belfast newspaper writing in the days prior to the fixture: 'One forward change is also probable, as good reports from old Trafford regarding George Best could earn the former Boyland player his first cap.' Another journalist penned, 'I applaud the selectors for choosing George Best, the Manchester United colt for inside left.'

George's roommate for the pre-match stay in Manchester was John Napier who was on the books of Bolton Wanderers. 'He was six months older than me' recalled John, 'and we both had trials with the Northern Ireland schoolboy team when we were fifteen. I made it and George did not – unbelievable. I asked him what they had said to him and he replied that they had told him he was "too small and got knocked off the ball". George was very quiet and the night before the game we just talked football.'

With both sides vying for the country's youth championship, an enthralling encounter was expected from the youngsters but according to one of the match reports available from the game, it was considered 'disappointing'. The English boys, although showing much promise in mid-field, floundered in front of goal. Even although they were to take the lead as early as the fourth minute, when Stokes in the Irish goal allowed something of a lob-cum-cross by Hall on the left wing to drop over his head and into the net. The goal could in fact have been an equaliser, not the opening goal, if a shot from Guy, running onto a through ball from George, had only been a few inches lower.

Following a lob into the English goalmouth by Corbett, Morris miss-kicked his clearance and the ball fell to Guy who headed towards goal, only to see Craven clear off the line. At the opposite end, Corbett was finding the lively Hall something of a handful and with the England Number Eleven once again getting the better of him, the full-back was relieved to see his 'keeper clear the immediate danger'.

Despite the Irish attacks being only in 'fits and starts', George was a constant danger to the English defence 'showing cleverness with the ball when Ireland began to enjoy more of the game and a pass to Warburton looked promising until Guy first-timed the ball high over from the wing's cross'.

As the second half got underway, England came close to increasing their lead, with Hall once again at in thick of things. Racing through the Irish defence, he drew Stokes from his goal, but as the ball headed towards the vacant goal, Watson managed to get back to clear the immediate danger.

A second goal was soon to materialise, but it was scored by the visitors in the 58th minute following a free-kick some 20 yards from goal. Nicholl, preparing to shoot, stepped over the ball allowing Warburton to follow through to send a low shot past Roper. Both sides had the opportunities to secure victory, Guy shooting over from a pass by Norris, Leach shooting wide with only Stokes to beat and then in the closing minutes, Mansfield created the opening only to see Hall blast the ball way off target and then right at the death, Norris fired over the bar when in a good position. But even at this level, George caught the eye, with another report of the game stating, 'Certainly the class of new cap and inside left George Best of Manchester United and the composure of centre-half John Napier (Bolton) deserved more.'

England: Roper, Craven, Stringer, Grummett, Morris, Bennett, Mansfield, Healey, Leach, Bruntlett, Hall.

Scorer: Hall

Nothern Ireland: Stokes, Corbett, McCurley, Nicholl, Napier, Watson, Warburton, Reid, Guy, Best, Norris.

Scorer: Warburton

Attendance: 4,000

Wales Youth vs Northern Ireland Youth

19 May 1963

Eight days after winning his first Northern Ireland international cap, albeit at Youth team level, George was celebrating scoring his first international goal in the home country's championship fixture against Wales at Aberystwyth. If there had ever been any doubts as to his natural ability by those who ran the game at international level, then this particular fixture went a long way towards convincing those doubters, while adding a few new admirers to his ever growing fan club.

Once again John Napier was a teammate and he recalled: 'That same year we played together against the Wales youth team in Aberystwyth in North Wales. I remember on the Friday before the game, my manager at Bolton Bill Ridding and coach George Taylor were taking me and George in their car and we would drive down to Wales. We picked George up on the way at his digs in Manchester and drove down with me and George in the back seat.' Once again, the conversation was limited, but George was to do all his talking out the pitch the following day.

With the game less than a minute old, Guy forced a corner, following good play by Reid, in what was the Irish lad's first attack. When the ball swung into the goalmouth it fell to the feet of the one of the smallest players on the pitch and George quickly despatched the ball past Park with a low shot. Wales were quick to retaliate and, with the wind on their backs, were soon putting the Irish goal under siege and it did look as though Lewis was going to snatch an equaliser, but Stokes dashed from his goal to flick the ball wide for a corner kick.

But as the game went on, there was little to judge between the two sides, although for a brief spell prior to the interval, it did look as if the visitors were going to increase their lead, but a combination of red-shirted bodies and the woodwork managed to keep the ball out.

In the early stages of the second half, it was again Ireland who looked the better of the two sides, although a mix up in their defence almost brought the equaliser, but the Welsh side were made to wait until the 59th minute before they were to eventually draw level, Evans creating the opening for Jones to score. For the remainder of the game both goals saw their fair share of action, but there was to be no further scoring as any opportunities created were shunned by both sets of forwards.

But what of George? 'Best's assurance in possession and precision passes were factors in further Irish Raids, and only safe handling and good anticipation by goalkeeper Park foiled two splendid efforts by the Manchester United colt', penned one correspondent. But George was also to miss the odd scoring opportunity, a header was well saved by Park not long after the interval, while another effort was shunned with the chance to redeem that particular miss coming right at the end, but once again the ball was sent wide of the post.

Another reporter at the game was to write: 'George Best scored and began a game that must have done him a lot of good in the selectors' eyes. An immaculate ball-player he seems assured of pulling on a green jersey many more times.'

Wales: Park, Lucas, D. Jones, Davies, Smith, Pearce, Hughes, Evans, N. Jones, Pugh, Lewis.

Scorer: Jones.

Northern Ireland: Stokes, Corbett, McCurley, Nicholl, Napier, Watson, Warburton, Anderson, Guy, Best, Reid.

Scorer: Best.

United Reserves vs Sheffield Wednesday Reserves

24 August 1963

'Our Central League side are eagerly looking forward to the new season' began the 'With the Reserves and Juniors' section in the *United Review* for the opening home fixture of the 1963/64 season against Ipswich Town. Going on to say,

> Last year's performance in failing to take the championship by only five points was really outstanding for time after time injuries and first team calls made it necessary to draft young players into the side before they had had the chance to gain experience usually necessary for this League which requires such a high standard of play.

The article went on to mention that 'The junior programme will be underway by the time these notes appear and the youngsters will have had the eagerly awaited opportunity of proving their ability and putting to the test the knowledge and experience gained in the pre-season training and coaching sessions. Although there have been one or two departures, most of last season's players will again be showing their paces and hoping – successfully we trust – to earn promotion to the senior ranks.' There was no mention to be found anywhere in relation to George. For that, we have to go to *United Review* No. 2, covering the game against Everton, where about a third of the 'Reserves and Juniors' page is taken up with a report on the Central League fixture against Sheffield Wednesday at Old Trafford.

It was a favourable start to the season on home soil for United's second string, the mixture of experienced and untried youth scoring four without reply. It was even more favourable as five of the eleven fixtures on that opening Saturday ended in draws.

Perhaps surprisingly, two of those who made the short journey from their Manchester homes a couple of hours before had been members of the United side that had lifted the FA Cup only a few weeks previously and, instead of lining up to face Sheffield Wednesday's senior side in a first division fixture at Hillsborough, they found themselves in front a more sparsely populated ground. 'In addition to Quixall and Giles being given places in the attack, we had Dunphy and Anderson who made only five appearances last season while Tranter, who played centre-half, had three and left winger Best was making his first appearance in this grade of football.'

United took the game by the scruff of the neck almost from the offset, but could not convert their superiority into goals and due to those missed opportunities, the visitors could perhaps consider themselves fortunate to go in at the interval only one goal behind. Mark Pearson, another experienced individual scoring that opening goal.

It wasn't all missed opportunities by the United forwards, as MacLaren in the Wednesday goal pulled off a couple of superb saves from Pearson, but any hopes that the visitors had of clawing themselves back into the game disappeared when their keeper was carried off injured just before half-time.

Although now reduced to ten men and with full-back Noble now between the posts, Wednesday put up a brave fight with the stand-in custodian turning in an excellent display, making superb saves from Anderson, Dunphy, Nicholson and George before his luck ran out. United scoring a further three goals without reply through Anderson, who also hit the post, Nicholson and an own goal by O'Donnell.

As the weeks passed by George could be found back among his teenaged friends in the United 'A' side, although looking through the 'United Reviews' for season 1963/64 his name seldom appears in the line-ups, although when it does, it was usually accompanied by mention of a goal.

For the match against Burnley 'A' on 30 November, we find 'wingers Best and Morton sharing the honours' along with a mention that he claimed a hat-trick. Then on 10 December a 10-1 victory over Tranmere Rovers 'A' team gave us 'a great goal from Best' and 'Best made it eight with a well-worked goal'. If we move on to April 1964 and the 'Review' for the match against Nottingham Forest, a few lines on the junior members of the playing staff mentions George, Willie Anderson and Wilf Tranter all having made their first division debuts, going on to add: 'The advancement of George Best has been almost meteoric. Dividing his time last season almost equally between the "A" and the "B" teams he gained a regular first team place during a most testing period.' Certainly a player for the future.

United Reserves: Briggs, Brennan, Lorimer, Nicholson, Tranter, Dunphy, Giles, Quixall, Anderson, Pearson, Best.

Scorers: Pearson, Anderson, Nicholson, O'Donnell own goal.

Sheffield Wedneday: Unkown.

United vs West Bromwich Albion

14 September 1963

There was no fanfare of trumpets, no shouting from the roof of the stand. Instead he emerged rather inconspicuously from the mouth of the tunnel, trying to merge unnoticed with his fellow teammates as he took the field for the first division fixture against West Bromwich Albion for his first division debut. Although he was followed onto the sacred turf by a posse of cameramen.

He wasn't, however, some unknown youngster, as those around Old Trafford were well aware as to his capabilities. They were not kidded by the scrawny, tousle-headed Irishman. This precocious talent had already made many sit up and take notice with his speed, box of tricks and uncanny balance while on the ball.

The apprenticeship had been served, with the juniors long since left behind, although playing for the youth team was still an option. The first division stage beckoned despite those hard-as-nails defenders waiting patiently for fresh-faced youngsters to come somewhat foolhardy onto the scene and straight into the end of a well-polished and well-used boot.

United, despite having won the FA Cup the previous season, were still some way from being a real force in English football again. Nevertheless Matt Busby believed in the players he had on the Central League side and was quite happy to give them their head rather than delve into the transfer market for some experienced replacements.

Ian Moir, Phil Chisnall and David Sadler had already given the team a youngish look, but it was Moir whose name was missing from the United line-up for the visit of West Bromwich Albion to Old Trafford on 14 September, a date that would become forever etched in the history of Manchester United Football Club. There was no record scoreline, stand-out performances or any incidents of note over the course of the ninety minutes, it was nothing more than the debut of a youngster by the name of George Best.

On that September afternoon, as he trotted out before a crowd of 50,453, he was simply 'George who?', a youngster drafted into the United side in place of the injured Ian Moir, with wing-half Nobby Stiles as his inside partner, replacing another medical room attendee in Denis Law. It was little different in *The Guardian* with their report simply saying, '... and G. Best, a seventeen-year-old former Irish schoolboy international, at outside-right for his first match.'

West Bromwich Albion, who also had a debutant within their ranks in the form of nineteen-year-old full-back Crawford. He had enjoyed a favourable start to the season and could be found one point behind United at the top of the first division, so the fixture promised to have something of an edge to it and, as the waif like Belfast boy tugged at his sleeves, the referee's whistle got the game underway. Had he been up against his fellow debutant then he might have enjoyed a more productive afternoon, instead he was to come face-to-face with the experienced Welsh internationalist Graham Williams, who was more than eager to give out a first-hand beginner's guide to first division football, showing little in the way of compassion to the mop-haired Irishman.

Indeed, a heavy tackle by Williams on Best did not simply subdue the debutant for a while, but also set the tone for the majority of the ninety minutes, as both sides resorted to unnecessary pettiness when it came to physical contact. On one somewhat mysterious occasion, Fenton was left flat out on the pitch with play fully 30 yards away, an incident missed by everyone, including the referee.

Both sets of half-backs out manoeuvred the inside-forwards of the opposition, and with Stiles finding it difficult adjusting to his more advanced role and Chisnall completely out of the game, United's thrust and productive play was somewhat stifled and their attack disjointed.

Charlton did much to lift the game and cause a threat to the West Bromwich goal, especially in the lacklustre opening forty-five minutes, moving across the front line in search of an opening, but it was akin to a soloist attempting to lift a complete orchestra out of mediocrity. Faced with the Albion debutant Crawford, he would have been better off remaining on the left and putting the youngster under constant pressure, which would surely have been more productive.

Due to Charlton's wanderings it did enable Best to seek refuge on the left flank when the going got tough on the right, away from the grinning Williams, but after a breather out of reach of the Welshman's studs and continuing harassment, he returned to show his determination and spirit as he took the ball to, and sometimes past, the experienced defender.

Best's play was often of a high quality and showed the definite hint of promise underneath the immaturity, although he would certainly have been more than happy to have been involved in what was to be the only goal of the game.

Following the goalless and totally forgettable opening forty-five minutes, with the only real threat of a goal coming when Stiles slammed the ball against the upright as he ran onto a Charlton through ball, it was still looking as though a 0-0 draw was going to be the outcome. Until the sixty-fifth minute when Best pushed the ball inside to Stiles who, in turn, squared the ball across the face of the Albion penalty area to the unmarked Sadler. Potter moved off his line but Sadler kept a cool head and directed the ball, left footed, past the advancing goalkeeper.

Play did improve slightly as the second half progressed but West Bromwich showed little capability of denting the United defence, while United themselves only showed flashes of what they were capable of and put the visitors goal under threat on the odd occasion. Slowly, the game faded rather disappointingly and many of the spectators made their way towards the gates long before the referee had even bothered to look at his watch and blow for full-time.

George Best had enjoyed his first senior appearance and gleaned much more than a few red stud marks from the close attention from Graham Williams, it helped that the reaction from the seasoned campaigners in the press box was favourable. In *The Guardian*, their special correspondent wrote:

> Young Best came in for some stern treatment by that splendid back Williams and twice sought refuge for short spells on the opposite wing where he faced Crawford. Best's football was occasionally of a high quality, but he also showed his immaturity and it says much for his spirit that he twice returned to the right wing to take on Williams again, who seemed intent on showing a disapproving crowd that there is no sentiment in football.

In the *Daily Telegraph*, Denis Lowe wrote of the 'valuable experience' that would be gained by 'the slim dark-haired lad of seventeen' who 'had a promising first league game as Moir's outside-right deputy. He showed good ball control and a subtle body-swerve, but will be happy to learn that few first division left-backs tackle with the power and accuracy of Welsh international, Graham Williams.'

But despite a favourable initial showing, it was back to the reserves the following Saturday afternoon, as Busby was more than happy to allow the prodigious youngsters progress to develop gradually.

Manchester United: Gregg, Dunne, Cantwell, Crerand, Foulkes, Setters, Best, Stiles, Sadler, Chisnall, Charlton.

Scorer: Sadler.

West Bromwich Albion: Potter, Crawford, Williams, Howe, Jones, Simpson, Foggo Cram, Readfern, Fenton, Clark.

Attendance: 50,453.

United Youth vs Barrow Youth
18 December 1963

Whenever the FA Youth Cup appears on the Manchester United fixture list, the success in those early years of the competition is always going to be mentioned, when the likes of Eddie Colman, Bobby Charlton, Geoff Bent, Wilf McGuinness, Alex Dawson, David Pegg, Albert Scanlon and the incomparable Duncan Edwards played their parts in claiming ownership of the trophy for the first five seasons of its history.

Trying to emulate such an achievement was an impossible task, but as the sixties unfolded, a new crop of youngsters were on the scene: Ian Moir, Nobby Stiles, Jimmy Nicholson, Phil Chisnal, who in turn made way for the likes of Bobby Noble, Willie Anderson, Albert Kinsey, David Sadler, John Aston, Jimmy Rimmer, John Fitzpatrick and George.

Having stuttered at the fifth round in the previous season, losing 2-0 to Sheffield Wednesday at Hillsborough, this latest crop of youngsters had their eyes set on glory from the offset. The draw for the second round of the 1963/64 competition (United were given a bye in round one) presented them with a favourable home draw against Barrow.

The Cumbrians were more than aware that they stood little chance of progressing in the competition and had only progressed into round two courtesy of the 4-2 replay victory over Chester at home following a 1-1 draw at Sealand Road, so they were more than content to travel to Manchester and simply enjoy the occasion. They were, however, to get more than they bargained for.

Some were surprised that it took United twelve minutes to break the deadlock, with George opening the scoring and then notched a second in the 28th minute denting the visitors hopes of perhaps pulling off something of a shock. Ken Morton scored twice to make it 4-0, followed by Republic of Ireland schoolboy internationalist Frank McEwan who was determined not to be out-done by George; he claimed a hat-trick between the six minutes leading up to the interval to give United an 7-0 interval lead.

Many expected the United youngsters to show their visitors some compassion during the second forty-five minutes, but they were not in the mood to do so. However within seven minutes of the second half getting underway, it was the visitors who were to claim the next goal; McBride penalised for handball and Knox scoring from the penalty spot. United, perhaps a little offended, proceeded to score a further six.

Albert Kinsey made it 8-1 in the 58th minute then, with the woodwork having been struck at both ends, Ken Morton made it nine as the Barrow youngsters longed for full-time and to be on the coach heading back up north. But before they could wash off the evenings grime and sweat they were to endure further torture.

McEwan took the scoring into double figures before Willie Anderson became the last member of the United front line to get his name on the score sheet and made it 11-1 with a quarter of an hour remaining. George claimed his hat-trick to make it twelve and then Morton rounded off the scoring with two more to make it fourteen.

By the time round three materialised, George had progressed to first-team status and perhaps his skill and panache was missed by his teammates, as they only managed to squeeze past Blackpool by the odd goal in five. He was also missing from rounds four and five, a 2-0 victory over Sheffield United and a 3-2 win over Wolverhampton Wanderers, both at Old Trafford.

Nevertheless, when it came to the semi-finals it was a more prestigious game as local pride was at stake, as well as a place in the final, and he was recalled to face Manchester City in both the 4-1 home first-leg and the 4-3 victory in the return, scoring once in the latter.

United: Rimmer, Duff, Noble, McBride, Farrar, Fitzpatrick, Anderson, Best, McEwen, Kinsey, Morton.

Scorers: Morton (5), McEwen (4), Best (3), Kinsey, Anderson.

Barrow: McGuire, Lappin, Russell, Hughes, Slowey, McKechnie, B. Knox, Marshall, Lappin, Pritchard, M. Knox.

Scorer: Knox.

Attendance: 5,487.

Manchester United vs Burnley

28 December 1963

Boxing Day 1963 had seen Matt Busby's team make the relatively short journey from Manchester to neighbouring Burnley for what was a first division 'double header', with the Turf Moor side due at Old Trafford two days later.

Having escaped relegation to the second division by the skin of their teeth in the extended 1962/63 campaign, United used the summer months to recharge the batteries, forget about the dismal days and weeks of the past year and concentrate on the new season on the horizon. Kick-starting the 1963/64 season in a way that they could never have imagined, with only two defeats in the opening thirteen games, compared to only three victories in a similar number of fixtures twelve months previously. Everton were soundly beaten 5-1 at Old Trafford on 31 August and Ipswich Town defeated 7-2 at Portman Road three days later. Denis Law's third goal of his hat-trick against the Suffolk side gave him seven for the season, with only four games played.

Everton were to gain revenge for their early season thumping with a 4-0 victory at Goodison Park on 21 December, forcing Matt Busby into making a handful of changes to his side for the trip to Burnley five days later. In came Quixall for Moir, Charlton was given the Number Nine shirt, and Shay Brennan was given a rare ninety minutes in what was now for him something of an alien position at outside-left. Sadler was left out altogether.

Those changes to position and personnel made little difference to United's performance, with the 6-1 defeat their heaviest reversal since October the previous year, when they lost 6-2 to Tottenham Hotspur. The sending off of Crerand making little difference to that defeat at Burnley.

For the Old Trafford return fixture Matt Busby had two days to contemplate his problems and team selection but, after much deliberation, he decided on only two changes and brought back the untried but highly-rated George Best back from his Christmas break for what was to be only his second first team appearance, thus taking over the Number Eleven shirt from Brennan. The other change to the line-up was the equally untried sixteen-year-old apprentice professional Willie Anderson, who was handed the Number Seven shirt for what was his league debut. Many considered this as something of a risk by Busby, commenting that if the highly-experienced Eleven that he had sent out at Burnley had failed to achieve anything, how could he expect the throwing of two novice youngsters in at the deep end, against a team who would have been bristling with confidence following the 6-1 win forty-eight hours previously, achieve anything.

By full-time Busby was proved right although, as the game began, it was Burnley who made the early running; virtually picking up from where they had left off forty-eight hours previously and stretching the United defence to its limits.

With only four minutes gone Lochhead, that thorn in the United side from two days previously, had come close to opening the scoring twice. His first effort saw Gaskell palm an ambitious lob round the post, while his second flew harmlessly over the bar.

Having weathered the early storm and worked their way back into the game, United soon took command of the game and in the eleventh minute also took the lead, when Elder, only recently back from injury, for some unknown reason attempted a pass back to goalkeeper Blacklaw. The full-back, however, totally misjudged it and the ball rolled invitingly to the feet of David Herd. Although in an offside position a mere half a dozen yards from goal, the pass from Elder played him on and he was certainly not going to scorn the opportunity, firing the ball past Blacklaw to give United the initiative.

Burnley almost equalised from the restart when Pointer hit the post with Gaskell beaten but, two minutes later, United scored a second. A corner from Anderson has headed towards goal by Herd and although Blacklaw managed to block the effort, he failed to hold the ball and Moore nipped in to fire home the rebound. Setters had the opportunity to make it three, but missed the ball completely when in a perfect position in front of goal. But that third goal was not long in coming, engineered by Crerand in the twenty-third minute. Having won possession in mid-field, the United wing-half set off towards the Burnley bye-line, he crossed into the penalty area, the ball was initially missed by Charlton but fortunately in ran through to George who swept the ball into the roof of the net.

The visitors continued to push forward as the second half got underway but were fortunate not to go further behind when Crerand unleashed a shot from well out, which Blacklaw did well to tip over the bar. But they could only keep up the offensive for so long and in sixty-sixth minute they conceded a second. Charlton worked his way along the by-line drifting past Elder, before setting up an easy-scoring opportunity for Graham Moore. The Welshman having little else to do than tap the ball home for his second of the game. Four minutes later, David Herd made it five. Crerand, once again the architect, slipping the ball through the Burnley defence and allowing Herd to thump the ball past Blacklaw.

It was a goal in keeping with play, leaving Burnley scrabbling for any crumbs of respect that they could salvage from the game and, with four minutes, remaining they managed to snatch something of a consolation goal when Lochhead nipped in to head an intended lob from Setters to Gaskell, into the vacant United net. Revenge was sweet and the United faithful headed for home, basking in the victory and talking about the lad from Belfast who had made more than a telling contribution to the afternoons proceedings. Rather prophetically Bob Ferrier in *The Daily Telegraph* wrote: 'Best is a young man whom Matt Busby praised highly in the autumn. He is a slight, dark, casual Irishman with lovely ball control and a fine feeling for the positional game, but he still has to learn when not to shoot. In twelve months' time we should hear a great deal from him.'

In *The Guardian* Eric Todd spoke of how Best and Anderson had, according to the United match programme, figured prominently in United's overwhelming victory against Barrow in a FA Youth Cup game earlier in the month, going on to write:

Did you ever see an American film in which a doting mother introduced her young and precocious son – named Wilbur as often as not – to a distinguished visitor, with the words: 'Say hello to the nice gentleman, dear.' And did not Wilbur stick out his tongue and say, 'You're stooped and I'm gonna make you sorry you came?' Well, Anderson and Best did something similar like that to Elder and Angus (apart from sticking out their tongues, and they may have done that too, for all I know). They were enthusiastic, impertinent, not without skill, and they kept going splendidly in the heavy going.

The Daily Telegraph's special correspondent was once again excited with what he had seen for the young Irishman: 'George Best, aged seventeen, playing in his second first team game, was the hero of the Old Trafford crowd. He gave a tremendous display of speed and artistry and rounded it off with a 25-minute goal.' Other headlines spoke of 'Busby's Starlets', 'United's Pep Kids' and 'Revenge By New Babes', with Edgar Turner in the *Mirror* speaking of 'the new Busby Beatles' and 'two pocket sized cheeky urchins'.

George was here to stay and kept his place in the side for all but two of the remaining seventeen fixtures, playing his part, as United scaled the dizzy heights of second place, four points behind champions Liverpool. The Merseysiders superiority clearly visible in their 3-0 victory when the two teams met at Anfield on 4 April. They had also won at Old Trafford 1-0. United however, were on the right track and it was only a matter of time before Busby guided his team back to the top.

Manchester United: Gaskell, Dunne, Cantwell, Crerand, Foulkes, Setters, Anderson, Moore, Charlton, Herd, Best.

Scorers: Herd (2), Moore (2), Best.

Burnley: Blacklaw, Angus, Elder, O'Neill, Talbut, Miller, Morgan, Pointer, Lochhead, Robson, Price.

Scorer: Lochhead.

Attendance: 47,834.

10

Barnsley vs United

15 February 1964

Having won the FA Cup in 1963, strangely as the underdogs, beating Leicester City 3-1 thanks to goals from Denis Law and a David Herd double, there was a determination within the ranks to return to Wembley and retain the trophy. In the third and fourth rounds of the 1963/64 competition, positive steps had been taken along the road that would see Wembley Way as the final destination with five goal encounters against Southampton at the Dell (3-2) and Bristol Rovers at Old Trafford (4-1).

In round five it was another away draw with third division Barnsley standing between United and a place in the quarter-finals. With the slag heaps as a somewhat strange back drop it wasn't the inspiration and goals of the usual suspects, but yet another promising display from the youngster from Belfast who had sat in the Wembley stand alongside his father on that May afternoon and watched United lift the cup, dreaming of what it might be like to take part in such an occasion.

Barnsley, for all their grit and determination were never really in the hunt and above the 4-0 scoreline on the match report for the *Daily Telegraph*, the headline: 'Cup-Holders Heading for Another Final' to it all. But it was another headline – 'Boy Best Snatches Glory' – that captured the imagination.

Denis Law stole the MOM award with his typical enthusiastic display coupled with a goal, but it was the performance of George who claimed two of United's four goals (depending on what reports you read) capturing the headlines and rave notices from spectators and members of the press alike. It was his goal that set United marching towards the last eight. According to Gerry Loftus 'it wasn't a big money player who set Manchester on the winning way, but seventeen-year-old Irish winger George Best. With his two-footed scheming, body swerves and rare anticipation he was always a menace to the home defence and scored the first goal.'

According to Denis Lowe, another member of the press pack "Matt Busby's discovery, the slim seventeen-year-old Best, has the look of a born footballer.' George began the move that lead to his opening goal, pushing the ball out to Tony Dunne, then immediately running off towards the penalty area. When the ball came over Denis Law chested it down and with a back-heel flick found George, who was on hand to ram the ball home.

Woeful finishing by the United front line saw the score remain at 1-0 until two minutes into the second half, when George was once again in the thick of things, with some superb footwork setting up Denis Law.

At 2-0 it was more or less game over but a question hung over, not so much the game, but the actual goal scorers. According to Denis Lowe in the *Daily Telegraph* (and one or two other statistical records): 'Law had two goals himself (forty-seven and fifty-six minutes) and also furnished the passes for those by Best (25) and Herd (49).' But after studying another seven reports they credit George with scoring two – the 25th minute opener and the fourth in the 55, 56 or 57th minute. The mystery is perhaps solved by Gerry Loftus who wrote, '... and in the 57th minute Best completed his afternoon of glory. Cutting in, he finally shot from a narrow angle with Law following up to make certain.'

Un-credited reports state, 'Law was in his element. As spearhead of the Old Trafford front line he scored once and laid on goals for Herd and Best,' going on to add, 'Best registered his second goal from a pass by Stiles.' Another stated, '... and young Best added a fourth in the 55th minute.'

We will go with the majority.

Law's ability to spot the half chance, something few players were capable of, supplied Herd with the opportunity to score United's third and, by the time United recorded that, fourth goal. They were toying with their opponents.

George had only six first team appearances under his belt, but already the footballing public were sitting up and taking notice of this slimly built youngster who showed a maturity out with his tender years, skill and determination that many of his elders could only dream about and that certain something that placed him apart from the majority of others who plied their trade in the football league and indeed on the European front.

Barnsley: Williamson, Hooper, Brookes, Wood, Winstanley, Houghton, Sheaville, Kerr, Leighton, Byrne, O'Hara.

United: Gaskell, Brennan, T. Dunne, Crerand, Foulkes, Setters, Herd, Stiles, Charlton, Law, Best.

Scorers: Best (2), Law, Herd.

Attendance: 38,076.

United vs Sunderland

29 February 1964

Being in the crowd for that 1963 FA Cup Final, caught up in its unique atmosphere, seemed to have something of a prolonged effect on George and, having broken onto the first team scene, he seemed to be determined to get his feet on that lush green turf as quickly as possible and if it meant playing to a higher standard than he was expected to, or going as far as to carry the team on his own, then so be it.

His two goals had disposed of Barnsley in round five, setting up a quarter-final tie with a much stronger Sunderland and even a mid-week European Cup Winners Cup tie against Sporting Lisbon a matter of days before. When he performed a little below that high standard that he had already set himself, there was little anyone could do to dim his appetite.

Second division leaders Sunderland came to Old Trafford totally unfazed by either the occasion or the hype that surrounded the new seventeen-year-old star in the making. Their 20,000 supporters who had made the journey from the north-east did so in a confident mood, something that spread from the terraces onto the pitch injecting the Sunderland players with adrenaline that fired them into taking a two-goal lead over their hosts.

Lead by the monolith that was Charlie Hurley, who maintained a tight grip on the ever dangerous Law, Sunderland took the game to United with a confident swagger and completely outshone their more illustrious hosts in the opening period which sprang to life around the twenty-fifth minute mark. Sixty-three hospitals were tuned into the game and the fast-flowing action-packed encounter was a far superior tonic than anything a doctor could have prescribed.

Crerand came close with a long-range effort, Sharkey just failed to get on to the end of Mulhall cross, Law missed a golden opportunity when the ball diverted to his feet off a defender, then Crerand fired narrowly over but it was not until four minutes before the interval that the deadlock was broken. Usher sent a tantalising cross into the United penalty area where Gaskell simply flapped at the ball, missing it completely, allowing Mulhall to run in a head home.

Five minutes into the second half it was 2-0. George Herd robbed Setters in midfield and the ball found its way out to Crossan who moved down the left as the United defence appealed for a non-existent throw in rather than attempting to tackle the advancing Sunderland inside-left. Cutting inside, he was allowed to continue towards goal, he drove the ball high into the United net past a wrong footed and helpless Gaskell. But United were suddenly back in the game within five minutes, when Hurley headed past his own goalkeeper who had moved from his goal in an attempt to deal with a centre from Crerand. Their joy was short lived as four minutes later Crossan reinstalled Sunderland's two goal advantage from the penalty spot after having been tripped inside the area by Brennan.

For a time, it was Montgomery in the Sunderland goal who stood between United and a hoped for victory. Charlton shot straight at the Sunderland 'keeper, then he somehow managed to block a Setters header from only 2 yards out. In the 78th minute Law headed wide from under the crossbar, before David Herd missed the target completely. A Crerand cross was to find Law but his header hit Montgomery in the face before being scrambled clear as the match slowly ticked away from the cup holders.

With four minutes remaining and Montgomery still in something of a daze, United won a corner which was taken by George. He swung the ball over and Charlton rose above everyone else to head home to make it 3-2. Few had left the ground, happy to be later home than normal if it meant witnessing a memorable United fight-back and, with less than three minutes remaining, their delayed departure was made worthwhile.

In the *Daily Express* Terence Elliott wrote:

> George Best, the kid from Belfast, the so-modest boy with a dimple and a blush, made nonsense of mighty men like Charlie Hurley, the Sunderland pin-up giant in one shattering moment with seconds to go.
>
> From desperately battling Norbert Stiles to Denis Law, who found himself faced once again with a wall of blue yet pushed the ball to the right and Hurley moved too late ... as the blur that was seventeen-year-old Best came into view. And outside left Best, from inside right hit that teetering ball true and firmly into the gap that Jim Montgomery and his teammates had left unguarded. The Cup holders were saved.

'Boy Best nips in to rock giants' was the preceding headline.

In *People* the headline screamed 'Kid Winger Saves Busby Men' and Len Shakleton, himself not too bad a footballer, scribbled: 'Best, seventeen-year-old man of the hour, day or week, made the replay possible. The youngest kid on the field, he stole this show with a tremendous equaliser. He fastened on to a bobbling ball just inside the box and let fly a drive that bypassed half-a-dozen Sunderland defenders and crashed into the corner of the net.'

In the Roker Park replay, there were no repeat heroics from George, but there was a dramatic finale with Bobby Charlton grabbing a last-gasp equaliser with only two minutes of extra time remaining to level the scores at 2-2. In the second replay at Huddersfield Town's Leeds Road ground there was no nail-biting finish or late goals, only United once again having to chase the game after going behind in the 48th minute. Their reply was swift and brutal. Equalising almost immediately from the start, they hit Sunderland with five goals in a devastating twenty minute spell to leave the gallant Sunderland side stunned with no way back into the game, their strength sapped away on the rain sodden pitch.

Despite the 5-1 success, there was still no return to Wembley, as West Ham United running out comfortable 3-1 winners in the Hillsborough semi-final.

United: Gaskell, Brennan, T. Dunne, Crerand, Foulkes, Setters, Herd, Stiles, Charlton, Law, Best.

Scorers: Hurley (own goal), Charlton, Best.

Sunderland: Montgomery, Irwin, Ashurst, Harvey, Hurley, Elliott, Usher, Herd, Sharkey, Crossan, Mulhall.

Scorers: Crossan (2), Mulhall.

Attendance: 63,700.

But what of the enigma that was George Best?

For many of those out with the Salford environs, he was still relatively unknown. Match reports were basic and straight-to-the-point summaries, only dishing out the merest details: 'seventeen-year-old George Best from Belfast ...' is about as good as it got. But gradually, the public became more aware of his presence on the football field. They were becoming inquisitive.

Television coverage was limited to say the least. The FA Cup Final was the staple diet for many so it was word of mouth or, as the teenagers appearances totted up, the newspapers began to realise that they could perhaps shift a few more copies on the back of this waif of a lad who's name was suddenly on everyone's lips.

In a team of established international stars – the fiery goal-scoring machine that was Denis Law, the Munich-surviving Bobby Charlton, the now integral part of the United machine the inspirational Pat Crerand and the other familiar red-shirted hero's – George Best was beginning to create a niche for himself.

Not every performance captured the headlines most, to be honest didn't, but suddenly out of nothing there would be a flash of brilliance leaving a defender, or more likely defenders, feeling and looking embarrassed and the packed throngs of spectators on the terracing left open mouthed, leaving everyone wanting to know more about this red-shirted leprechaun.

The *Express* went a considerable way to constructing something of a 'pen picture' of the new name among the footballing headlines, sending Ray Purcell in search of the Manchester United youngster in order to reveal something of his identity. Under the heading 'The Boy who Kept United in the Cup' Purcell wrote,

> He looks like a thin-faced Beatle, but George Best doesn't have to sing for fame and fortune. At seventeen he has found another way to the top – football. A boy among men of his team, he scored the last-minute goal which saved Manchester united from defeat and kept them in the Cup. Yesterday George was taking it easy in this dig, enjoying a game of cards with his landlady's teenage son.
>
> George Best is a slight lad – 9st 7lb. He looks no older than his years; a dark handsome boy, black hair cut in Beatle-style, wearing tight grey trousers, brown Cuban-heeled, elastic sided boots. But you could pick him out in a crowd as an athlete, long-legged, very quick, light on his feet.

Having written a little on his home life in Belfast and his eventual signing for United, Purcell continued,

> He moved into the semi-detached corporation house in Chorlton-cum-Hardy where he digs with reserve goalkeeper Ronnie Briggs. Ask him what it is like to live the schoolboys dream and play for United and he says, 'Oh, it's great to be playing with the big stars...' and Best's sentence trails into silence which says that he's still a bit awkward about mixing with them. When he does, confusion can rise among outsiders: 'What's this lad, mascot or just an autograph hunter?' said someone who saw Best with the team.
>
> Manager Matt Busby says with feeling: 'This lad has the lot. Not only is his temperament perfect for the job but he has complete confidence.' With all this, George's biggest fan is his landlady: widow Mrs Mary Fullaway. 'He's a grand lad, no trouble at all,' she says warmly. And George blushes. 'George doesn't smoke or drink, eats everything I serve up and is a real pal to my own eighteen-year-old boy, Stephen,' says Mrs Fullaway. George grins, 'I do eat a lot. Matt Busby told me I could eat everything I like – and that includes lots of chicken, steaks and chops.' And just to prove the point, he also helps himself to a couple of chocolates.
>
> George's fame is spreading: 'I get fan letters most days. This morning two girl fans knocked at the door and presented me with this,' he said, holding up a teddy bear dressed in United's red

and white. But he has no time to spare for girls. 'I relax by playing ten-pin bowls or snooker. I don't go to dances – I can't twist or shake – but I do collect pop records.' He can afford to these days. He is on the junior players' basic rate of £12 a week – but there are bonuses. Last week his pay cheque was £25. Next Thursday it will be around £100.

Whatever the size of it George Best's payday drill is the same: Off to the bank to cash the cheque, take out £4 for his landlady, a few pounds for his own living expenses, something more to send home to his parents – and the rest goes into his savings account.

Ask him about that last-minute goal with which he saved United's bacon and he says modestly: 'The ball just dropped at my feet and I hit it hoping it would go into the net.' Well it did!

Wales vs Northern Ireland

15 April 1964

Following his match-saving goal against Sunderland in the FA Cup quarter-final tie at Old Trafford George was widely tipped to win his first full Northern Ireland cap, with the press revealing that 'the Irish selectors will watch the outside-left on Saturday and if he lives up to his fast-rising reputation he will be in Ireland's team to meet Wales on 15 April.'

Watch him they did and they certainly must have liked what they saw as the speculation proved correct and George, still a month short of his eighteenth birthday, found himself included in *The* Northern Ireland side to face Wales at Swansea on 15 April. 'In the lively Irish team Best, of Manchester United, will be playing for the first time' wrote Albert Barham in *The Guardian*, continuing: 'Although the fact that Crossan is his partner should ease for him some of the tension which must come from such an ordeal.'

Barham, a seasoned United observer, should have been well aware that the debutant would certainly not be struck down with stage fright, as the packed terraces of Old Trafford had been an ideal platform upon which to serve his apprenticeship. Pulling on the green of Ireland would be little different than wearing the red of Manchester United but, then again, perhaps George was a little subdued by the occasion or perhaps, more to the point, haunted by the spectre of Graham Williams the West Bromwich Albion full-back once again rearing up in front of him on a debut day.

George certainly wasn't out of his depth, following his rave notices for his United performances and for the fact that both the Wales and Northern Ireland sides had an average age of under twenty-three, but the rain sodden pitch certainly did little to help him display his wide array of skills.

Wales, with six former Swansea Boys' players in the side and fielding something of an experimental eleven due to World Cup fixtures looming on the horizon, went behind in the eighth minute. Goalkeeper Sprake only managed to half clear a corner, the ball falling kindly to Braithwaite who chipped the ball back into the penalty area where McLaughlin headed home.

Wales equalised in the twenty-third minute through Godfrey, picking up the ball after a neat chip over the head of Magill by Jones, but on the half an hour they were again to find themselves a goal behind. Braithwate again in the thick of things, crossing the ball towards the Welsh goal where both Wilson and McLaughlin waited, but it was the former who was to beat Sprake with relative ease. A minute before the interval it was 3-1, Harvey brushing past half-hearted Welsh challenges to blast the ball past Sprake with a shot on the run.

However, the Welsh goalkeeper wasn't simply involved in the game by picking the ball out of his netting as he pulled off a couple of fine saves to keep the scoreline at something of a respectable level. The first when a shot from George hit him on the knee, the other when he stopped a Wilson effort with his foot.

Graham Moore was certainly much more involved in the game than his Manchester United teammate, twice coming close to scoring, but it was one of his miss-kicks in front of goal that saw Davies nip in to prod the ball past Jennings for the second Welsh goal in the sixty-second minute. Davies indeed had the opportunity to snatch an equaliser for Wales on not one but two occasions, but wasted them both as Ireland held out to secure a victory amid the terrible playing conditions.

Not the most memorable of debuts, or indeed ninety minutes for George Best, but having more or less just set foot on the footballing ladder it was something of an achievement for one so young to break into the international set-up after so few first team appearances.

Wales: Sprake (Leeds United), R. Evans (Swansea Town), G. Williams (West Bromwich Albion), Johnson (Swansea Town), England (Blackburn Rovers), Hole (Cardiff City), B. Jones (Swansea Town), Moore (Manchester United), Davies (Norwich City), Godfrey (Preston North End), C. Jones (Tottenhamd Hotspur)

Scorers: Godfrey, Davies.

Northern Ireland: Jennings (Watford), Magill (Arsenal), Elder (Burnley), Harvey (Sunderland), Neil (Arsenal), McCullough (Arsenal), Best (Manchester United), Crossan (Sunderland), Wilson (Falkirk), McLaughlin (Swansea Town), Braithwaite (Middlesbrough)

Scorers: McLaughlin, Wilson, Harvey

Attendance: 10,434.

Swindon Town Youth vs United Youth

27 April 1964/30 April 1965

Few youngsters, unless you play for Manchester United that is, can go from first division and FA Cup fixtures to the international stage and then back down to FA Youth Cup level in a matter of weeks, but that is the rollercoaster season that George experienced as he began what was to be a career of similar high's and low's.

There had been audible complaints when Matt Busby fielded Duncan Edwards in similar circumstances a decade before, but Swindon Town were content to accept the challenge of facing the United Youth side, George and all, without the hint of objection. Neither was there any hint of inferiority within the Swindon ranks in having to face the five times FA Youth Cup winners.

Some 17,000 flocked to the County Ground for the first-leg of the final in anticipation of a memorable evening's entertainment, or were the majority there to lay claim to having seen George Best play in the flesh in the fledgling days of his Manchester United career? It mattered little as they were indeed treated to a thrilling ninety minutes, reported in one source as being 'hard, fast, [with] a fair showing of team work and some remarkable individual performances.' The latter without any shadow of doubt coming from the visitors who had the likes of David Sadler, Willie Anderson as well as George within their ranks, all of whom could admit to having already played at first division level, the boy from Belfast being something of a veteran compared to his teammates.

But despite that experience, it was the home side who took the lead in the thirty-second minute through Don Rogers, upon whom Swindon relied more than United did George. A cross-field ball from Walker was collected by Rogers who immediately raced past three united defenders before hammering the ball past Rimmer from an acute angle.

If some of those on the packed terracing were there only to see George then they were certainly not disappointed as, despite showing remarkable skills, he came close to scoring on three occasions on either side of the interval. Hicks in the Swindon goal being equal to all three, pulling off a trio of outstanding saves. Sadler and Kinsey both had opportunities to open United's account but again Hicks kept them out while, at the opposite end, Rogers blotted his copybook in the fifty-second minute when he missed a golden opportunity to put Swindon two in front, shooting wide when it looked easier to score. It was a miss that he was to regret.

George, who had come close to scoring early on with a header that Hicks did well to save, was 'the most polished player on the pitch' according to Alan Williams in the *Daily Express*, and it was his goal that was to the leave the outcome of this final dangling on a string. Taking a pass from McBride, George let fly with a right footed shot and although the hero of the hour, Tony Hicks, managed to get a hand to it, he could do little else in preventing the ball from entering the net.

So, at 1-1 it was everything to play for, with the Swindon Town camp hoping that the possibility of playing four games in six days as being just a little too much for even George, keeping their fingers crossed that the man (boy?) who was involved in every dangerous United move would perhaps be missing for the second-leg. But their luck was out, as having played against Nottingham Forest on the 25th, in the first-leg of the Youth Cup Final on the 27th and for Northern Ireland two days later, George did pull on the red Number Eight shirt and run out with his teenage friends at Old Trafford for the second-leg against Swindon on the 30th and if he was feeling tired, he certainly did not show it.

Swindon adapted their tactics accordingly, playing with an extra defender, in the hope that if they could keep George at bay and under control there was always the chance of a breakaway goal and the possibility of springing a surprise on the much fancied United. George had flown into Manchester on the morning of the game and ran around Old Trafford as though he had simply arrived back following a relaxing two weeks on holiday, causing even more problems for Swindon than he had done in the previous ninety minutes.

United looked nervous in the opening exchanges and for the opening half hour, the game could easily have swung either way but gradually the experience of the United lads, along with the individual brilliance of George, began to shine through. 'Rarely this season, in any class of football have I seen a finer example of genuine teamwork. I can pay United no higher tribute than that" purred Eric Todd in his rather lengthy match report for a youth team fixture in the *Guardian*.

Heavy rain had made playing conditions far from ideal but it made little difference to United once they got into full swing, they almost found themselves a goal behind as early as the first minute when Peapell shot wide following a corner. Eleven minutes later United thought they had made the breakthrough with Kinsey blasting the ball home but, after having given the goal, the referee changed his mind upon noticing the linesman's raised flag.

Subdued pressure from the visitors kept United's defence on their toes for fifteen minutes, Rimmer doing well to keep out Rogers, but having weathered the storm and with only three minutes remaining until the interval it looked as though George was about to open the scoring as he dribbled round the stranded Hicks but, to the surprise of everyone present, he put the ball wide of the goal. A minute later however, he made amends for his uncharacteristic miss by setting up Sadler who hit a fierce shot on the turn to give United the advantage.

Duff had to kick clear after Rimmer failed to hold a shot from Plumb as the second half got underway then the United 'keeper did well to save from Walker as Swindon pushed for an equaliser but, they were soon to find the game and the trophy slipping away from them as Sadler notched his second in the fiftieth minute.

Swindon did pull a goal back in the 67th minute through Walker, following a Rogers free-kick but, any thoughts of a comeback lasted only three minutes when George once again became the provider, teaming up with Anderson before teeing up Sadler for his hat-trick.

Peapell was booked for a foul on George probably more out of frustration than anything but, it mattered little and ten minutes from time the result was put beyond all doubt when Aston claimed a fourth.

At the final whistle an unsuspecting observer would have thought that United had won the Football League, not the FA Youth Cup, as thousands of supporters invaded the pitch caught up in the spectacle that they had just enjoyed.

United: Rimmer, Duff, Noble, McBride, Farrar, Fitzpatrick, Anderson, Best, Sadler, Kinsey, Aston.

Scorer: First leg: Best.
   Second leg: Sadler (3), Aston.

Swindon Town: Hicks, Foscolo, Ling, Griffin, Brown, Prosser, Rogers, Peapell, Plumb, Tabor Walker.

Scorer: First leg: Rogers
    Second leg: Walker

Attendance: First leg: 17,000
    Second leg: 25,563

Chelsea vs United

30 September 1964

For many the step up from being nothing more than an unfamiliar face in the reserve/youth team set up to suddenly finding yourself thrust into the first team spotlight and unable to walk unnoticed through the crowds swarming around the turnstiles and main entrances to grounds on a Saturday afternoon never materialises or, if it does, it can be something of a long drawn-out process. While for others it can only be a fleeting moment, a rare opportunity to relate to others at a much later date: that you once graced the first division stage.

For George however, there was never any doubt in the minds of those who watched him progressing through the United junior ranks that he was a youngster who would surely emerge as a first team regular and not look out of place alongside the already established all-international cast that was Matt Busby's Manchester United.

Having established himself in the United first team during the season of 1963/64 by making twenty-six appearances and scoring six goals – those first division appearances being more or less evenly split between the Number Seven and Number Eleven shirt – George kicked off the 1964/65 campaign on the United left wing in a destructive forward line that also included John Connelly wearing Number Seven, Bobby Charlton at Eight, David Herd at Nine and Denis Law at Ten. A front five of potential goalscorers that few, if any, could match. With such a talented quintet there could be a considerable battle to capture the headlines in the nation's press, if they were so concerned, but it was slowly becoming obvious that one individual was, by his own natural ability (at this moment in time at least), going to out-do the rest.

For Manchester United, the 1964–65 season had got off to something of a poor start, drawing three, losing two and winning only one of the opening half dozen fixtures, leaving them uncomfortable in the bottom half of the table. Then suddenly, as if something somewhere clicked, there was a run of fourteen games unbeaten, all victories except for a goal-less draw at Burnley. George made his contribution to this sudden upsurge in fortune, but it was Denis Law whose name was the most regular to be found on the score sheet, and indeed the headlines.

However, at the end of September the trip to the bright lights of London saw the spotlight fall on the United Number Eleven, a number that was beginning to haunt countless defenders as that was all they saw, the two white number ones on the back of the red shirt as it ghosted past them scurrying down the touchline and heading towards goal.

On the morning of 30 September Chelsea stood atop the first division seventeen points from their ten games, United were in fourth, four points behind. By 9:45 p.m. that Wednesday evening the challengers were two points closer thanks to the performance of one individual. 'Brilliant Best Breaks Chelsea Grip after McCreadie Slip Up', 'Star Best Tops Law' and 'Chelsea manager Tommy Docherty says: "Fantastic – That's Super Best"' were only three of the headlines that summed up those ninety-minutes in south London. 'Young George Best was the "thing" of

Stamford Bridge last night.' wrote Ken Jones in the *Mirror*, continuing with, 'At the end of the match the crowd stood and acclaimed him. They gave him their hearts because he had won them with every bewitching swerve, every flick of his magic feet. The nineteen-year-old Best, Manchester United outside-left and a bundle of brilliance, amazed the fans as much as he bewildered Chelsea's defence. Ken Shellito, England international back who played Best calmly despite the torture, raced to him at the end to acclaim his skill.'

Unbeaten Chelsea, already being tipped as championship favourites by some were found wanting and although having played some good football in the games prior to this particular fixture, did not have the individual brilliance that their visitors could muster neither did they have the composure or the experience to combat and stifle the threat and the genius that United presented.

Stamford Bridge was filled to overflowing and, within thirty seconds, the home side showed why they were sitting above the rest at the top of the first division as Hollins forced Pat Dunne into producing a notable save, leaping high towards his post to grasp the ball in mid-air. Two minutes later Venables out foxed Charlton to set up Tambling with another effort that came close to opening the scoring.

Play quickly swung to the opposite end and from a Herd centre, amid a flurry of activity around the Chelsea goal, the ball crossed the line only to see the 'goal' disallowed for off-side against Connelly. The game was still to pass the five minute mark.

The opening half hour continued to produce plenty of action but no goals, although opportunities and half chances did materialise. A Law header tested Bonetti, as did a rasping shot on the run. Murray was forced to the ground with a strong Crerand tackle after tricking his way past Charlton and Tony Dunne, while Pat Dunne once again rescued United with a superb save from Houseman.

In those opening exchanges it was a game that could have swung either way then, in the thirty-second minute, the deadlock was finally broken. As United pressed forward Eddie McCreadie, Chelsea's Scottish international full-back, attempted a back-pass but stubbed his toe on the Stamford Bridge turf as he did so and up popped George, quickly slipping the ball past Bonetti before anyone could react. The blue-shirted defender slumping to his knees as the United players celebrated.

George swung over a corner kick from which Charlton rattled the Chelsea crossbar, while Chelsea pressed forward searching for the equaliser. Murray fired into the side netting, then Foulkes cleared practically off the line. Charlton brought Bonetti to his knees, as did George and as half-time approached it was United who looked the stronger of the two sides, although the game was far from over.

David Herd had the opportunity to secure United's advantage in the 69th minute latching onto a loose ball after Bonetti failed to hold a rasping drive from Crerand but the United Number Nine, with the goal at his mercy, ballooned the ball high over the bar, much to his embarrassment.

United's second goal eventually materialised in the 73rd minute when George sent a tantalising high ball into the Chelsea penalty area. Bonetti simply palmed the ball into the air, allowing Law to leap like a salmon and headed into the unattended Chelsea net. The contribution by George to United's success was immense, constantly bewildering the Chelsea defence with an array of bewitching dribbles. In the *Sun* Peter Lorenzo wrote: 'Not for seasons have I thrilled to such a spectacular display. And this when Denis Law, in my view Britain's number one, was on the same field.'

At full-time it wasn't just Shellito who wanted to congratulate George on a notable performance, as both John Hollins and Barry Bridges made a bee line for the unassuming United Number Eleven as he walked head down off the Stamford Bridge pitch.

Back with the report of Ken Jones, the *Mirror* scribe penned: 'It was over. But who can forget it? Best's devastating application of touchline skill brought memories of young Stan Matthews and Garrincha. It topped a quality performance by United.'

Matthews, they said, kept his top performances for the London audiences whereas George was to care little where the venue was, whether large or small, he would delight the crowds at will.

Chelsea: Bonetti, Shellito, McCreadie, Hollins, Hinton, R. Harris, Murray, Tambling, Bridges, Venables, Houseman.

United: P. Dunne, Brennan, T. Dunne, Crerand, Foulkes, Stiles, Connelly, Charlton, Herd, Law, Best.

Scorers: Law, Best

Attendance: 60,769

Some spoke of George 'commanding an almost hypnotic influence' over the near 70,000 Stamford Bridge crowd and on the eve of his third international appearance he was heralded as 'Northern Ireland's greatest gift to soccer since the legendary Peter Doherty', the article going on to say, 'In appearance and physique (5 foot 8 inches, 9st 11lb) this frail looking lad looks more suited to be a pop singer than a professional sportsman. Beneath the fragile exterior lies a streak of steel.'

The experts go into rapture about him. Jimmy Murphy, United's assistant manager said: 'Best ranks alongside Duncan Edwards as the finest player for his age I have ever seen.' Johhny Aston, ex-United and England full-back, says, 'I played with Tom Finney at the same age. Tom wasn't as good as Best is today.' Gigi Peronace, Italy's world-travelled talent scout said, 'He is the finest young winger in Europe. In a year he will be the finest in the world.'

Borussia Dortmund vs United

11 November 1964

Europe wasn't exactly an obsession with Matt Busby, neither did it hang around his neck like an albatross. It was simply a dream, albeit an unfulfilled one, but the belief was there that one day he would guide a Manchester United team to success in Europe. Hopefully it would be in the prestige European Cup but, if not, a victory in either the European Cup Winners Cup or the Inter Cities Fairs Cup would not be shunned upon.

The masterful Spaniards of Real Madrid had taught United something of a lesson in that inaugural campaign of 1956/57 after Busby's team had sent shockwaves across the continent with those remarkable victories at the Maine Road, home of neighbours Manchester City, against Anderlecht 10-0, and that memorable 3-0 defeat of Athletic Bilbao overturning the 5-3 first-leg defeat in Spain.

In the 1957/58 tournament United were on track to meet Real Madrid once again but, this time in a one-off final. However, the Munich air disaster brought an end to those hopes and dreams with United's rather inexperienced and somewhat makeshift side, thus losing 5-2 on aggregate to AC Milan in the semi-final.

United returned to the European scene in season 1963/64 following their 3-1 FA Cup success over Leicester City at Wembley and, having disposed of the current holders first division stable mates Tottenham Hotspur with a 4-3 aggregate win in round two of the European Cup Winners Cup, it looked as though a European trophy was at last within Matt Busby's grasp. More so following the 4-1 quarter-final first-leg victory over Sporting Lisbon. However, it was not to be as the Portuguese trounced United 5-0 in the second-leg.

The Inter-Cities Fairs Cup was perhaps the lesser of the three European competitions but, it was played in the same competitive spirit as its more glamourous relations despite the opposition not being exactly stand-out names in continental football. In the first round of the 1964/65 competition United were drawn against the Swedish side Djurgardens IF in the away first-leg 1-1, but making no mistake with a 6-1 victory at Old Trafford.

In that second-leg tie, George had 'taunted and tormented' the Djurgardens right-back Jan Karlsson throughout the game, so much so that he Swede simply got fed up with it all and brought George down to concede a penalty in the 67th minute. George was to rub more salt in the wounds with five minutes remaining when he scored United's sixth of the night and hammered the ball home from 18 yards.

When the draw was made for round two United were paired with a familiar opponent in the form of Borussia Dortmund, having met them previously in the first round of the 1956/57 European Cup. On that occasion United won by the odd goal in five at Maine Road, before holding out for a 0-0 draw in Germany. This latest meeting was to turn out rather differently.

Prior to the first-leg in Germany United had scored fourteen goals in four games, seven of those coming against a hapless Aston Villa at Old Trafford. Dortmund were well warned as to what to expect although, to be fair, Matt Busby's side, although confident, could not approach the game in a relaxed fashion as only a fortnight previously the Germans, like United, had sat at the top of their League table. And, in all honesty, the visitors were far from relaxed in the opening minutes looking somewhat nervous with misplaced passes, coupled with some neat football from the home side.

United however, were soon to settle down proving to be a completely different class to Dortmund with one major telling difference: George, the name that jumped out of every newspaper report as the press waxed lyrically over United's devastating 6-1 victory. 'They're Back – Busby Men Take Europe by Storm' shouted the *Mirror*, 'Fantastic United' proclaimed the *Express* and others followed suit with the likes of 'Triumph of Manchester United'. But there was another: 'The Best Way to Conquer Europe', but this did not refer to Matt Busby's tactics on the night, nor the football that United played in order secure such an emphatic scoreline. It was reference to an individual who led Dortmund a merry dance while entertaining the crowd, among whom were a number of British servicemen, with his wide array of footballing skills. Underneath the report read,

There were fantastic scenes at the Red Earth Stadium here tonight when hundreds of spectators left their seats five minutes before the end of this magnificent display by Manchester United.

Spearheaded by a group of fifty RAF servicemen from Cologne, 80 miles away, proudly brandishing a massive Union Jack, they surrounded the touch-line waiting to crowd the pitch and acclaim the new masters of Europe.

Hundreds of them grappled for the honour of carrying that slim wisp of an Irish lad George Best shoulder-high from the field after an out-of-this-world display of individual brilliance.

His bewildering footwork, astute football brain and the manner in which he utterly destroyed this Borussia defence almost single handed made him a hero.

There were similar plaudits in all the other reports: 'What a wonderful night for Manchester United. What a wonderful night of triumph for the magical teenager George Best' and 'The youthful Best delighted even the Germans in the 25,000 crowd with his brilliant footwork' were only two.

After an uncertain opening five minutes United settled down, Stiles pushing forward to join in the attacks, Charlton going close on two occasions, before Herd opened the scoring in the 12th minute. A forceful shot from Charlton was blocked by a German defender but, the awkward spinning ball was brought under control by Law who then slipped it to Herd, his volleyed shot going underneath the body of the diving goalkeeper.

It was a goal that instilled confidence into the United side, allowing the likes of Charlton, Law and George to beat defenders at ease. But despite enjoying the bulk of the possession, there was to be only one more goal before the interval. Herd snatched the ball from the feet of left-half Sturm before sending Charlton away, his forceful run towards the Dortmund goal finishing with a thunderous drive that crashed off the underside of the bar before crossing the goal line.

Five minutes into the second half it was 3-0. Having wormed his way through the German defence George calmly placed the ball past Wessel, prompting two Dortmund supporters to turn to the press box and in broken English say, 'Best is best.' A minute later a mistimed tackle inside the United penalty area by Crerand on Kurrat in the 52nd minute saw the lead reduced when the up-ended Kurrat beat Pat Dunne from the spot. There was little hope of Dortmund getting back into the game as George constantly toyed with them, holding them under a spell, working his way through their defence time and again.

With United comfortable in their lead the game lost some of its sparkle as it progressed but there were still more goals to come. With fifteen minutes remaining George, out on the left, saw the raised arm of Denis Law and measured his cross perfectly for the blond-headed Scot to jump and nod home for Number Four. Three minutes later it was 5-1, Law sprinting down the right and beating two defenders before cutting the ball back to Charlton who, with the defence in disarray, skipped past another tackle before hammering a right-footed shot past a helpless 'keeper.

George rattled the crossbar and then six minutes from time passed to Charlton who scored his third of the night and United's sixth with a shot into the roof of the net, rounding off a performance considered by Frank McGhee in the *Daily Mirror* as one that 'no other Manchester United team has ever topped.'

While the media scribbled furiously as regards to George's contribution to victory in Germany, the player himself was his usual modest self. Terence Elliott of the *Daily Express* managed to get a few words with him before he caught a flight from Dusseldorf to Switzerland to meet up with his Northern Ireland teammates prior to a World Cup preliminary round tie. The man of the moment was to say: 'I didn't even hear the crowd most of the time and, to me, it was just a game of football that I really enjoyed.'

In the Old Trafford second-leg the German's fared slightly better, conceding only four without reply with George again a thorn in their side and following the demolition job on Dortmund, many felt that it was a forgone conclusion that United would now go on and win the competition.

Drawn against Everton in round three they drew 1-1 at Old Trafford but, turned the tie around at Goodison Park winning 2-1. The quarter-final first-leg tie took United to Strasbourg where they hit five without reply but, amid a carnival atmosphere second-leg when United were presented with the League championship trophy and Denis Law with his European Footballer of the Year award, the rather dismal 34,188 crowd failed to see any goals.

It was the Hungarians of Ferencváros who now stood between United and a place in the final. There was to be no goal fest at Old Trafford, or indeed in Hungary, with United taking only a one goal advantage into the second-leg following a narrow 3-2 win. With the return leg ending 1-0 to the home side a third match was called for to determine who would earn a place in the final and, with Matt Busby losing the toss of a coin, it was back to Hungary for that decisive ninety minutes.

With United trailing 2-1 George dribbled past six Hungarians, one of them twice, but was to fall over the 'keeper as the ball trickled towards the empty goal, allowing a defender to step in and clear. Shortly afterwards Herd missed another easy chance and the opportunity was gone. Ferencváros, the eventual cup winners, were through.

Borussia Dortmund: Wessel, Cyliax, Redder, Kurrat, Paul, Sturn, Yoash, Brungs, Beyer, Konietzka, Emmerich.

Scorer: Kurrat

United: P. Dunne, Brennan, T. Dunne, Crerand, Foulkes, Stiles, Connelly, Charlton, Herd, Law, Best.

Scorers: Charlton (3), Herd, Law, Best.

Attendance: 25,000

United vs Burnley

20 February 1965

The FA Cup has always conjured up memorable moments. A white horse trotting, or at least attempting to, across a Wembley turf smothered in supporters, Stanley Matthews inspiring Blackpool to victory in 1953 and of course Manchester United, the first of Busby's three great sides gaining the upper hand against that same Blackpool side in 1948, a game still regarded as one of the best final's played under the twin towers.

20 February 1965, was nothing more than the day of the fifth round ties, with two victories required by any team aspiring to reach the final, which was then regarded a momentous occasion in any players career. On this particular Saturday afternoon, it wasn't so much the outcome of the Lancastrian 'derby' encounter that would be remembered but a snapshot by a pitch encroaching photographer that would be used time and time again to portray the enigmatic footballer that was George Best. Mention the game and you would little more than a blank stare but mention the photograph and you would get instant recognition from those familiar with the player and the period.

Perhaps that last statement reads wrongly and I should have written about two photographs, not one, as United's first goal in the 2-1 victory over Burnley also epitomises one of football and Manchester United greats in Denis Law. When you read about the goal you will know the one I mean.

Burnley had held their hosts to a 0-0 draw at Turf Moor back in early October and lost by the odd goal in five at Old Trafford the previously Saturday, but in the anything-could-happen FA Cup it was certainly not odds on that United would find a place in the quarter-finals.

United began the game strongly but Burnley were prepared for the onslaught ensuring that Lochhead, Bellamy and Harris augmented their defence, ensuring that there was no clear route to goal for the advancing red shirts. Whether they were intent on holding United to a draw and taking them back to Turf Moor for a replay, was more than a distinct possibility in those opening minutes, but it was a considered option that was soon to be forgotten about when the visitors rather surprisingly took the lead.

With only seventeen minutes gone, Bellamy and Smith were involved in taking a short corner, over the ball came into the United penalty area where it struck Foulkes on the head. Pat Dunne in the United goal was caught unawares but managed to divert the ball onto the crossbar, only to see it rebound out to Lochhead who nodded it into the unguarded net.

Stiles found his way into the referee's notebook following fouls on Irvine and Lochhead, while Law had also been spoken to strongly by the referee, both incidents restricting their contribution somewhat in terms of physical effort. United's overall contribution had already been relatively restricted with a Bill Foulkes shot from 25 yards in the 51st minute, their only worthy attempt on goal up until that point.

There were audible groans from around the stadium when Lochhead once again had the ball in the net but thankfully on this occasion an infringement by Irvine saw it disallowed, although the groans from those same individuals were again heard when a mix up in the Burnley penalty area saw the ball sneak towards the goal-line, Blacklaw only managing to claw the as it was about to cross the line.

Best was giving the Burnley defence some testing moments but his ball control could not be converted into scoring opportunities by either him or his teammates. One excellent opportunity going amiss as he delayed shooting with the word 'goal' already on everyone's lips.

As the game progressed it was beginning to look as though it was going to be 'third time lucky' for Burnley, their solitary goal enough to ensure their passage into the sixth round of the competition. For eighty-five minutes they had frustrated their hosts, forcing many to abandon their seats and places on the terracing, disappointed with their afternoon's entertainment. It was a grave error on their part.

Let Hugh McIlvanney take up the story with his report in the *Observer*:

> Best, United's young Irish outside-left, had apparently developed minor difficulties with his left boot. He had been carrying it in a hand for some seconds before he used the stockinged foot to hit over a cross from the right wing.
>
> Until then, Burnley's massed defence had been surviving almost comfortably. Suddenly they were in a crisis. From Best's cross the ball had bounced threatingly around the Burnley goal and, as a shot was beaten out, it spun high in Law's direction but apparently out of his reach.

But Law was no ordinary footballer. He was the 'King' of those massed in front of him on the Stretford End and his adoring public stood open mouthed as suddenly the blond-headed Scot launched himself into mid-air like some circus acrobat and as if suspended by an invisible thread above the 6-yard line, sending his over-head kick high into the roof of the net past Blacklaw's outstretched right arm. A replay at Burnley in mid-week was now on everyone's thoughts but they, like those now heading home by foot or on public transport, were wrong.

Best, still with one boot grasped in his hand, picked out Crerand with a cross from his booted foot and from the left wing and the Scot, not renowned for his scoring, drove the ball towards goal from all of 30 yards, deceiving Blacklaw by bouncing in front of him and into the back of the net. Despite the brilliance of Law's late equaliser, the *Observer* ignored the Scot and opted for 'Bootless Best's Rescue' as their headline to precede McIlvanney's match report.

The bootless winger caused much debate following his extraordinary performance, with an article by Howard Booth stating that George should not have been allowed to play with only one boot on. Match referee George McCabe said of the matter:

> The first thing I noticed was Best bending down on one knee as if to replace the boot. I assumed that was what he would do and my attention immediately went back to the game which was in a very tense state. It was sometime later when I noticed that Best was carrying the boot. I looked at my watch and it was nearly full-time. Looking back I suppose I should have ordered him to put the boot back on but the game was poised in such a state that I could not relax for one second.

Booth went on to quote the Association Football Law 4, which degreed that 'football boots must be worn at all times and the referee should not allow one or a few players to play without wearing football boots when all the other players do wear them.' Three independent referee's all said that they would not have allowed George to continue without his boot on. As one said, 'Suppose United had been defending and Best, in his own area, had stopped a shot with the boot he was carrying? What's the answer to that?'

United: P. Dunne, Brennan, T. Dunne, Crerand, Foulkes, Stiles, Connelly, Charlton, Herd, Law, Best.

Scorers: Law, Best.

Burnley: Blacklaw, Smith, Elder, O'Neill, Talbot, Miller, Bellamy, Lochhead, Irvine, Harris, Latcham

Scorer: Lochhead

Attendance: 54,000

Sunderland vs United

11 December 1965

Season 1964/65 saw Manchester United claim the first division title for the first time since 1956/57, with dreams of a League and Cup double only thwarted by Leeds United by a solitary goal in semi-final replay. The re-building of the side since the Munich air disaster had been completed and it now ranked alongside that fabled side and that of Busby's first post-war trophy winning season, but it was now time to move onto that other level, achieving even more success on both the domestic and European front.

In the League, there was once again an indifferent start with four victories and four defeats, in the opening dozen fixtures. But, in something of a mirror image of the previous season, results suddenly changed for the better with a ten match unbeaten run, which was to see George in breath taking form as November moved into December. The Irishman scoring six goals over the course of five games.

United hit championship form with a 5-0 hammering of Leicester City at Filbert Street, where George began his formidable run, before notching a couple in the 3-1 victory against Sheffield United at Old Trafford. There was a solitary goal in the 3-0 home win over Everton, but it was against Sunderland at Roker Park that George was to really capture the headlines in a devastating display.

Being faced with the likes of Bobby Charlton and Denis Law, never mind George Best being thrown into the equation, was often the call for drastic measures to be taken and, reportedly, Sunderland had spent the majority of the previous few days working on various tactics and game plans in order to combat the threat posed by their more illustrious visitors. Unfortunately those plans were thrown into complete disarray after only three minutes when their right winger Hellawell was forced to go off with an ankle injury but, it was a move that seemed to boost their resilience, forcing United to search deep in order to secure victory.

Surprisingly, it was the ten men of Sunderland who, while still debating about bringing on a substitute, took the lead in the 5th minute. Charlton made a meal of a bouncing ball, it broke towards Martin and the Scot took a couple of steps before unleashing a shot from 25 yards out which flew past the impotent Dunne and into the roof of the net.

Three minutes later Sunderland were back to full strength but somewhat against the run of play, United were soon to draw level. Stiles directed a long low pass towards the Sunderland penalty area and, before anyone could react, George was onto it in a flash powering the ball past a helpless McLaughlan from all of 20 yards.

With United having found their feet following that 15th minute equaliser, play began to flow from end to end and in the 35th minute the Sunderland defence was once again caught out. Charlton did all the running, allowing George to score from close in.

To say that George was leading Sunderland something of a merry dance is an understatement as the first half saw him operating mainly on the right while the second saw him mainly on the opposite flank. In between times he could be found making an impromptu appearance in the centre-forward position. Like the elusive Pimpernel the Sunderland defenders chased him all over the pitch but to little avail much to the satisfaction of Ashurst, the man deployed in marking, as it meant he wasn't to endure facing the mop-headed Irishman for the whole ninety minutes.

As George continued to wreak havoc across the Roker Park pitch the outcome of the match was soon to be decided as the hour mark approached. A rather clumsy challenge by Foulkes on Moore saw the Sunderland man carried off, once again reducing the home side to ten men. On this occasion it was for good and then, five minutes later, a Denis Law cross was flicked on by Crerand towards Herd and the United centre-forward had the simple job of tapping it over the line for United's third.

It was a goal that for many sides would have seen the raising of the white flag but Sunderland to their credit simply rolled up their sleeves and continued to press the United defence and were rewarded for their persistence with a second goal, Martin heading past Dunne for his second of the afternoon. As much as many would have seen as deserved, an equaliser failed to materialise.

According to reports, from a time when match-winning performances from opponents were greeted with much acclaim rather than abuse, the Roker park crowd were appreciative of George's contribution to the ninety minutes. That same report carried the following: 'Even with eighteen other internationals on view – and thirteen of them cost £536,000 in transfer fees – nobody reached Best's magnificence.' Many of the headlines told much of the same: 'United take Cue from Best', 'Sunderland Fall to Lively Best' and, the most emphatic: 'Best Runs Riot'.

Sunderland: McLaughlan, Irwin, Ashurst, Harvey, Hurley, Baxter, Hellawell, G. Herd, Moore, Martin, Mullhall. Substitute: Elliott for Hellawell.

Scorer: Martin (2).

United: P. Dunne, T. Dunne, Cantwell, Crerand, Foulkes, Stiles, Best, Law, Charlton, D. Herd, Connelly. Substitute: Aston.

Scorers: Best (2), Herd.

Attendance: 37, 417

18

Benfica vs United

9 March 1966

Having avoided relegation by a hairs breath in 1962/63, it was a complete turnaround to end the 1963/64 campaign as runners up to Liverpool. Twelve months later they were to go one better; clinching the championship for the first time in eight years. A notable feat really, considering the decimation of the team at Munich and the re-building that had been necessary. The triumph was perhaps more of a testimony to the work done by Jimmy Murphy in those dark days in the early months of 1958.

Unlike when the championship success of 1956 brought the invitation through the Old Trafford letter box inviting Matt Busby's team to take part in the European Cup produced much debate and divided loyalties and indeed a request to refuse the invitation outright, the competition was now well established and an integral part of the first division champion's fixture list.

So it was a buoyant Manchester United who gratefully embraced the European Cup once again. The European Cup Winners Cup and pre-season friendlies against top European sides were all very well but the European Cup was the icing on the cake and the trophy which drove Matt Busby on during those bleak times in 1958.

By the time the opening European Cup preliminary round tie to Helsinki came round United were languishing in thirteenth place, four points behind leaders Burnley and against the Finnish amateurs. United struggled despite Herd opening the scoring after only thirty seconds. Connelly added a second fifteen minutes later, but a mistake by Gaskell let the home side back into the game ten minutes before the interval, but Law was to restore the two goal advantage three minutes later. Twenty minutes after the break Helsinki might have scored thrice, but it was not until thirteen minutes from time that they finally broke down the United defence for a second goal which kept the tie alive.

In the Old Trafford second-leg, coming on the back of an uninspiring 4-2 defeat by Arsenal, United offered their visitors little in the way of hospitality other than food and drink at the after match dinner, securing their place in the first round proper with an emphatic 6-0 victory.

By the time United travelled to Germany to face Vorwaerts they had climbed to seventh, although still remaining five points behind early leaders Liverpool. In Berlin, a game played on a bone-hard pitch and in freezing conditions, United acquitted themselves well and a superb goal from Denis Law and another from John Connelly gave them a two goal cushion to take into the Old Trafford home leg. Here the East German's showed little to convince anyone that they were about to cause an upset and be a threat to United's European ambitions. Something that was clearly confirmed by David Herd's two first-half goals.

United took their foot off the pedal with the four-goal aggregate advantage and with eight minutes remaining the German's pulled a goal back. As slow hand-claps echoed around the stadium, United re-awoke and with a minute remaining, Herd claimed his hat-trick to give United a 3-1 victory.

There was now something of a break until the first-leg of the quarter-finals where United found themselves given the rather daunting task of facing the Portuguese side Benfica. In the Old Trafford first-leg, with the capacity crowd still settling down, United should have taken the lead following a foul on George. The ball was floated the ball into the Benfica penalty area and, amid a crowd of players, Herd's header beat the 'keeper but bounced off the post and was eventually cleared to safety. At the opposite end, amid a rather frantic pace, the counter attacking of the visitors almost saw them snatch the early advantage as Eusebio tested Gregg from all off 35 yards. Law shot into the side netting and then stumbled through on goal while Costa Pereira in the visitors goal did well to keep out Herd and Charlton, the former on two separate occasions.

But after half an hour it was Benfica who silenced the Old Trafford crowd by taking the lead. A Eusebio shot was deflected for a corner and, taking the kick himself, he floated the ball into the area where Jose Augusto rose to head past Gregg.

Undeterred by this set back United immediately set off in search of the equaliser and a Connelly pass saw a flick from Law going inches wide of the post. Seven minutes later the ball did go past the correct side of the post when Herd pounced on a pass engineered by George and Law, before whipping it past a surprised goalkeeper.

As half-time beckoned, United gained the advantage. Charlton gathered a weak clearance following a corner from George and curled the ball over towards the 6 yard area where Law brought it down with one foot before scoring with the other.

In the second half United continued to put pressure on the aging Benfica defence and on the hour they finally managed to increase their lead. Connelly was impeded by Germano and from Cantwell's free-kick Foulkes, playing in his twenty-first European tie, dived forward through a mass of red Benfica shirts to head home.

A two goal advantage should have been United's, but they let their guard slip in the 70th minute, when Torres was on hand to knee the ball over the line after Gregg had fumbled. The United 'keeper redeemed himself somewhat as the minutes ticked away when he tipped a 35 yard shot from Eusebio over the bar, with another effort from the same player flashing past the post as the visitors sought an equaliser.

United hung on to their slender one-goal advantage, something that many felt would not be enough to see them progress in the competition, as the Portuguese side were unbeaten in a European tie at the Estadio da Luz (Stadium of Light). Indeed none had even managed a draw, such was the task in front of United as they flew out from Manchester airport.

Busby and his troops were prepared for a daunting night in Lisbon, but they had been instructed to 'keep cool and attack', responding to their manager's request in emphatic fashion, stunning the 75,000 raucous Portuguese supporters into astonished silence with a display equal to any in the competition's history. United catching their host's cold, hitting them with three goals in quick succession in an unforgettable fourteen minute spell.

With only seven minutes gone, Pinto fouled Charlton out on the left wing and from Dunne's curling free-kick into the Benfica goalmouth, George nipped past Germano to head home as the 'keeper attempted to get his fingertips to the ball. Four minutes later George once again had the ball in the net having taken a pass from Charlton, but a linesman's flag denied him a second.

A second goal did come in the 12th minute, this time with no hint of offside. A long clearance was headed by Herd into George's path and taking the ball in his stride, he swerved between two defenders before placing an angled shot past the helpless Pereira.

Three minutes later, Law crossed from the left and in a race for the ball between the now goal-hungry George and Connelly, it was the latter who made it fractionally before his teammate going on to beat Pereira for United's third. As the frantic pace began to slow George had the chance of a hat-trick in the 28th minute, but his powerful shot went narrowly wide.

Only once in the opening twenty minutes did Benfica offer a hint that they had the ability on the night to gain any advantage over their guests as the United defence, well aware of the danger that Eusebio on his own could create, kept a tight grip of things at the back. Indeed, it wasn't until the 52nd minute that Benfica managed to break down that United defence, but even then it was an own goal that gained them a scrap of respectability, Shay Brennan lobbing the ball over the head of goalkeeper Harry Gregg.

With thirteen minutes remaining United scored again when Crerand, the mid-field creator, streamed into the Benfica penalty area before rocketing the ball past Pereira. 4-1 and Benfica were well and truly beaten, something that their supporters sensed, with many beginning an exodus from the vast area as United, not content to rest on their laurels, continued to press forward. There was an even greater surge towards the exits two minutes before time after Charlton added a fifth, dribbling past the now overly harassed Pereira with ease.

It had been a display of master-class brilliance, minutes of football that would be shown again and again in years to come – perhaps not in its entirety, but at least in the form of the five goals. It was proclaimed as 'United's greatest display in Europe' and few would argue, only that dramatic encounter against Bilbao with the 'Babes' at their prime could come close. But it was also the game that threw George onto a much bigger stage.

His name was now shouted, whispered and acclaimed at football grounds throughout the length and breadth of Britain, but it had been relatively unknown at the likes of the Bernabeu, the San Siro and of course Benfica's Stadium of Light. That was, until now. As George left the scene of this latest triumph a pitch invading Benfica supporter approached in search of a souvenir. An autograph was far from his mind, as he produced a knife and quickly cut off a lock of hair from the stunned man of the moment. Another supporter presented him with a budgerigar. Others were merely content with simply getting close enough to obtain his autograph.

In the *Daily Express* under the headline: 'George Best Baffles Benfica', Desmond Hackett wrote, '… and Best so bedevilled the muscular men of Benfica that finally the crowd were compelled to applaud his brilliance and his impudence.'

After the game, with the Portuguese newspaper 'La Bola' christening him 'Um Beatle', George admitted, 'We were lucky at the start, but they could not stop us from then on.' Going on to add, 'This was the most momentous match of my career and I can honestly say that I did not feel any nerves.'

Benfica: Costa Pereira, Cavem, Cruz, Coluna, Germano, Pinto, Augusto Silva, Eusebio, Torres, Jose Augusto, Simoes.

Scorer: Brennan (Own goal).

United: Gregg, Brennan, Dunne, Crerand, Foulkes, Stiles, Best, Law, Charlton, Herd, Connelly.

Scorers: Best (2), Charlton, Connelly, Crerand.

Attendance: 75,000

Manchester United were not totally reliant on George Best; there were ten other players making up the team and many would argue that the goals of Herd, Law and Charlton won more games than the individual brilliance of the merlinic Irishman. But having brushed aside Benfica many thought that the European Cup was at long last within United's grasp. But such hopes were severely dashed when George suffered a knee injury at Leicester City on 9 April, a matter of days before United were due to play Partizan Belgrade in the first-leg of the European Cup semi-final.

George travelled to Belgrade and, following a training session, Matt Busby told the waiting press, 'I know this is a calculated risk, but I feel I must take the chance. I am playing the lad because I feel we have a chance of making a bit of history by winning the European Cup and the FA Cup (they were due to play Everton in the semi-final ten days later), in one season.'

Risk it certainly was as George struggled through the majority of the match, wrenching his knee going up for a high ball and playing the final quarter of an hour as nothing more than a passenger as United lost 2-0. It was his final appearance of the season, a cartilage operation pencilled into his diary. United's dream was nothing more than that, as in the second-leg against Partizan there was little inspiration and a solitary goal was all that United could muster. In the FA Cup Everton went to Wembley on the back of a 1-0 victory. It was United's third consecutive defeat at this stage of the competition.

19

Chelsea vs United

5 November 1966

A 1-1 draw between United and Chelsea at Old Trafford in mid-October was perhaps the result most expected as United had yet to lose at home, while the visitors were unbeaten on their travels. It was a result that left United in sixth place, with fifteen points from their twelve games, four places below the Londoners and three points behind early first division leaders Stoke City.

By the time the return match appeared on the fixture list just under a month later Chelsea were leading the pack, four points ahead of United, who had a game in hand. It was still early days, but the meeting between the two sides at Stamford Bridge was already a crucial fixture in the chase for the championship.

Disregarding current form many would have put their money on a United victory or, perhaps if they were of a slightly more cautious nature, on a draw. Mainly due to the fact that, since the war, Chelsea had only managed to gain the upper hand against Matt Busby's side in eight of the previous thirty-nine fixtures. That total of successes was to remain the same following this latest encounter in south London.

Was there something about Stamford Bridge, or was it the London air, that inspired George and his United teammates? Or for this particular encounter on Bonfire Night, did George decide to incorporate his own brand of fireworks?

Experience was to be a telling factor in the outcome of this particular fixture as Albert Barham of *The Guardian* made his readers aware:

> Manchester United, with effortless grace and the majestic assurance born of wide experience, gave Chelsea a 3-1 spanking before the biggest crowd at Stamford Bridge this season. United contrived, enjoyed and benefited from superiority of numbers – in defence when need be, more often than not in midfield, and certainly always in attack. But that perhaps puts the case too baldly. It does not tell of the genius of Best.

'Genius' was now a word commonly linked with George, having quickly replaced others such as 'the boy from Belfast' and on a stage – a stage that every aspiring star wanted to tread – he treated the Stamford Bridge audience to a virtuoso performance.

Some said that United won this game by default but a look at their starting eleven reveals that there was no Denis Law, already the club's leading scorer with twelve goals from the same number of games. His place taken by a player more familiar in a Number Eleven shirt – John Aston. Pulling on the Number Eleven shirt must have seen some of Law's DNA rub off on his replacement, as the son of a famous father was to score twice in the 3-1 victory.

The opening exchanges had been something of a cat-and-mouse affair but three minutes before half-time United, inspired by Crerand, opened the scoring. The Scottish international wing-half moved down the right, ignoring the challenges from Chelsea defenders, before shooting for goal. Strangely the usually competent Bonetti allowed the ball to slip from his grasp and Aston was on hand to nudge the ball over the line.

It was never going to be the goal that would decide the outcome of this fixture, that was to come on the hour and it was a goal worthy of winning any game at any level. A goal that had even those men in the press box drooling.

'Best at his impish, irresistible best, managed a goal of stunning brilliance' wrote Bryon Butler in The *Daily Telegraph* following that second United goal. Perhaps words that Eddie McCreadie, the man given the task of marking George that afternoon, might well have agreed with. The Chelsea full-back's predicament was highlighted by Albert Barham in *The Guardian*:

McCreadie faced, not for the first time, the problem of how to contain Best. Does one really seek to up-end him as often as possible, as McCreadie tried on Saturday? Such a policy, when it fails, makes the back appear rather foolish, lying on the ground as the skimpy figure, black locks billowing, skips away to create more havoc.

Or does one stand-off, watchful and ready? McCreadie tried that too, and lost out. He stood, head thrust forward, glaring, poised to pounce. Best out-thought him, flicked the ball sideways with his left foot to Sadler, bounded forward, and was lost to McCreadie. Back came the precise pass and Best, denying himself the pleasure of a second to steady himself, though he had created time enough and space shot and beat Bonetti for the finest goal of the match

'The Best of Best' proclaimed Ken Jones in the *Sunday Mirror*, writing:

It was one of those moments that not even the tricks of memory can polish into something more marvellous. It was there to see, to savour, to enthuse over – the genius of George Best, Manchester United's Irish international.

For seconds that must have seemed an age to Chelsea full-back Eddie McCreadie he was still, his body keeled over at an incredible angle, his right foot poised like a wand over the ball. Then Best was away, sprinting for a return to the pass he had stabbed to the feet of David Sadler.

An incredible shot hit off the wrong foot, swept past a bewildered Peter Bonetti and a capacity crowd at Stamford Bridge were suddenly living lavishly with the greatness of it all. It was more than just a great goal. It was absolute proof that in the ultimate it is the magic of the individual that makes the game live.

In The *Sunday Telegraph* David Miller penned,

A few times a season, with luck, you see a truly great goal which has everyone on their feet in a thunderclap of noise – last season, Charlton's against Spurs and Greaves's in the return match. Today it was George Best with one in a thousand which, with an hour gone, finally drove home the realisation to the packed cosmopolitan crowd that here was a talent, collective and individual that Chelsea do not begin to possess, Osgood excepted.

From Hugh McIlvanney in the *Observer*:

It was the class of Best, Charlton and Crerand that was the heart of United's victory, and the other two would admit grudgingly that Best's was the most spectacular contribution.

He spilled his genius through the grey, sodden afternoon with the profligacy of a man who has come to regard the miraculous as the common currency of his game and crowned it all with a goal of unforgettable virtuosity. Perhaps Delilah could have done something about him. Certainly he seems beyond the powers of any defender in Britain.

Chelsea had no one to match the artistry of Pat Crerand, never mind that of George, his pin point passing a telling factor in the final outcome. Sadler too was much involved, while the experienced Foulkes won everything directed in Hately's direction. But if George was the headline artist then it was the supporting act of John Aston who earned the plaudits with his two goals, the second of which came in the 73rd minute. Best, yet again, slipping the ball towards Aston who once again rounded Kirkup before picking his spot and calmly placing the ball wide of Bonetti.

It was a goal that ended Chelsea's hopes of grasping something from the game as they had pulled a goal back a few minutes earlier through Hollins, whose speculative shot flew over the defenders heads and went in off the post with Stepney momentarily deceived.

Chelsea: Bonetti, Kirkup, McCreadie, Hollins, Hinton, Harris, Boyle, Baldwin, Hately, Cooke, Tambling. Substitute: Houseman for Tambling.

Scorer: Hollins

United: Stepney, Brennan, Noble, Crerand, Foulkes, Stiles, Herd, Aston, Sadler, Charlton, Best. Substitute: Anderson.

Scorers: Aston (2), Best.

Attendance: 55,958

20

West Ham United

6 May 1967

United's 3-0 victory over a mid-table West Ham United on 1 April 1967 saw them retain their two-point advantage at the top of the first division, keeping challengers Nottingham Forest and Liverpool at arm's length. The shock 2-1 home defeat at the hands of second division Norwich City in the FA Cup, a repeat performance of the Canaries 1959 success at Carrow Road, was something of a blessing in disguise. As it allowed Matt Busby's team to give their championship challenge their full concentration.

With George in devastating form – 'Best Baffles Leicester' cried one headline following United's 2-1 victory at Filbert Street in late November, then a fortnight later at Anfield it was 'Liverpool cannot better Best' as the table topping United held the third place Liverpool to a 2-2 draw – it was only a handful of draws as 1966 moved into 1967 that prevented the Old Trafford side from running away with the championship.

Although surrendering their leadership to Liverpool they were soon to reclaim pole position and that 3-0 victory over the 'Hammers' was once again instigated by the Belfast boy, it was only a couple of late goals from George and Denis Law that finally secured victory against a gallant West Ham side.

As April moved into May and the season edged towards its final couple of fixtures United's advantage had been increased to three points, with Nottingham Forest now the club tugging at their shirt tails. Liverpool, despite having a game in hand, were now seven points behind. With two games left to play the pressure was on Forest as they had to rely on United dropping points, while maintaining the pressure on the leaders by notching up victories in their own final two fixtures.

On the penultimate Saturday Forest made the long journey to the south coast and Southampton while United also travelled south, London bound, heading for the east end and the fiery cauldron of Upton Park where West Ham sought revenge for their recent defeat at Old Trafford.

Hundreds had found themselves locked out of the compact Upton Park ground, finding a much different way to pass an hour and a half, the temperature on the east London streets simmering away before totally boiling over. Whereas on the pitch the action watched by a post-war record crowd of 38,424, it took a mere two minutes for the radios at the Dell to crackle out the news that 'Manchester United have taken the lead against West Ham'.

The United support was in no doubt as to where the League title was heading, with cries of 'Champions' echoing around the ground well before kick-off. The breakthrough after two minutes only cranking up the volume. Denis Law sent the ball through for Stiles to run onto, but the diminutive half-back found his route to goal blocked. The ball broke loose and as Burkett hesitated, Charlton was onto it in a flash, lashing the ball past a helpless Mackleworth for a sensational opener.

It was only the beginning of a majestic afternoon for Charlton, as he surpassed even his crowning performances for England almost a year previously a few miles up the road as Alf Ramsey's side moved towards World Cup glory. He had the ball at his command, sending it at pin-point accuracy wherever he chose and in one instance, turned past seven opposition players with the same move.

With seven minutes gone, United scored a second. Aston swept past Burkett and, from his cross, Crerand headed past a helpless Mackleworth and by the 10th minute it was 3-0. Foulkes challenged the West Ham second choice 'keeper as the ball swung in from an Aston corner kick and the ball slipped from the custodians grasp. The United defender reacted quickest and wasted little time in prodding it over the line.

3-0 in front, with two of the goals coming from half backs, showed the determination of the visitors to get forward at every opportunity and ensure that the title race did not stretch out until the final Saturday of the season. However such a scenario was never going to materialise as a fourth goal was added in the 25th minute leaving the Nottingham Forest supporters, who had made the long journey to the south coast, wishing that they had stayed at home. At least they could have switched their radios off!

As the West Ham goalkeeper picked the ball from the back of his net for the third time that afternoon, all hell broke out on the terracing behind, with vicious outbreaks of fighting between the two factions of supporters, resulting in police and ambulance men struggling among the flaying arms and feet in order to extract blood stained casualties and hooligans from the pushing and swaying throng.

United's fourth goal saw Stiles push the ball inside the full-back, allowing George to gather it before Charles knew what was happening. The Irishman swiftly slipping the ball from his right foot to his left, before shooting under the once again helpless Mackleworth.

Half-time gave the home side some breathing space, but there was little in the way of a break for the now harassed police, as no-man's lands developed on the terracing and a steady stream of youths were marched away from the trouble spots and out of the ground.

West Ham caught their visitor's cold as the second half got underway. Left-back Charles, who had been left bewildered by George for United's fourth goal, gained something in the way of recompense when, after continuing to move forward as the United defence retreated, he beat Stepney from all of 25 yards for a goal that was never going to have any bearing on the outcome of this particular game. The ball going under the body of the United 'keeper, who appeared to have been unsighted, although he was also late in getting down in his attempt to save.

There was certainly no fight back from the home side, as United continued to dominate, knowing that the title was in their grasp and it came as no surprise that their lead was increased further in the 63rd minute. Charles, back in his defensive role, managed to push the ball out of play for a corner as Law threatened, but as the resulting kick was lifted towards the West Ham goal by Stiles, the Hammers full-back was adjudged by referee Spittle to have pushed Law, the official immediately pointing to the spot. Up stepped Law, 5-1.

That was basically that. Game, set and match, as Forest were now on the end of 2-0 defeat on the south coast. West Ham did mount the odd attack, Peters forcing a save out of Stepney with a header from a Moore free-kick, but United continued to toy with their hosts. They were determined to take the title in a style befitting the champions crown and, with ten minutes remaining, they increased their goal tally to six.

George had already come close to claiming that sixth but Mackleworth was, on this occasion, equal to his effort. Minutes later however, the 'keeper failed to hold a centre from George and as the ball broke loose, Law sprung forward to blast the ball high into the vacant net.

Sensing that the full-time whistle was not too far away, players from both sides were more than content to keep the ball and themselves on the side of the pitch adjacent to the tunnel and, well aware of the situation and the impending pitch invasion, the referee gave the players fore-warning prior to blowing for full-time.

Within seconds of the shrill blast echoing around the East London ground, the pitch was covered in supporters of both teams and they were still roaming around the ground and surrounding area for whatever intentions, as the champagne corks popped merrily in the visitor's dressing room.

So United were champions with one game still to play, a fixture that saw Stoke City visit Old Trafford as bridesmaids on the big day, holding the title winners to a goal-less draw in front of just over 61,000 jubilant supporters, as Matt Busby's team were presented with the first division championship trophy for the fifth time under his guidance, but a record seventh all told.

'Our greatest aim is to win the European Cup next year' proclaimed Matt Busby amid the celebrations in the packed Upton Park dressing room, a trophy that had remained in his sight since he first took Manchester United into Europe despite the reservations of some and a trophy that had taken on a much more significant meaning since that Thursday afternoon in Munich.

West Ham United: Mackleworth, Burkett, Charles, Peters, Heffer, Moore, Redknapp, Bennett, Boyce, Hurst, Sissons. Substitute: Hartley.

Scorer: Charles.

Manchester United: Stepney, Brennan, Dunne, Crerand, Foulkes, Stiles, Best, Law, Sadler, Charlton, Aston. Substitute: Ryan.

Scorers: Law (2), Crerand, Charlton, Foulkes, Best.

Attendance: 38,424.

George vs Manchester City Magistrates Court

Early December brought the news that George had been 'slightly hurt' in a car accident. Going by the report:

> Twenty-one year old Best was driving his Jaguar car in Victoria Avenue, Blackley, Manchester, when it was in collision with another car.
>
> He was taken to hospital with a slight face injury but went home to his lodgings in Aycliffe Avenue, Chorlton-cum-Hardy after treatment. United's manager, Mr Matt Busby, said later: 'He is alright and he will be playing tomorrow. He just got a slight knock trying to avoid a cat or something.'

George was indeed fit enough to travel with the rest of the United players to the north-east for the match against Newcastle United, but the accident did have repercussions with an appearance in front of the Manchester City magistrates with the true (?) story of the accident being revealed. This lead to a six-month driving ban.

In court it came to light that George was returning home at 3.30 a.m. on 8 December (the game at St James Park was on the 9) when he ran into the rear of a parked car, which had its parking light on. The owner was to find his car some 30 yards further down the road from where he had parked it. George's Jaguar was 35 yards away from the car owner's home. Due to the extent of the damage to George's car the brakes could not be examined, but the car was said to be in good condition.

According to George's lawyer: 'The position was that the engine was set very fast. He failed to see this parked vehicle until the last minute. When he turned away to his offside he actually put his foot down to go round it and he obviously misjudged it or the speed of the car caused him to collide with the rear of the parked vehicle.'

Despite claims that a ban would affect his business interests, George was banned from driving for six months, fined £25 and ordered to pay £2 4s costs. He was also later fined by the club.

This was not George's first driving offence as the court was told that in March 1966 he had been fined £3 and his licence endorsed for exceeding the speed limit. In November 1966 a further speeding offence saw him fined £8, with another endorsement. Then, in 1967, he had been fined £10 and his licence again endorsed for driving without due care and attention.

As for the cat, it was never mentioned at all during the court case, as it is very doubtful if it ever even existed.

21

Arsenal vs United

24 February 1968

Manchester United were first division champions again with their title success once again offering them the opportunity to finally lay their European Cup ghost to rest. There was also the urge to finally vault the FA Cup semi-final hurdle and make the somewhat allusive final, while also looking towards retaining the first division championship flag.

The 1967/68 season started favourably, sharing the FA Charity Shield with Tottenham Hotspur following a thrilling 3-3 Old Trafford draw, Pat Jennings outdoing George with a goal. The Northern Ireland 'keeper launching the ball downfield from his Stretford End goal, then watching it bounce over Alex Stepney's head and into the net at the Scoreboard End. In the first division, despite the 3-1 opening day defeat at Everton, United went the following eleven unbeaten. A run that saw them sit in second place behind Liverpool by the turn of the year they were top, three points in front, an advantage that was soon reduced to two points, with Leeds United overstepping Liverpool as the nearest challengers.

By January many felt that the title race was already over with United in first place and set to regain their position as England's top club. The newspaper headlines confirmed their superiority above the rest of the pack, with George vying his club on a regular basis for a share of those same headlines. One week it would be 'Brilliant Best Again', the next 'The Incredible Best'. They changed little from week to week.

Capturing the headlines was, by now, something that came naturally to George. As easy as drifting round a hapless or, more to the point, helpless first division defender. Those in opposition found it difficult to handle his rapidly increasing brilliance but off the field the members of the press who followed United around the country and on to foreign fields had no difficulty whatsoever in conjuring up words of approval, nor were their headline writers stuck for inspiration if George had once again turned on that moment or, most likely, moments of magic.

As mentioned elsewhere London had that special appeal to George. Manchester was always home but the capital had that little bit extra, something that inspired George onto a different level. A moth attracted to the brighter lights, fluttering busily rather than a more leisurely flight of fancy.

Highbury in February 1968 was one of those afternoons. George turned on his brilliance, while the pen pushers drooled in unison. 'Highbury – the Best Place to be' appeared in the *Sun*. 'Best's genius confounds Arsenal at Highbury' lead David Lacey's report in the *Daily Telegraph*, with the likes of 'Best livens the gloom', 'Best steals the shows' and 'Best's genius snatches points from Arsenal' could be found elsewhere. The story was the same and they couldn't all be wrong!

Manchester United's season was gathering momentum, rapidly. The FA Cup was out of the way at the first hurdle, losing to Tottenham Hotspur 1-0 after extra time in a third round replay at White Hart Lane following a 2-2 draw at Old Trafford. On the European Cup front United had, once again, reached the quarter-finals by beating Hibernians of Malta and the Yugoslavs of Sarajevo. Gornik Zabrze lay in wait four days after the visit to north London.

In the League a 2-1 defeat at Burnley, the only first division fixture that afternoon, prevented United from increasing their advantage over second placed Leeds United. The Yorkshire side, now a point behind but with a game in hand. Liverpool in third place were five points behind the leaders, while opponents Arsenal languished in eighth, twelve points behind.

This Highbury encounter had the makings of a feisty encounter if the events of the Old Trafford meeting back in October had anything to do with it, as that particular encounter between the two sides did considerably more than simply bubble over, with both Denis Law and Ian Ure given their marching orders following a running on-field battle. Both players were booked in the 23rd minute following an exchange of blows after Law reacted to a rash Ure tackle then, with only seven minutes remaining and play nowhere near them, Ure aimed a kick and Law threw a punch, leaving the referee with little alternative than to send both players off. George was also fortunate not to have enjoyed an early bath after throwing punches at an Arsenal defender.

The stage was set for what would possibly be a tempestuous ninety minutes. It was perhaps a blessing that Ure was on international duty with Scotland, while Law had been ignored by his country and led a Charlton-less United out at Highbury for the 100th League meeting between the two sides, leaving the previous confrontation to nothing more than the memory. But this was a game that left, despite being of much importance to both sides, United needing the points and Arsenal needing a confidence booster, it was somewhat diluted as the home side had a Football League Cup Final against Leeds United and a fifth round FA Cup tie against Birmingham City on the horizon. United, as mentioned, had the trip to Gornik in their sights.

Arsenal began well and, with slightly more luck, could have taken the lead. Simpson headed the ball to Armstrong and took the return with a searing volley that, had it been a foot lower, would have beaten Stepney rather than fly narrowly over the bar. Prior to the interval both Gould and Sammels went agonisingly close but by that time, United were already in front.

Having weathered those early Arsenal attacks with relative ease and slowly built up the momentum that was to eventually win them the game, the opening goal came in the 23rd minute when George outpaced Storey, his marker for the afternoon, as they both chased a long Stepney clearance. The ball landed near the touchline and George, with the Arsenal defender inside him. Suddenly the ball was flying towards the Arsenal goal, catching Furnell by surprise and leaving the 'keeper helpless in his attempt to stop it from entering the net. What had actually happened was debated by many of those present as how the ball had gone from the wing to the back of the Arsenal net was something of a mystery. As it transpired Storey, under pressure from George, had over hit his attempted back pass to score an own goal.

Perhaps frustrated at being denied a goal to celebrate his boutique business having been awarded a £15,000 mail order catalogue contract, George set matters right ten minutes into the second half by scoring a goal that left no one in any doubt as to how it had materialised or who had scored it. A centre from Kidd on the left picked out Law almost on the penalty spot who, with canny accuracy, nodded the ball down back towards George's feet. There appeared to be no route for goal with the Arsenal defence en-masse in front of him but, with a dummy to the right, George swerved inside turned and took the ball a couple of paces forward through the gap that had suddenly materialised before hitting the ball into the top-right hand corner of the Arsenal net from around 20 yards out. Furnell's reflexes were nowhere near quick enough to prevent the goal.

With the two-goal advantage, despite there still being half an hour or so remaining, United were content with their lead and were more than happy to see out the game and pulled John Fitzpatrick, wearing the Number Nine shirt in place of Bobby Charlton, back into a more defensive role alongside Nobby Stiles.

Arsenal did enjoy some midfield control through McLintock and Simpson but they were no match for the visitors who recorded the first success for the away side at Highbury for more than a year. But then again, not every side has a match winner in the form of a George Best. As one observer wrote:

> By his own brand of imagination, unparalleled talent and cheek. Best made the two goals that tightened United's grip on the League championship at precisely the time it might have begun to weaken. The match was full of Best's splendid works: sprinting for a ball half a minute from time when, with the match in the bag and a punishing struggle coming up on Wednesday, worried fans were yelling at him to take it easy; accelerating from nothing to top speed on a postage stamp and once drawing eight nervous Arsenal players with him on – as it turned out – a harmless expedition to the corner flag.

The victory is perhaps best summed up by another uncredited report which contained: 'United won without extending themselves largely because they had on tap the genius of George Best.'

Arsenal: Furnell, Storey, McNab, McLintock, Neill, Simpson, Jenkins, Gould, Graham, Sammels, Armstrong. Substitute: Court

United: Stepney, Dunne, Burns, Crerand, Sadler, Stiles, Best, Kidd, Fitzpatrick, Law, Aston. Substitute: Ryan.

Scorer: Best (2).

Attendance: 46,417.

22

United vs Real Madrid

24 April and 15 May 1968

For a fourth time Manchester United found themselves in the semi-finals of the European Cup, 180 minutes away from the ultimate goal of a place in the final of European footballs top competition. A tournament that back in 1956 Matt Busby had been advised to forget about and refrain from entering. A trail blazing venture that some felt would never take off. It was now a dream waiting to be fulfilled.

The honour of becoming the first British side to win this prestigious tournament had been denied to Matt Busby and his players, it was captured instead by his friend Jock Stein who had led his totally home grown Celtic side, all of whom were born within a 30 mile radius of Glasgow, to the title of European Cup winner's the previous year after defeating Milan in Lisbon. Busby's more cosmopolitan eleven were now more determined than ever to claim the crown of being Europe's best.

The draw for the opening round of the competition which was to see the final played at Wembley, an incentive that appealed to the United players just as much as any amount of money offered as a bonus, paired United with the unknown and certainly un-taxing Hibernians of Malta. A draw which left the United loving residents of the Mediterranean island really believing in Father Christmas.

In the Old Trafford first-leg, United were far from impressive and had they been up against a much stronger side then they could well have found themselves encountering a few problems. As it was, the visitors were restricted to only a few attacking moments and United treated the game as something of an advanced training session thus wining the tie with a comfortable 4-0 scoreline. There was never going to be any danger of losing the second-leg on the sand-covered pitch of the Gazira Stadium but, in a heat of eighty degrees, the nearest United came to increasing their lead was to hit the bar on a couple of occasions. Play moved frequently from end to end but Stepney had only one real save to make, while the most exciting incident came when Stiles fouled Priviterr which led to a scuffle among the players. This stirred the crowd into a frenzy and brought mounted police into action down the touchline. But there were to be no goals and United went through thanks to the four they scored at Old Trafford.

Round two paired United with the equally unknown Yugoslavian side Sarajevo who, although unable to match United for skill, they more than made up for it in brawn and were content to distribute body-jarring tackles and outrageous trips with much regularity. It was certainly a testing ninety minutes for United in the Kosevo Stadium and, in the end, they were indeed fortunate to come away with a 0-0 draw.

At Old Trafford Sarajevo found themselves behind after ten minutes, John Aston scoring after Crerand worked his way down the right before slipping the ball inside to Kidd who in turn crossed for Aston to head home. United added a second in the 63rd minute, when Crerand found

Aston and the outside-left's cross was headed against the bar by Foulkes. The ball appeared to go out of play, but was hooked back into the goalmouth by Burns and George was on hand to fire the ball home.

By this point the visitors had been reduced to ten men after Prljacea had been sent off for scything down George from behind and had been more than happy to resort to tripping, tackling late and body-checking anything in a red shirt. But it was not just the Sarajevo players who were guilty of foul play as George lashed out at goalkeeper Muftic, who seemed to be doing little more than attempting to help him to his feet after he had seen his header saved by the 'keeper. The referee ignored the Yugoslav protests and it was shortly after this that Prljacea took out his own form of revenge.

'His own brand of imagination, unparalleled talent and cheek' is perhaps an excellent description of George from his particular period of his career. He was no ordinary footballer that was clear to all who watched him at close quarters. His extraordinary talent was something that came naturally and nerves were not something that formed part of his CV, clearly illustrated prior to the European Cup third round first-leg tie at Old Trafford against Polish champions Gornik on 28 February.

It was 7.17 p.m. and kick-off was less than half an hour away but George was not in the Manchester United dressing room. He was several yards away standing, somehow completely unrecognised, at the supporters crammed refreshment bar under 'B' Stand, enjoying a carton of tea with best mate Mike Summerbee. Tea finished, a quick 'see you later' and he was off to finally get changed for the European tie. Ninety minutes later, he had guided United to a 2-0 first-leg victory. That was George.

Gornik's goalkeeper Kostka was all that prevented his team from being on the end of a heavier defeat, so much so that the twenty-seven-year-old mining engineer received one of the biggest ovations ever given to an opposition player at Old Trafford, as he left the field at the end of the ninety minutes.

The balance of play was clearly reflected in the fact that United had twenty-two corners to Gornik's solitary one. However, it was not until the 61st minute that Kosta was finally beaten when George's low centre was turned into his own net by centre-half Florenski. Kidd added a second, giving United something of a safety cushion with a minute remaining, scoring from close range.

The second-leg in Poland almost never took place on its scheduled date as United arrived in Katowice amid a blizzard, with the snow already lying deep on the ground and Matt Busby considering asking for a postponement. Despite the sub-zero temperatures the game did go ahead with United more than happy to abandon their usual free-flowing football for a more defensive game with a disciplined performance as the 100,000 crowd created a unique atmosphere with klaxons, fireworks and a seemingly constant wall of noise.

A snowstorm swirled around the ground during the first forty-five minutes, as United battled the conditions as much as they confronted their opponents. But their rear-guard was finally breached in the 70th minute when Stepney was pulled up for taking to many steps with the ball and although the resulting free-kick was beaten out, with the whole United team lined across the face of the goal, the ball was immediately returned into the area and Lubanski thundered the ball home via the cross-bar. United held on to go through 2-1 on aggregate.

And so United exchanged the biting wind and snow covered Katowice for the more pleasant and familiar surroundings of Spain, with the semi-final draw pairing them with old adversaries Real Madrid. Both sides had changed dramatically since that last semi-final meeting back in 1957 when United lost 5-3 on aggregate as Matt Busby's team had of course been decimated on the runway at Munich, while the Spanish champions no longer had the likes of Santamaria or Di Stefano or Puskas. Gento was now the only remaining link to the Madrid side of old. Bill Foulkes and Bobby Charlton were United's survivors.

Matt Busby would have preferred either Benfica or Juventus, the other two semi-finalists, but having beaten Real Madrid in the Bernabeu 2-0 back in September 1962 and 3-1 at Old Trafford the previous December, he at least knew that the Spaniards were beatable and that his team, now much stronger than that of six years previously, could go all the way to the Wembley Final. However, much would depend on the first-leg in Manchester.

It was an evening ideal for football with a cloudless sky revealing a golden glow as the evening sun went down. The flags around the ground fluttered in the faint breeze as 63,000 supporters settled down to enjoy ninety minutes that would go some way in determining which team could begin planning for a trip to Wembley at the end of May. It was an evening, and a stage, ideal for George to climb off his pedestal as Britain's top footballer and propel himself onto an even greater platform as the best in Europe. As if he needed any encouragement.

But for every headline that George grabbed following United's 1-0 victory there was another offering a word of caution, or more to the point, proclaiming that the solitary goal advantage would not be enough to see Matt Busby's team through to the final. 'It's not enough, Matt. Best hits great goal – but what about those misses?' came from the *Sun*, while the *Guardian* went with 'Manchester United Given Frail Lead by Best'. The *Express* decided on 'Best Raps Slim Lead', *The Telegraph*: 'Best Puts United One up with One to Play', but added below, "Slender Advantage may not be Enough'. The *Mail* had 'United Miss the Two Goal Target', with *The Times* being the most blunt and to the point: 'Manchester United toil for meagre reward.'

The experienced European campaigners of Madrid set their stall out in the hope that while keeping things tight across the back they could perhaps catch United on the break but it was the home side who threatened first in the opening minutes, Betancort, the Madrid 'keeper diving across his goal to keep out Aston's header following a cross from George. From the ensuing corner Crerand, not the most noted of strikers, could only stand and look as his shot hit the woodwork with the 'keeper beaten.

Prior to the match and from the first whistle the tension was obvious, a ticking time-bomb waiting to explode and George certainly did his utmost to release the pressure on his teammates and lighten the mood of the crowd. Shortly after Crerand's attempt at goal he plucked the ball from mid-air before shooting narrowly over then, minutes later, forcing Betancort into making a fine save.

United continued to push forward, Madrid seemingly content to soak up the pressure and wait for the chance to catch their opponents on the break. Kidd blasted high over the bar when in a good position after Crerand, George and Charlton engineered the opening, while Aston tantalised Gonzalez and fed his fellow forwards with an array of crosses. George was rather unceremoniously upended by Zoco as he drifted through the Madrid defence, then Aston was again denied as that opening goal simply failed to materialise.

Ten minutes from the interval, United finally gained that sought after advantage. Attacking the scoreboard end of the ground, Aston chased down the left after Kidd's long pass and, managing to regain possession having monetarily lost the ball after getting the better of Gonzalez, he pulled it back from the by-line towards the penalty spot where George calmly picked his spot and hammered the ball let footed high into the roof of the Madrid net. A thunderous,effort that no goalkeeper would have seen, never mind could have stopped. Old Trafford exploded as the net bulged and a frightened cat that had somehow strayed into the ground ran the length of the pitch, hoping for safety in the packed Stretford End.

A minute after the restart Sadler headed on a Charlton corner and Kidd nodded the ball onto the underside of the bar. 'Goal' screamed the crowd as the ball bounced precariously onto the line but Bakhramov, the Russian linesman who played a crucial part in awarding England's third goal in the 1966 World Cup Final, stood with his flag down on the touchline. He was clearly not willing to get involved in a second controversy on English soil while the referee, amid twenty frantic appealing players, awarded a free-kick for a foul on the Madrid goalkeeper

United should certainly have punished their visitors more severely as, despite their dominance, countless scoring opportunities were shunned with Kidd possibly being the worst offender. Madrid, to their credit, never allowed themselves to be flustered but seldom departed from their methodical football, Stepney having been not been tested once in the opening forty-five minutes. But, despite this, those on the Old Trafford terraces were more than aware of the dangers that could well materialise from the white-shirted Madrid players as the minutes ticked away.

Much to their relief Stepney kept his goal intact despite long periods of inactivity with United taking that solitary goal advantage into the second-leg. As the supporters made their way home at full-time the talk was not about the team's success against the Spaniards, but whether or not that one goal would be enough to take them through to the final. Few were confident.

Few present on the night were aware that George's actual contribution to the ninety minutes had been severely hampered by an ankle injury sustained some four weeks previously. This was something that had required constant treatment over the course of the days leading up to the game. In the second half the ability to play to his usual ultra-high standard lessened considerably and he was seen to drift out to the flanks with more regularity than normal, something that was certainly not tactical, merely an attempt to get away from the more physical midfield. His usual relaxed play, prior to a sudden burst of pace was also clearly missing.

'I was knackered' he was to say later in the bar of his favoured watering hole, The Brown Bull in Salford.

The ankle wouldn't take it. Every time I tried to go, it let me down. I can really sympathise with Denis now. For months, every time he came in after playing, either his ankle or his knee was up like a balloon. It's enough to take the heart out of anybody. Then tonight, when Denis seemed to be winning the battle and going a bit like his old self again, I had this lot.

When they drag on for weeks like this and you can't shake them off, you begin to get depressed.

And so to Madrid. Ninety minutes from a place in the European Cup Final, or ninety minutes for yet another European adventure to end in tears. It was perhaps also Matt Busby's final opportunity to get within touching distance of that most coveted trophy and for Bill Foulkes and Bobby Charlton to complete the job that they had begun with their much lamented teammates more than a decade previously. The United manager had been disappointed with the Old Trafford outcome in the fact that his team had not scored more goals, but went on to say 'I think we can still win it.'

Busby also feared that opening half hour in Spain, a period when he considered his team would suffer an onslaught from the home side, backed by their partisan, voracious support. Denis Law was unfit and United fielded the side that had lost to Sunderland the previous Saturday, a defeat that cost them the retention of the first division title and a game in which George had been risked, and scored, despite his ankle problems.

In those opening thirty minutes in the Bernabeu cauldron, the United mid-field trio of Crerand, Sadler and Charlton were over-worked as the white shirts looked to have a distinct numerical advantage, swarming around the arena like men possessed. Nobby Stiles also had his work cut out coming up against Amancio, the Madrid Number Nine, a talented individual who had missed the first-leg at Old Trafford. Had he played, it was considered that he would have made quite a difference to the outcome.

In the 4th minute, Madrid forced a corner and Shay Brennan had to head clear from underneath the crossbar. Four minutes later and another corner, Amancio headed against the bar, then Stepney did well to stop a 30 yard drive from Sanchis. But United weathered those opening thirty minutes, with the volume of the Madrid crowd dropping a few decibels, while the United contingent scattered around the vast bowl and those nervously listening on the radio back home relaxed slightly, a little confidence even beginning to seep into their thoughts. This however, was only momentary, as two minutes over that half hour, disaster struck.

Following yet another Madrid attack, the Italian referee signalled for a goal kick to United only to have his attention attracted by a flag-waving linesman, who forced him to change his mind and give the home side a free-kick two yards from the corner flag for obstruction against John Aston. Amancio swung over an inch perfect cross towards the near post and up jumped Pirri to move in and head home.

Five minutes prior to the interval the game exploded into life as Stiles brought down Amancio with a vicious tackle. On the resumption of play after a stoppage of three minutes Gento, playing his 83rd European tie, cavorted some 30 yards down the left after Brennan failed to control the ball before sending a searing left-footed drive past Stepney and into the back of the United net.

Although now two down United managed to catch Madrid on the rebound, pulling a goal back two minutes later when Charlton, alone in front of goal, was robbed by Zoco. But to everyone's surprise, the Madrid half-back's pass back was completely misplaced and rolled past his own 'keeper to give United a life line. Despite this confidence shattering blow, United were dealt a bit of luck a minute later when Dunne hit a high ball forward and Kidd moved in but was beaten to the ball by Zoco. The Spaniard however, sliced his attempted clearance past his own 'keeper to level the score on aggregate.

There was barely time to catch your breath and with only seconds of the half remaining, the ball again found its way into the back of the net. Gento again involved hammering the ball low into the United goalmouth and as it rebounded from a crowd of defenders, Amancio pounced and sent the ball wide of a helpless Stepney. Deflated, United made their way to the dressing rooms where they were reminded by Matt Busby that they were only a goal behind on aggregate, although still requiring two goals to win the tie outright. George was also vocal in his thoughts, telling his teammates 'We're as well losing 10-1 as 3-1. Let's have a real go at them.'

The second half saw a revitalised United, thoughts of that goal which could rekindle the flame pushing them forward at every opportunity and forced Betancort into making numerous saves. A quick break by Crerand in the 57th minute saw the ball swung towards the somewhat subdued George who took the ball round his man, only to see his shot cannon off the fortunate 'keeper. A minute later Crerand himself shot narrowly over, which was followed by a Kidd header being saved at full length by Betancort.

After twenty-eight minutes of that hectic second half, United achieved the breakthrough they sought. Crerand, the man behind most of United's forward surges, once again moved forward and his high, inviting cross from the left was headed on by George. This allowed Sadler to beat the Madrid 'keeper from close range. It was now 3-2 on the night, but level on aggregate. Could United achieve the impossible, or would they simply be content to go into a third meeting in Lisbon two nights later against the Spaniards?

Sadler's goal had a surprising demoralising effect on the home side and their heads drooped, shaken that a game they had earlier thought was safely within their grasp, was now suspended by a mere thread. Their attacks lacked the determination of those during those first forty-five minutes, while United continued to look positive in everything they attempted, sensing that perhaps success was indeed within their grasp. Their attitude being rewarded thirteen minutes from time.

Crerand took a long throw down the right, George moved almost effortlessly past Sanchis and Zoco and took the ball to the touchline before pulling it back diagonally for an on running colleague. However, it wasn't to feet renowned for scoring goals, but to those belonging to centre-half Bill Foulkes who had somehow momentarily disregarded his defence role and moved forward to supplement the United front line. With the calmness of his more attack-minded teammates, the veteran warrior turned the ball into the far corner of the Madrid net.

The night was United's. Wembley here we come.

Although not George's finest hour by a long shot, he was a crucial part in United's march to the final. Would he find the occasion and the big Wembley stage a more inviting platform for his talents?

First leg:

Manchester United: Stepney, Dunne, Burns, Crerand, Sadler, Stiles, Best, Kidd, Charlton, Law, Aston.

Scorer: Best.

Real Madrid: Betancort, Gonzalez, Sanchis, Pirri, Zunzunegui, Zoco, Perez, Jose-Luis, Grosso, Velazquez, Gento.

Attendance: 63,200.

Second leg:

Real Madrid: As above except Amancio for Jose-Luis.

Scorers: Pirri, Gento, Amancio.

Manchester United: As above except Brennan for Dunne, Dunne for Burns, Foulkes for Sadler, Sadler for Law.

Scorers: Zoco (own goal), Sadler, Foulkes.

Attendance: 120,000.

'George Best, Manchester United Star, Killed in a Car Crash' were the words that sent supporters into a panic, forcing telephone lines to the club, newspaper offices, police stations and countless other places into melt down as the rumours circulated around Manchester and beyond. George in the meantime, oblivious as to what was going on, stood chatting to his girlfriend Jackie Glass in his Edwardian boutique, his gleaming white S-type Jaguar standing outside.

It wasn't until his girlfriend's father suddenly barged through the shop doorway, showing great signs of relief upon discovering that both his daughter and George were both safe and well, that George was made aware of the ongoing rumours. Such was the price of fame.

But that fame, that also saw George named as the youngest precipitant of the 'Footballer of the Year' award with over 60 per cent of the votes, had also earned him his fortune as he declared, 'I could retire tomorrow and have no financial worries for the rest of my life. But I want to do something for my family back in Belfast first. My dad wants a pub and I've told him to look around. Money doesn't have the same significance for me as it did' he continued. 'I've just paid £45 for a suede coat and I might not wear it again. My dad, a Belfast shipyard worker, would think I am bonkers. A pound is still a lot of money to him.'

But looking back to his early days at United he said, 'When I think how near I was to forfeiting all this, I can only shake my head.'

23

United vs Newcastle United

4 May 1968

Having been crowned first division champions in 1967, Manchester United had set themselves a twin target for the following season. One was defending their newly won title, while the second was to finally scale the heights on the European front, exorcising the demons of the past which still haunted the Old Trafford corridors and adding 'Champions of Europe' to the ever growing list of domestic honours.

The 1967/68 first division campaign had begun somewhat erratically with a 3-1 defeat at Goodison Park, albeit their only defeat in the opening seven fixtures but with four of those other opening fixtures drawn it left United in ninth place, three points behind early leaders Liverpool. Unabashed and shaking off the summer cobwebs United welcomed Law back to the fold, the blond-headed Scot having missed three of those opening fixtures and a run of five victories soon had them level on points with their Merseyside rivals, with the added cushion of a game in hand.

Two defeats in three outings rocked the boat, but it was only a gale rather than a hurricane amid a sea of calm and an unbeaten run between 11 November, when they defeated Liverpool 2-1 at Anfield in a crucial top of the table clash, and 3 February saw them leading the pack three points in front of Leeds United while still enjoying the benefit of having that game in hand.

There were distractions away from the first division title race, the forthcoming European Cup Final semi-final ties against Real Madrid now firmly entrenched in the minds of supporters and players alike. But that was the future and the championship chase was now and this, for the time being at least, was the number one priority.

Four defeats in six outings during February and March were certainly not the form of potential league champions and the last defeat of that quartet, a 3-1 reversal by neighbours City at Old Trafford was, although unknown at the time, to prove crucial in deciding the outcome of the title. Following that defeat a glance at the League table on the evening of 27 March saw United effectively in third place, even although they had the same number of points as Leeds United and Manchester City – forty-five from thirty-three games. Making goal average now an important ingredient in the mix, while that previously held game in hand had now also disappeared.

Stoke were beaten 4-2 at the City ground, but Liverpool claimed some sort of revenge when they left Old Trafford win a 2-1 victory. Easter weekend saw Fulham beaten 4-0 at Craven Cottage and 3-0 in Manchester, with a 2-2 draw at Southampton sandwiched in between. United were back on top. With only four fixtures remaining, in United's case at least, Leeds United and Manchester City were breathing down their neck – determined not to be shaken off, both were on forty-nine points, United were on fifty-two, but the two challengers had played two games less than United.

Nerves had now well and truly set in. City lost 1-0 to Chelsea, while Leeds beat Tottenham 1-0 twenty-four hours later. Saturday 20 April saw United beat Sheffield United at Old Trafford by a solitary goal, while Leeds defeated West Bromwich Albion 3-1. City were held to a no scoring draw by Wolves. Stoke City beat Leeds on 23 April, but City kept a tight hold of United's shirt tails with a 1-0 win over Sheffield United two days later. With the finishing line in sight, two points from the 2-0 defeat of Everton on 29 April saw the Maine Road side clamber over their cross-town rivals on goal average (2.03 against 1.55). That edge being achieved as much in the Midlands as it had been in Manchester, as United's defence disintegrated at the Hawthorns, where West Bromwich Albion hit the reigning champions for six, United managing only three in reply.

Two games remained, 180 minutes that would determine in what area of Manchester the first division championship trophy would reside for the next twelve months. No matter how United fared against the north-east duo of Newcastle United and Sunderland, victory for City in their remaining fixtures – Tottenham Hotspur and Newcastle United, both away would see the title end up at Maine Road. With two home fixtures, United had the advantage. Or did they?

On the afternoon of 4 May, there would have undoubtedly have been a sprinkling of Manchester City supporters among the 59,976 at Old Trafford, some of whom might have been unable to afford the fare and admission that would have taken them to White Hart Lane so deciding instead upon a cheaper option for their Saturday afternoon entertainment. Cheering on Newcastle United against their cross-town rivals.

The Geordies were mid-table, posing little threat to a United side hell-bent on snatching the title from their neighbours grasp and it was to take them a mere ten minutes to settle down and crack open the black and white striped defence.

It was reported that prior to this vital encounter Matt Busby approached George, in the knowledge that his inspirational forward had been voted 'Footballer of the Year' and requested that he 'turn on something special'. George was never one to disappoint.

Injury to Denis Law had brought his season to a premature end while the robust, hard-tackling Nobby Stiles was also missing, forcing United to depend more on style rather than strength, something they were capable of doing, especially with their Irishman at his rampant best. If United had an Achilles heel, it was their defence, but this was to be an afternoon when the rear guard was seldom troubled.

Knowing what was expected off them, it took United only nine minutes to take the lead. A throw in from Crerand to Gowling saw Denis Law's replacement side-step past Clarke before chipping the ball into the Newcastle goalmouth where Kidd rose majestically to head home.

As the game would wear on, the fragility of the Newcastle defence became so obviously apparent, offering little in the way of cover for McFaul stationed between the posts behind them, and thirteen minutes later United were two in front, as George grabbed the game by the scruff of the neck.

A half-hearted clearance at the near post by a Newcastle defender went behind for a corner and from Bobby Charlton's flag kick, Pat Crerand headed the ball down to his left and George hammered it home from eighteen yards giving McFaul no chance.

Having been slow to react to the rasping drive which had beaten him moments earlier, McFaul now faced George from a mere 12 yards as the United man placed the ball on the penalty spot after Kidd had been sent tumbling to the ground by Robson as he prepared to shoot, following yet another Charlton corner. This time despite having a clear view of the ball, the 'keeper had little chance in saving his fellow countryman's kick as it flew high into the roof of the Newcastle net.

To the surprise of many the visitors somehow managed to stem the almost constant flow of attacks on their goal, keeping United at bay for the remainder of the first half. Forty-five minutes that had the home support bubbling, but at the same time failing to command their total attention as the events further afield at White Hart Lane and Elland Road were of equal importance. As the teams changed ends, Leeds were a goal in front against early first division leaders Liverpool, while City were also a goal in front down in London. United could do little more than continue as had done in the opening half.

Ten minutes after the restart, George made it 4-0, claiming his hat-trick from the penalty spot, after being tackled clumsily from behind by Winstanley. McFaul once again left grasping at thin air. Even the most pessimistic of supporters knew now that there was no way back for Newcastle United on this occasion. They were also aware that no matter how many United scored, it was going to make no difference at all to the first division table as the news had filtered through that City had scored again and were now 2-0 in front.

George was giving Winstanley a torrid time leading to the rather inexperienced Newcastle centre-half being replaced by the more seasoned Iley with twenty minutes remaining. It made little difference. In the *Sunday People* Paul Doherty wrote, 'George Best boldly led the one-way procession with bursts of devilment and dynamite that might have given him two hat-tricks, not one. He put on a show for nonplussed Newcastle of the qualities which have won him his title [Footballer of the Year] and also made him a masterful marksman – though, surprisingly, this was the first hat-trick of his League career.'

With victory all but assured, there was now an opportunity for United to attack the goal average that Manchester City held and on the hour mark the portable radio's in Leeds and north London crackled that United were now 5-0 in front. Kidd claiming his second of the game, once again climbing above everyone else to head home as a Charlton corner was flicked on by Sadler. Those City supporters in the Old Trafford crowd made their way to the exits, knowing now that they would not witness a defeat for those despised red shirts that afternoon, but they were content in the knowledge that their own team were in little danger of losing their lead at White Hart Lane.

Five minutes later United were six in front, David Sadler finishing off a superb move orchestrated between Gowling and Charlton with the United number left-half powerfully driving the ball home from the left-hand corner of the penalty area. If that sixth goal brought the curtain down on the afternoon's events at Old Trafford, despite some twenty-five minutes still to play, there was still much attention paid to the goings on elsewhere.

Leeds were still a goal in front against Liverpool and City were holding onto their 2-0 advantage in London. A hush suddenly fell over Old Trafford as news filtered through that Summerbee had added a third for City and with only sixteen minutes remaining, it was unlikely that Tottenham could claw anything back and derail the light blues' titles aspirations.

It was 4.35 p.m., five minutes remaining at the grounds around the country, all ears on the radios, play out on the Old Trafford pitch was of secondary importance. 'There's been a goal at Elland Road. It's now Leeds 1 Liverpool 1'. 'There has also been another goal at White Hart Lane, where Tottenham have pulled a goal back. Spurs 1 City 3'. Around Old Trafford there was a definite buzz.

Two minutes later Liverpool went 2-1 in front, but there was to be no late rally from Tottenham. It was now all down to the final game of the season and it was with heavy hearts that the United supporters made their way out of Old Trafford, up Warwick Road or across the Ship Canal, as having witnessed such a mediocre performance from Newcastle. They knew in their heart of hearts that there was little possibility of City not being able to claim a victory when they needed it most.

So City travelled to Newcastle on the morning of 11 May, with Sunderland making the journey from the north-east to Manchester to face United. Ninety minutes of football that would determine the destination of the first division championship for season 1967/68.

Sunderland took the lead in the 14th minute and added a second twelve minutes before half-time, George managed to claw one back seconds before half-time. On Tyneside, it was 2-2.

Try as they did, United failed to breakdown the Sunderland defence as the game drifted into something of an ill-tempered affair. Busby withdrew Foulkes and sent on Gowling in an effort to save both the game and the championship, but to no avail. Newcastle scored a third against City, but the visitors scored two themselves, running out 4-3 winners. In the end, a draw would have been suffice for them to claim the title.

For United there was still the European Cup, but could they lift themselves enough to overcome the likes of Real Madrid, when lesser opponents had caused them problems during the season?

Speaking about his 'Footballer of the Year' award George said, 'I can hardly believe it. I think it's fantastic to have won this title after only four years in soccer. I couldn't have picked a better time to score my first hat-trick. I feel great, apart from the City result.'

Manchester United: Stepney, Brennan, Dunne, Crerand, Foulkes, Sadler, Best, Kidd, Charlton, Gowling, Aston. Substitute: Fitzpatrick.

Scorers: Best (3 inc 2p), Kidd (2), Sadler.

Newcastle United: McFaul, Craig, Clark, Burton, Winstanley, Moncur, Sinclair, Scott, Davies, Elliot, Robson. Substitute: Iley for Winstantley.

Attendance: 59,976

24

Benfica vs Wembley

29 May 1968

This should certainly not have been Manchester United's first appearance in a European Cup Final, cruel fate, poor performances and bad luck decided otherwise. It was however, the end of a long drawn-out journey, tearful and tiring but there was compensation in the fact that this particular final had been scheduled for Wembley, allowing the majority of the north London stadium to be over ran by United supporters.

Once the initial excitement of having overcome the mighty Real Madrid had diluted thoughts immediately spiralled into overdrive like a 'fast-forward' button being pressed overly hard, moving through the next fourteen days at the click of a finger with visions of Wembley's twin towers and the Portuguese champions Benfica looming large from the mist. 'Where are we going to get tickets? How will we get there?' were the questions asked as a sudden cold sweat sent a shiver down the spine. United were in the final, it's at Wembley, we have got to be there. Indeed. The biggest game in the lifetime of the vast United support and what if you couldn't get a ticket?

In what was a completely different era, completely alien to many today, owning a season ticket was akin to having something really special. Something that only a select few owned and something that was envied by thousands of others. Those who were among the fortunate few could lie in their beds at night and sleep easy. No recurring nightmares of all your friends laying their hands on a ticket for the European Cup Final and you being left without. No huge laughing face with a handful of tickets, pushing them towards you but, just as quickly grasping them back and disappearing into thin air. No, they were ok. They were on their way to Wembley.

For the rank-and-file supporters it was down to the good old programme token scheme to ensure their passage through the Wembley turnstiles. In each *United Review* there was a printed token, which had to be cut out and glued to a token sheet. Similar tokens from reserve and youth team programmes were often thrown into the equation to test the loyalty of the huge support. Programmes were only sold inside the ground, no going to Old Trafford picking up a programme and going home. However, if you were unable to go, you could always arrange for a friend to buy a programme for you. There was no restriction on how many you could purchase. Away programmes would also find their way into the mix, sometimes asked for as further proof of your loyalty.

It was an equally testing time for the players and their manager. With each passing day the pressure grew as newspapers and magazines wanted a few minutes of their time. George was especially in demand, his name was on everyone's lips – none more so than those of the Benfica players and training staff.

No one fancied Benfica to win: 'Manchester United hottest favourites for years' proclaimed the *Guardian* and although United's 5-1 victory in Lisbon a mere two years previously was still fresh in the memory, the threats posed by the likes of Coluna, Torres, Simoes and of course the extremely talented Eusebio could never be ignored. On the other hand, many in the Benfica camp would not sleep soundly as the recurring nightmares of a tousled-haired Irishman weaving past defenders as if on a ski slope appeared with an unwanted regularity.

'The responsibility for cracking the (Benfica) defence falls on the slim shoulders of Irish Will o' the Whisp George Best' wrote Bernard Joy in the *London Evening Standard*, going on to say:

> Best will be shadowed by Fernado Cruz and this is a clash which will put the heralded Stiles-Eusebio affair into the shade. Cruz, who was nearly sent off in the last round against Juventus, is a hard, ruthless warrior. Manager Matt Busby reckons that Best is the finest winger he has known in forty years of football because of "his tremendous heart", but I think Best will need the help of Italian referee Concetto Lo Bello as well as his courage.
>
> Bets destroyed Benfica with a magical display in the opening fifeen minutes of the 1966 quarter-final and will be the priority for the defence.

The threat of Eusebio was certainly not ignored but Nobby Stiles had enjoyed previous successes against the Benfica talisman, although the United man certainly did not go along with the idea that it would be the same again on their next meeting. He did however say as regards to the head to head: 'Still, there is one consolation, I'd rather play against Eusebio or Amancio or any of them than have to face George Best. You should see what George does to me in training. Splits me in two, he does. It gives you heart that some poor character has to try and deal with him.'

United travelled south to their pre-match headquarters at Egham, Surrey, hopelessly unable to escape from the media glare that followed their every move. Opponents Benfica were also closely monitored but nothing like that of United, the story of their initial journey into European football, the disaster of Munich and now within touching distance of their holy grail filling page upon page of the national newspapers.

'United for the Crown', 'The Big Night For Busby and United' and 'United's Moment of Truth' were only three of the many headlines in the run up to the game, building a pressure cauldron at the feet of Matt Busby and his team. But the United manager and his players did not need to read the newspapers in order to know what was expected of them. Neither did Busby have to indulge in any long winded pre-match team talk. The past took care of that.

There was a mass exodus from Manchester on the morning of 29 May, although many had travelled in the days leading up to the final determined to make the most of this special, possible one-off occasion. Many made the journey south without tickets, hoping that the streets of London were not paved with gold, but with those much sought after pieces of paper that would ensure their passage through the Wembley turnstiles. Making their fortune in the capital was of no concern whatsoever, there were more important matters at hand. Central London soon became a mass of red and white, few cared that United were to play in blue, and the colourfully bedecked supporters soon became just as big an attraction for the tourists camera's as the sights of the city itself.

Touts were out in force but their prices were beyond the pocket of most as they were asking up to ten times the actual face value. Frustrated by the actions of those wide-boys, even although they were accustomed to their Mancunian counterparts, some supporters decided that enough was enough and in their desperation to get inside the ground, they ganged up on the rouge ticket sellers and relieved them of their wares by force. One seller was not simply relieved off his tickets, but also had his shirt ripped off before fleeing for safety across one of the car parks.

Back in Belfast the fryers of the 'Golden Eagle' fish and chip shop were silent, a 'Closed' sign hung on the door as the owners were among those in the packed to the rafters Wembley. 'We are closing shop because this is one game we just couldn't miss' said Mrs Ann Best. 'Anyway, nobody will be wanting fish suppers. The streets of Belfast will be deserted during the game.' She went on to add. 'It will be United by 3-1, and George will score one of them. Just you mark my words.'

Her husband Dickie was slightly more cautious:

This definitely the big one for George. I went to Madrid and it was a terrific thrill when they got through to the final. But this is the final mountain. I believe United can climb it, but it's not going to be easy.

Maybe they were a wee bit lucky in Madrid. This will be a really hard game to win because Benfica area great side.

But I am doing the double – Sir Ivor and United.

With the terrace anthems echoing around Wembley, the vastly outnumbered followers of Benfica all but inaudible, the noise reached a crescendo as Bobby Charlton lead out his team from the bowls of the stadium, smartly kitted out in their white track suit tops and out onto the Wembley turf. This was indeed the moment of truth.

As could perhaps be expected, the opening minutes were somewhat subdued, a rather dull mundane affair, with neither side contributing to the glamour of the occasion. Peter Lorenzo in the *Sun* described it as a 'foul-ridden, destructive session with muscle so much more miserably prominent than method.' George, his reputation going before him, was singled out for preferential treatment and twice in successive minutes he was chopped down by the muscular Cruz. When he switched wings, hoping for a little reprieve from the underhand tactics of his tormentor, the equally cynical Humberto was happy to add to the already accumulated bruises.

With eleven minutes gone, the first scoring opportunity fell to Benfica. A bad pass by George, meant for Crerand but intercepted by Torres, allowed the tall Benfica forward release Eusebio. Gliding past Stiles and then Foulkes, the 'Black Panther' let loose a speculative right-footed drive from all of 25 yards, the ball crashing off the underside of Stepney's cross-bar, immediately silencing the United support.

Due to the game still being in its infancy referee Lo Bello appeared to be somewhat reluctant to quell the over-zealous, often malicious, tackling. Although often punishing the rather petty infringements that were an early feature of the game, by both sides it must be noted, but with twenty minutes gone his patience finally snapped and he booked Humberto for one foul too many on the now irate George, relentlessly shadowed by one defender or another wherever he went across the wide expanse of Wembley turf. At least half a dozen times in the first half George was chopped unmercifully to the ground, a painful reminder of his status within the game and perhaps the tactics of the Portuguese harbouring on revenge for his performance in Lisbon some two years previously. 'It was crude, but it was certainly effective' Albert Barham was to write in *The Guardian*.

George at one point thought he had gained the perfect revenge, latching onto a through pass from Crerand, before lifting the ball over the head of the advancing goalkeeper and into the empty net. He was denied the moment by a raised linesman's flag for offside.

Appearing to be everywhere, George was helping out in defence one minute, then moments later prompting his fellow forwards. On one occasion he lost the ball in a tackle but immediately harried and retrieved it from a Benfica defender, dribbled past three before passing with the outside of his foot to Kidd. On another, he quickly reacted to a rather poor throw out from Henrique, robbed the unsuspecting defender before closing in on goal but the angle was tight and his shot hit the side netting. Neither was he immune to teasing the Benfica defenders with some tongue in the cheek play. With two white shirts standing in front of him, he casually flicked the ball into the air before sending it into the Benfica penalty area. He could even be seen to dribble round the referee when the official got in his way.

To the relief of many the first half quickly drew to a close. The game far removed as to what had been expected, but as the second forty-five minutes got underway, it was to be simply more of the same as Cruz once again sent George sprawling. The game was suddenly transformed in the 53rd minute, the intimidation and underhand tactics, by both sides suddenly cast aside by the game's opening goal.

Tony Dunne found Sadler, whose lob into the Benfica goalmouth saw Charlton, unmarked, rise like a salmon from the water to flick the ball with his head. His strands of hair seeming to act as some sort of catapult, propelling the ball past the stranded Henrique. An eerie silence enveloped the ground for a mere second or two before Wembley erupted. United were in front. The game was awoken from its slumber.

George suddenly squirmed his way past three mesmerised defenders before releasing a powerful drive from just inside the penalty area that was to prove too hot for Henrique to hold, the ball rolling invitingly to the feet of Sadler, but hesitating slightly, with the goal invitingly in front of him, his shot hit the unsuspecting Benfica goalkeeper and went behind for a corner. George himself could have ensured victory, once again dancing past various white shirts but as he attempted to take the ball round the goalkeeper, it was to be one touch too many and the chance was gone.

They were misses that were to prove costly as seven minutes later Benfica drew level, their experience seeping through. A deep, right wing cross from Augusto towards the far post and the towering Torres, was nodded back across the United goal towards the unmarked Graca who shot past Stepney with ease.

The expectations of earlier now turned into fear. The United support was again silenced. Thoughts of victory began to fade. Could the dream suddenly become a nightmare?

Indeed with only three minutes of normal time remaining it looked as if the game had spun on its axis and the trophy was heading for Portugal and not the north-west of England, as Eusebio surged through on goal. Having collected an excellent pass from Augusto, with the United defence in disarray, he bore down on Stepney's goal and was suddenly one-on-one with the United 'keeper. With no disrespect few would have put their money on the green clad custodian as the Benfica legendary forward pulled back his foot, unleashing a powerful drive. But Eusebio had gone for power rather the accuracy and shot right at Stepney, who managed not simply to block the ball, but to hold it, much to the amazement of everyone. None more so than the white shirted Number Ten.

If there was a defining moment in the game, then this was it.

Extra time beckoned for those tired, energy sapped legs. Busby and his opposite number, Otto Gloria, along with their backroom staff were on the pitch massaging those tired legs and minds for the thirty crucial minutes ahead. There was no need to play those additional thirty as midway through the first fifteen the final outcome was in no doubt. United found some inner strength and grabbed the initiative. Three minutes into extra-time Stepney sent a long hopeful clearance downfield, the ball back-headed on by Kidd to George who slipped the ball between the legs of one defender before dribbling round the advancing goalkeeper and slipping the ball into the empty net. The goalkeeper chasing back in a futile attempt to prevent the goal, ending up beside the ball in the back of the net.

Two minutes later it was 3-1. A Charlton corner was headed towards goal by Sadler, Kidd diverted it closer, but his effort was blocked by Henrique. Fortunately it came straight back towards Kidd and he again headed for goal, the ball this time lopping over the head of the 'keeper and into the net. Benfica were now demoralised, resigned to defeat and this was well and truly confirmed two minutes later when Charlton latched onto a Kidd cross to fire the ball high into the Benfica net.

That was it and the celebrations began. United were Kings of Europe.

Manchester United: Stepney, Brennan, Dunne, Crerand, Foulkes, Stiles, Best, Kidd, Charlton, Sadler, Aston. Substitute: Rimmer

Scorers: Charlton (2), Best, Kidd.

Benfica: Jose-Henrique, Adolfo, Humberto, Jacinto, Cruz, Jaime-Graca, Coluna, Jose-Augusto, Torres, Eusebio, Simoes. Substitute: Nascimento.

Scorer: Graca.

Attendance: 100,000.

25

United vs Estudiantes

16 October 1968

Crowned 'Champions of Europe' less than five months previously on a balmy May evening in north London, United now had the opportunity to add to their seemingly ever increasing list of honours, enhancing that previously mentioned title with another: 'Champions of the World'. A title no other British club could lay claim to.

European football had been an adventure, a ground-breaking journey initially denied them by the authorities but it was a demand that Matt Busby ignored, taking on that new challenge like a duck to water, his team using its experience of previous friendly sojourns against teams from other countries to good advantage. But South America was an entirely different kettle of fish, the tempestuous fixtures against Atlas of Mexico in the early fifties while on tour of the United States coming to mind when the two-legged affair against Estudiantes drew close.

Some felt that Busby was wrong in taking his club into a competition that had seen Glasgow Celtic, European Cup winners of the previous season, going into the World Club Championship blind and blissfully ignorant as to what lay ahead. As it was, their two fixtures against Racing Club of Buenos Aires being more akin to a mini-war than a football match. The Hampden Park first-leg saw Celtic win 1-0, only to lose the Buenos Aires return 2-1. With a play-off necessary in Montevideo, they were involved in something best described as a shambles with six players sent off – four Scots and two Argentineans. Celtic ultimately lost 1-0 and in the aftermath every Celtic player was fined £250 while the Racing Club players received £2,000 per man and a car.

United were well aware of what they were getting into and were advised by many to give the games a miss. Respected columnist Brian Glanville wrote: 'The best way to prevent the incidents which will no doubt disfigure Wednesday's world championship match between Estudiantes and Manchester United, in Buenos Aires, would simply be not to play it.' The journalist going on to say: 'No one in his senses believes that the ultimate winners of such matches will be the best club team in the world, if only for the fact that they take place long after the moment when each proved itself the best in its respective Continent.'

Despite the 7,000 mile, twenty hour, journey Matt Busby was confident of success: 'If we can keep out of trouble in the first-leg'. This was despite an indifferent start to their League campaign, where they could only claim three victories from their last eight first division fixtures. Many suspecting an aging team and vulnerability within their defence as being the major cause for this decline.

The first-leg of the confrontation against the South Americans was akin to a blind date – something you were going into through choice, although might be regretted later, while being totally uncertain as to how the whole thing would pan out. It also turned out to be a match that the Estudiantes players appeared determined to win at all costs. Memories of the sometimes over physical confrontation between England and Argentina at Wembley in the 1966 World Cup

Finals were well to the fore, with Nobby Stiles singled out for preferential treatment long before the first blast of the referee's whistle.

Bilardo, a doctor by profession, butted Stiles, cutting his eye, in the 14th minute and proceeded to kick out at any United player he came into contact with. Stiles was also punched by Togneri and suffered double vision for most of the game. Pachame gashed Charlton's right shin with an over-the-top tackle, the same individual felling George with a sly off-the-ball punch. Suarez made a point of showing the United players what type of studs he preferred and didn't so much as tackle them, as simply run straight into them.

Many must have thought that United, at times, were playing with twelve men as trainer Jack Crompton was frequently on the pitch and they would certainly have welcomed an additional player as they struggled at times to contain the home side as they attempted to get the better of their hosts with long through passes and high balls into the middle of the defence.

United, despite the oppositions tactics, played well and might have returned to Manchester with a draw. They went behind in the 29th minute, when Stepney missed a swirling corner and Conigliaro headed the ball into the net. Ten minutes later they thought they had equalised when Sadler flicked home a low Charlton free-kick, but having at first signalled a goal the referee changed his mind after talking to a linesman. Photographs were later to show that perhaps the decision was the correct one, with Bill Foulkes looking very much in an offside position.

But it was another incident that denied United their draw, coming ten minutes from time when Nobby Stiles was sent off. Having been booked earlier in the game for 'standing too close to Bilardo', he was then flagged offside as he moved forward to join the attack. Raising his arm in a dismissive gesture was taken as an offence by the referee, who surprisingly sent him off.

George had little opportunity to rescue United, never mind display his wide array of skills as he was too closely marked. When asked 'what was the most irritating thing that the Estudiantes players did to him?' he replied, 'Everything'. 'I didn't go for 70-40 balls, let alone 50-50 ones. And I don't think that makes me a coward. You couldn't live out there. I'd like to hear one of their team talks. They must spend hours thinking up different places to pinch you.'

Following the ill-fated trip to South America it was once again suggested that United should withdraw from the competition as a form of protest due to the treatment they received in Argentina, along with the opinion that the second-leg at Old Trafford would simply a repeat of the Celtic – Racing encounter.

Busby however, had other problems as he was struggling to find eleven fit men. George, Foulkes, Morgan, Kidd, Law and Dunne all carried knocks, as did Fitzpatrick who did not appear in the first-leg tie while Sadler was a major doubt. Stiles was of course suspended.

The Estudiantes officials laid a wreath at Old Trafford in the uneasy truce prior to the second-leg, with United on a reported £2,000 a man if they should win. It would be the hardest ever bonus that any of the players would ever have to play for.

It was never a gentlemanly affair, but it was far removed from the over-physical encounter of the first-leg. Tackles went from the acceptable to the totally unacceptable and peace reigned for the majority of the match. But perhaps the fact that Estudiantes scored within five minutes of the start had much to do with this.

A free-kick was awarded to Estudiantes when Foulkes was adjudged to have his foot up too high in a challenge with Coniglari. Taken by Madero, the ball floated over the heads of the rather static United defence, allowing Veron to ghost in at the back post to head past the unprotected Stepney.

After something of a poor start, while continuing to keep their cool, United kept plodding away in the hope that they could make that vital breakthrough. Crerand settled into having a good game, although Charlton was soon to become frustrated due to lack of support from his fellow forwards, while Kidd, through frustration due to being unable to get close on goal, as much as inexperience, adapted something of a shoot-on-sight policy.

George came close to equalising, as did Charlton and Sadler, but his reputation went before him and he was well policed with Malbernat, Madero, Suarez and Medina keeping a close watch while picking off passes in his direction with relative ease. Just before the interval, Stepney kept United in with a shout making what was, in reality, his only real save of the night, when he turned a shot from Conigliario over his crossbar.

Perhaps a more telling incident to the eventual outcome came just before half-time when Law, chasing yet another opportunity, crashed into goalkeeper Poletti – an accident that was to require four stiches to a gashed shin and lead to his eventual substitution.

United continued to chase the game in the second half but it was now more in hope than anything else the Estudiantes defence, standing firm, keeping their opponents at bay with relative ease, masters of their craft, well tutored in both the football and underhand tactics.

George was restricted with practically every step he took and, as in the first-leg, he was rarely allowed the opportunity to shine, to suddenly create that little bit of genius that would unleash the shackles that he and his teammates encountered and rescue a game that was slowly slipping away.

The unruly play that had blighted the first-leg of this tie and Celtic's free-for-all the previous season, had failed to materialise, although there were the odd petty fouls that you could see in any Saturday afternoon in a first division fixture. That was however, until ten minutes from time when the blue touch paper was suddenly lit and the game exploded into the spectacle that many had expected.

Although clad in all white the visitors were obviously far from virginal, reverting to underhand tactics as if at the snap of the fingers when the ball had left the red-shirted United player and the eyes of the crowd and those of the referee and his assistants were elsewhere and it was such an incident that tripped the switch of the already ticking time-bomb.

From the right touchline, directly in front of the main stand, George sent a cross soaring towards the Estudiantes penalty area and with the ball in mid-flight, he was caught, unfairly by Medina. Having refrained from rising to the bait throughout the entirety of the first-leg and the eighty minutes of the second, the George's temper finally snapped and he immediately sprang to his feet before swinging a right hook in the direction of his assailants head. In an earlier incident when he had been spat in the face had resisted any form of retaliation and simply patted the offender on the cheek. His response on this occasion was a mixture of anger and frustration.

Medina went down like a pantomime villain and rolled around the Old Trafford turf as if hit by a snipers bullet as around him, all hell broke loose. 'We want a riot' chanted the crowd, a thin line of police all that separated them from the pitch, as players from both teams became involved a pushing and shoving confrontation, with the odd punch also exchanged. There was little option for the referee, who although not having witnessed the incident took the word of his linesman and sent off both players. Medina, perhaps a little aggrieved, his sending off more to keep the peace both on and off the pitch, failed to take his punishment and attempted to get hold of George once again before getting restrained by the linesman and one of the Estudiantes backroom staff.

George could have no complaints as he had only minutes earlier kicked out at one opponent and punched another. 'He had a go at me and I retaliated. I can't say any more. He hit me on the lip,' was his after match comment. One correspondent however, sympathised with the offender writing: 'I can excuse, to some extent, George Best who, in the heat of the moment and at a critical time of the game, forgot himself to such an extent that he struck an opponent in retaliation. Best is still a comparative youngster, who comes in for tough handling in every game he plays.'

As the game struggled to regain some form of normality, United managed to make the breakthrough when yet another free-kick, taken by Crerand, found its way to the feet of Morgan who moved in to score with three minutes remaining on the clock. It was surely too little too late.

Along with the two minutes official time remaining, the referee was to add on an additional eight due to the forty odd free-kicks and time wasting throughout the game, United, with nothing to lose, surged forward more in hope than anything else and just as the Yugoslavian referee raised his whistle to his lips to signal the end of the game, Kidd fired home a Morgan cross. Everyone in the ground thought it was the winning goal on the night, levelling the match on aggregate. Unfortunately, it was not to be, as the official indicated that he had blown before the ball had crossed the line.

The jubilant Estudiantes players celebrated as the crowd booed and jeered, but the defeat left bitterness in the mouths of the United players, with Alex Stepney giving Pachame a backhanded slap to the face as the Argentinean stood on the touchline applauding the losers from the pitch!

The victors, unmoved by the hostility towards them, actually wanted to do a lap of honour with the trophy but were prevented in doing so by the police, who feared that the feelings of the home support would bubble over the fencing around the pitch.

United: Stepney, Brennan, Dunne, Crerand, Foulkes, Sadler, Morgan, Kidd, Charlton, Law, Best. Substitute: Sartori for Law.

Scorer: Morgan.

Estudiantes: Poletti, Malbernat, Suarez, Madero, Medina, Bilardo, Pachame, Ribando, Conigliaro, Togneri, Veron. Substitute: Echecopar for Ribando.

Scorer: Veron

Attendance: 63,500.

George had come a long way since that initial appearance against West Bromwich Albion. Gone was the shy, reserved and softly-spoken youngster and in his place we had the confident master craftsman with the world at his feet. How far, and indeed how much, he had changed was perhaps captured by Kenneth Wolstenholme in his book *The Pro's*:

> The once shy Belfast boy, who at first could not get used to the bright lights of Manchester, is the first to admit that he got to like them a little too much. The Beatle-hired Manchester United and Northern Ireland soccer sorcerer quickly established himself as a genius on the football field.
>
> The adulation showered on him by the younger fans, especially the female ones, matched his talent. They screamed every time he touched the ball. They invaded the pitch to touch him as he walked off. They waited for hours outside the ground just to see him. They flocked to his boutiques. They kept vigil outside his house. For he was just a wonder footballer. He was the with-it Mod. One of them. And the kids loved him for it.
>
> 'It was overwhelming, before I got used to it,' admits George. 'I loved it. Who wouldn't? Everyone loves to be loved. The more they screamed for me, the more I played up to it.' Only one man spotted the change coming over George – Sir Matt Busby, the Manchester United manager and the man who spots all the dangers at Old Trafford. He had seen the signs as George became accustomed to the sweet taste of life. The 'boyo' with the soft brogue, long hair, and sharp clothes was the idol of young Manchester – and he meant to cash in.

There were discotheques, there was dancing, and there were 'birds'. Georgie Best – the lad who was so homesick when he first came to Manchester that he hopped it back to Belfast – got to like them all.

As soon as training was over he would dash to his favourite discotheque. From then on it was records and girls. Tomorrow's training slog was a day away. Gradually this sort of life began to tell. George was still a fine player, but the edge began to dull. He still had great talent, yet it wasn't showing where it was most needed – on the field on match day.

Matt Busby could have called Best into his office and bawled him out, or given him some fatherly advice. Busby, always the master tactician, did neither. He had an idea that George would not take kindly to a lecture from one of 'the older generation'.

Matt just let it be known to Best that his way of life was a perfect short cut to ruining a great career – and dropped him. George said, 'My first reaction was one of shock. Then I was annoyed. How could they, how dare they, drop me? I dosed myself with self-pity.' That experience did it. George turned from the fun-loving gadabout to the fun-loving grafter.

Says George, 'I still love records and all that jazz. And I still love the birds. But soccer is my living – and nothing is allowed to interfere with it.' From that moment of truth, George has never looked back. Success has heaped itself on to his lean shoulders and none of it has turned his head.

Wolstenholme continued,

He regards the ball as his own property. But his dribbling skill can carry him through the tightest defences. If he has a flaw in his game, it is his sharp temper. Often he had turned round and ruined an otherwise faultless display with a fit of petulance. He admits: 'I hate myself for it, but I don't seem able to help it. It just proves that I am still young and that I still have a lot to learn. I do realise that I have a duty to the youngsters who look up to me. The youngsters make their own idols, and they copy them. They go around and claim that if it is good enough for George Best it is good enough for them.' He added, 'That is why I try to lead a proper life. It is my duty to do so, to do a little bit towards setting a good example. I hope I will not encourage anyone to take the wrong course.'

Having got the worst of Best out of his system, the best of best may still be to come.

26

Birmingham City vs United

8 February 1969

Manchester United's 1968/69 first division campaign was something of a struggle despite getting off to the perfect start with a 2-1 victory over Everton at Old Trafford (in which George claimed the opening goal), with only a further five victories in the following nineteen fixtures up until the turn of the year. Half a dozen were lost, with the other eight drawn, with a further downside being the fact that of the opening twenty fixtures, nine had seen United fail to score. They sat 16th in the table, a distant seventeen points behind leaders Liverpool.

So it was with some relief that the FA Cup made its appearance on the fixture list, although the third round trip to fourth division Exeter City was a potential banana skin. Thankfully however, it was bypassed without any problems courteously of a 3-1 victory. Round four raised an even more daunting prospect against third division leaders Watford, albeit the draw had given United home advantage, but true to form, they struggled, having to fight back from a goal down to snatch a replay at Vicarage Road. Denis Law, having secured the replay, was also responsible for United's passage into round five, scoring both goals in a 2-0 victory.

Second division Birmingham City were United's fifth round opponents five days after disposing of Watford, the trip to St Andrews no more looked forward to than that to Vicarage Road, as results in the league had continued to be poor, with only one victory in the last five.

In *The Sun*, Peter Lorenzo wrote of how the Birmingham City supporters 'must still be wondering how their team escaped a six-goal beating'. Going on to write, 'In everything barring goals, United were so impressively superior and better organised. Four times in the first-half United's forwards contrived to miss chances. They increased the ratio in the second half.'

Tons of snow had to be removed from the St Andrews pitch before play was possible, but the near perfect underfoot conditions were severely hampered in the second half following a torrential rain shower which began just before the interval. At all added to the spectacle that this cup-tie created.

The opening forty-five minutes was devoid of goals, but not incident, and the home side could well have found themselves three goals behind in the space of three minutes, but luck and excellent goalkeeping from Jim Herriot kept United at bay. Kidd crossed the ball from the right, but the 'keeper saved well from Law's header. Ninety seconds later, a dreadful pass along his own 18 yard line by Martin gave Law another opportunity to get his name on the score sheet, but once again Herriot was the equal of his fellow Scot. The third opportunity saw Morgan head against the bar from a Crerand cross.

Birmingham City caused United few first half problems, but it wasn't until the 63rd minute that they were to find themselves a goal behind. A splendid Crerand-Dunne-Kidd move ended with the latter sending a perfectly flighted centre into the Birmingham penalty area where Law rose to head superbly past Herriot to give his side the advantage. Something they should have had at least forty minutes previously.

But it was a lead they held for only three minutes. Birmingham substituted Beard for Thwaites and within ninety seconds the newcomer had equalised. Wylie started the move with a high centre towards Pickering, the former Everton and England forward rising above Steve James to nod the ball towards Beard who rammed the ball past Stepney. It was a goal totally against the run of play.

Within three minutes Kidd, who had frequently troubled the Birmingham defence, burst through on his own and having drawn Herriot from his goal clipped the ball over the advancing 'keeper only to see the it hit the angle of the cross-bar and post. George then had a shot saved by the overly active 'keeper, before Kidd headed over an unattended goal.

With eight minutes remaining and the game heading towards an Old Trafford replay, United scored what looked to be the goal that would take them into the quarter-finals. Bobby Charlton sent in a low cross from the left and George 'pirouetted like a ballet dancer to ram in a brilliant goal'.

Continuing his report in *The Sun* Peter Lorenzo wrote, 'But three minutes later Best, unquestionably became the angriest footballer in Europe when Gloucester referee David Smith adjudged him to have handled the ball from a throw-in just inside the United penalty area. Best continued his angry protest after the ball had rocketed into the back of the net.' 'Oh, George!' proclaimed the back page of the *Daily Mirror*, while the *Daily Mail* headline read: 'Best's Blunder Robs United' with the disgruntled player saying, 'It was never a penalty.' The referee however, took a completely different view and commented, 'I saw the incident clearly. Best brought his knee up and then followed through with his hand to strike the ball. Several of the players saw the incident as clearly as I did.'

George was well to the fore in the replay headlines, but it was a case of 'Birmingham Routed by Artistry of Law and Best' rather than anything negative. He wasn't to get his name on the score sheet however, only as a member of the supporting cast. In the *Times*, Geoffrey Green wrote, 'This was a night when Law became the passionless executioner, with three goals, and when Best, of whom there is no possible rival in the British game, revealed the whole range of his intense individuality and limitless artistry. He, especially, was on fire last night after Birmingham had taken a lighting lead after only four minutes – a possible fore-runner of disaster for United.'

He continued, 'But United, or rather Best, were not prepared to compromise the future. Suddenly they began to spread their wings like eagles, as they had done a fortnight ago in the first match at St Andrews.'

Birmingham stunned Old Trafford into silence with that fourth minute strike. Pickering forcing a corner, then rising high to head Vincent's kick square to Greenhoff who nodded past Stepney. Inspired by this goal, the visitors continued to take the game to United, with their forward line stretching the defence with considerable ease.

But in a devastating ten minute spell, which saw United score thrice, the game was suddenly turned on its head. Fitzpatrick, not noted for his attacking tendencies, exchanged passes with Charlton and Crerand, taking him into the Birmingham penalty area where he was upended by Beard. From the resulting penalty kick, Law netted with ease.

It was now that George came to the fore. Beating four men in a mazy, snaking dribble, during which he lost and regained the ball twice, he eluded a fifth challenge but was to see his eventual shot rebound off the post. The mesmerizing of the Birmingham defence continued with Martin being booked for kicking out at George as he lay on the ground, then he added to the punishment when he pulled down a high clearance, swept past Martin with a dip of the shoulder before supplying the pass that was to see Law put United 3-1 in front. Crerand having scored the second in between times, hooking home a Morgan pass from an acute angle.

The second half was something of a repetition of the first. Charlton combined with Law for the Scot to claim his hat-trick with fifteen minutes remaining. Kidd made it 5-1 from a Crerand cross. Summerill pulled one back for Birmingham City before Morgan rounded off the scoring following a seventy yard run through the Birmingham defence.

It was George at his best and United back to their free-scoring days of old.

First Game:

Birmingham City: Herriot, Martin, Green, Page, Robinson, Wylie, Vincent, Greenhoff, Pickering, Hockey, Thwaites. Substitute: Beard for Thwaites.

Scorers: Beard, Robinson.

United: Stepney, Fitzpatrick, Dunne, Crerand, James, Stiles, Morgan, Kidd, Charlton, Law, Best. Substitute: Foulkes.

Scorers: Law, Best.

Attendance: 52,500

Replay:

United: As above, except substitute: Sadler.

Scorers: Law (3), Crerand, Kidd, Morgan.

Birmingham City: As above except substitute: Summerill for Beard.

Attendance: 61,932.

27

United vs Rapid Vienna

28 February 1969

Having achieved success in any form of competition, you always aim to retain your title at the next opportunity. Manchester United were no different following their success in lifting the European Cup in 1968. Claiming the crown of 'World Champions' might well have been the next target on their agenda, but they most certainly wanted to win the coveted European Cup again twelve months down the line.

They were certainly given an ideal start in the retention of the trophy when they were drawn against Waterford from the League of Ireland, with the 10-2 aggregate win certainly not unexpected. Round two brought them up against old foes Anderlecht, the Belgians, on this occasion being able to keep the score down to a less than embarrassing 4-3 defeat on aggregate.

George, who had played against Waterford but had failed to get onto the score sheet, did not appear in either of the two games against Anderlecht due to suspension at the time of the first tie and an injury at the time of the second, this perhaps was the reason behind the closer than expected result. It could also be the reason that some 15,000 tickets went unsold for the first leg tie at Old Trafford.

Due to various injury problems and George's suspension against the Belgians, Matt Busby was more than happy to see his team into the next round of the competition, he was, however, slightly uninspired by the draw for the last eight as United were paired with either old rivals Real Madrid or Rapid Vienna. Strangely enough, it was the Austrians who were to stand between United and the semi-final, having defeated Madrid on away goals, proving that they were not a team to be taken lightly.

In *The Times* prior to the quarter-final fixture Geoffrey Green wrote, 'This, in fact, will be Manchester United's thirty-eighth match in Europe's senior club competition and they now take on Austria's most powerful representatives, a side dotted with internationals that beat famous Real Madrid in the last round. That in itself should underline United's present task, coming unfortunately at a moment that finds the Englishmen having to ride four vital cup-ties in the space of ten days.

'On the other hand, the contest has fallen at a time when Charlton and his men seem at last to have regained something of their peak form for the first time this season.' Thankfully that 'peak form' continued in that Old Trafford first-leg as the headlines were to reveal and United took a comfortable lead into the return fixture in Austria. In the *Daily Mail* it was: 'Magnificent, that United machine!', 'United Show the Form the World Loves' from the *Guardian*. 'Manchester United Break Down Rapid Resistance' said the *Times* and 'Goalkeeper Errors Help United Build Good Lead' could be found in the *Daily Telegraph*. But perhaps, the *Daily Express* and the *Sun* were closer to the reason behind United's 3-0 victory with their headlines: 'It's "Goodnight Vienna" as Best smashes two goals' and 'United March on into Europe by the Best Route'.

With injury and suspension, George had not enjoyed the best of seasons to date, if you excuse the pun, but against Rapid Vienna he regained some of the form and inspirational play that had become his trademark.

'Two goals from the twinkling feet of Best and one from Morgan, in his first European Cup match, gave Manchester United last night every hope of and confidence of reaching the semi-finals of the Champion's Cup, the trophy they won last season' wrote Albert Barham in his *Guardian* report. Many however, felt that it should have been more than three.

The Austrians managed to hold out for almost the entire first half, mainly through the leniency of referee Botic who denied United two rather blatant penalty kicks. First, Charlton was knocked to the ground by left-back Fak but to the surprise of everyone, the Yugoslav referee signalled for a corner. Seven minutes later, George wiggled his way through the Vienna defence and was bearing down on goal when Flogel fouled him just inside the penalty area. Again the referee simply waved the protest away. Just to show that he wasn't biased in any way, he ignored two blatant fouls by Crerand and Stiles, awarding free-kicks to United.

Minutes before the interval George put Denis Law through on goal only for Gebhardt to stick out a foot and divert the ball onto a post. The ball rebounded towards Morgan on the bye line who managed to pull it back wide of the diving 'keeper and into the path of George, who as quick as a flash pirouetted to beat Fuchsbichler in the Rapid goal.

As the second half got underway, Charlton had two opportunities to put the game beyond the reach of the Austrians when George and Brian Kidd placed the ball comfortably into his path, but on both occasions, he drove wide.

Thanks mainly to United's poor finishing and the brilliance of Austria's national goalkeeper between the posts, United failed to increase their advantage until the 67th minute. Bobby Charlton broke free some 50 yards from goal before passing to Kidd. Beating two men, the youngster slid the ball to Morgan and the ever improving former Burnley man scored United's second.

'Within minutes Best, the irrepressible, the dark haired magician who achieved so many sleights of feet, now set up a move with Stiles in midfield, took a perfect return, mesmerized three defenders, almost mesmerized himself as he lost the ball, and with his left foot hit the roof of the Austrian net.' Or do you prefer: 'Best twisted, turned, jinked, escaped lashing feet and thumping charges before he turned the ball into goal' or even: 'The final goal, in the 70th minute, was Best at his finest. Stiles chipped over the ball, Best delayed his shot, turning across the face of the goal, and it seemed his opportunity had gone, yet he turned calmly and placed the ball into the roof of the net.'

No matter which one captures your imagination the most, if was a typical George moment, 'a goal that only Best could score' tantalising the opposition and seducing the crowd, who were to obviously appreciate his brilliance more than his bewildered opponents. Kaltenbrunner was warned for a wild kick at George, while the unpredictable match official missed an Austrian defender punch him in the face. Such was the price of excellence.

That was it, except for some excellent saves from the Rapid goalkeeper, without whom the score would have been double and the second-leg a mere formality. As it was the 3-0 result was enough to see United into the semi-finals as they played out a 0-0 draw in the Prater Stadium.

George again entertained but failed to either score or assist in United's 100th European Cup goal. Neither could he conjure up anything in the San Siro when United faced AC Milan in the first-leg of the semi-final. John Fitzpatrick's sending off doing little to help the United cause in the 2-0 defeat. George barely rating a mention in any reports, with Hugh McIlvanney's summary stating, 'Best was roughly subdued all through by Anquilletti.'

Prior to the Old Trafford second-leg George was to comment, 'If we score in the first half, we've got a great chance. If we don't score before half-time, we're struggling.' And struggle they did. George was once again closely marked throughout the game, never allowed the space to dribble nor the time to shoot and it was not until the seventieth minute that the second-leg deadlock was broken. Bobby Charlton giving United a glimmer of hope after George had finally managed to manoeuvre past two defenders before side footing the ball for his captain to score.

Cudicini in the Milan goal had been felled by an object thrown from the Stretford end as the second half got underway, but the evening's high drama was not to materialise until ten minutes from the end. Crerand took a long pass from Charlton and sent the ball into the Milan penalty area. Law flicked it goalwards and it looked, momentarily, to have crossed the line before Santin and Anquiletti managed to hook it clear. The referee waved play on. The opportunity was gone and the tie was lost.

United: Stepney, Fitzpatrick, Dunne, Crerand, James, Stiles, Morgan, Kidd, Charlton, Law, Best. Substitutes: Rimmer, Foulkes, Sadler, Ryan, Gowling.

Scorers: Best (2), Morgan.

Rapid Vienna: Fuchsbichler, Gebhardt, Glechner, Fak, Berregaard, Ullmann, Fritsch, Kaltenbrunner, Grausam, Floegel, Soendergaard. Substitutes: Erovic, Lindmann, Traxler

Attendance: 62,726

28

United vs Queens Park Rangers
19 March 1969

He was overshadowed in the goal stakes by the man on the opposite wing, Willie Morgan, but when it came to the actual headlines, there was only one name emblazoned across those back pages: 'George Best Leads Rout of QPR', 'Best Leads United Romp', 'QPR Courage Beaten by Best Genius' were only a trio of the many that preceded the match reports of United's 8-1 trouncing of the London club.

For a team blessed with three former European Footballers of the Year, Manchester United were at times far from impressive, often relying on George to pull them out of the mire with a flash of genius, Denis Law to score the goals to win games and points and Bobby Charlton to pull the strings from mid-field. Neither had the Old Trafford faithful been spoilt with the sight of their favourites scoring goals during the 1968/69 season having witnessed, if they had attended all fourteen fixtures, only eighteen goals up until the visit of Queens Park Rangers on 19 March – only three other clubs had scored less at home. It was very hard to imagine that United were indeed champions of Europe.

Being anchored at the foot of the table did not auger well for any ninety minutes where Queens Park Rangers were concerned, a mere fifteen points from their thirty-five games. United, on the other hand had not won any of their previous five fixtures, so perhaps the Loftus Road side had thoughts of their first away victory of the season on the journey north. If they did, they were to be very much mistaken.

A little more self-belief from the visitors might have conjured up an entirely different scoreline. But despite starting the game well, they seemed somewhat reluctant to take the game to United and test their rather susceptible defence. Marsh and Glover missed simple opportunities while Stepney dealt competently with shots from Hazell, Glover, Watson and Ian Morgan, the United 'keeper, along with his centre-half Steve James, could also have been punished for some rather poor defending – a James back pass from 15 yards out simply rolled back towards Stepney and the 'keeper only just managed to beat Clarke to the ball, while the United custodian dropped a looping centre at the feet of Marsh, with only a frantic scramble managing to clear the danger.

It was, in reality, against the run of play when United took the lead on the half hour. A short corner from George was headed on by Aston and Morgan, at the back post lashed the ball home on the volley for his first League goal since joining United back in September.

If those who had turned up for this mid-week fixture (the 36,638 crowd the smallest of the season to date), felt deprived, perhaps short changed, in that opening forty-five minutes, they were still settling down for the second half, wondering what would unfold, when the game sprang to life within three minutes of the restart and they were treated to something special. As John Roberts wrote in the *Daily Express*, 'The wake was turned into a party by George Best'.

Having exchanged passes with Brian Kidd, George lost the ball, but Kidd regained possession before once again slipping a pass through to the Irishman. Teasing and impudently, George stood on the ball, practically inviting the Queens Park Rangers defenders to 'come and get it'. As two brave souls moved towards him, he pulled the ball back, deceiving the unsuspecting duo, while in the same fleeting movement fired the ball into the far corner of the net past Spratley. Even the referee appreciated this moment of skill, giving the goal scorer a pat on the back as he made his way back to his own half for the re-start.

It was only now that it seemed to dawn on United that the visitors were there for the taking but they were soon caught out once again by their rather non-existent defending, allowing Rangers to pull a goal back, Marsh scoring from a Glover pass. Glover, himself had also to come close to scoring, Stepney palming a net bound effort over the bar.

The Londoners joy and any expectations they had were short lived, as within a minute they were once again dazzled like a rabbit caught in a cars headlight but, for them it was George yet again who left them transfixed. Having picked up a pass from Stiles he rounded three opponents with ease, as only he could do before unleashing a powerful drive that left Spratley utterly helpless with a forceful right-footed shot.

There was now no way back for the visitors. Willie Morgan increased the lead, claiming his second of the night in the 74th minute, pouncing on the ball after George's corner kick had been deflected onto the crossbar. Then ten minutes later, the vulnerability of Queens Park Rangers was clearly in evidence when even Nobby Stiles managed to get his name on the score-sheet, scoring with a header. In between those two United goals, Leach and Glover had both missed ideal opportunities to pull their side back into the game. Neither however, would have changed the eventual outcome.

Three minutes from time Morgan claimed his hat-trick thanks to the sterling work of Denis Law who created the opening, the winger driving the ball home via the crossbar, but it wasn't quite game, set and match, although many had already decided that they had been given their money's worth, and had started heading for home. A move they were later to regret.

With two minutes still on the clock Law threaded the ball through to Kidd, who caught Spratley out of position with make it 7-1, and then in the final minute of the game with the Queens Park Rangers players almost begging the referee to blow his whistle and spare them any further pain or embarrassment, Aston rounded off the scoring with a fine 30 yard drive. A particularly pleasing goal for the United winger, as this was only his second first division appearance following his return to the side after breaking his leg back in September.

This 8-1 victory was by far United's best performance of the season, surpassing the equally emphatic 6-2 victory over Birmingham City in the FA Cup sixth round replay. The aggregate goal total of nine goals in one game equalled that from back in August, when Sheffield Wednesday won 5-4 at Hillsborough. It was also United's highest victory since their 8-0 trouncing of Yeovil Town in the FA Cup fifth round tie at Maine Road on 12 February 1949. It was also their first League 'double' of the season and their first League win since 18 January.

For Queens Park Rangers it was the individual brilliance of George, more than any other single facto that deepened their plight at the foot of the first Division table.

United: Stepney, Fitzpatrick, Dunne, Crerand, James, Stiles, I. Morgan, Kidd, Aston, Law, Best. Substitute: Ryan.

Scorers: Morgan (3), Best (2), Stiles, Kidd, Aston.

Queens Park Rangers: Spratley, Watson, Clements, Hazell, Hunt, Sibley, Morgan, Leach, Clarke, Marsh, Glover. Substitute: Keech for Clarke.

Scorer: Marsh.

Attendance: 36,638.

29

Sheffield Wednesday vs United

17 September 1969

George's mentor, Sir Matt Busby, had relinquished the post of manager of Manchester United, taking up something of a general office job, handing over the day-to-day running of the team to Wilf McGuinness, but not the title of 'manager', the former United wing-half considered worthy of only being called 'team coach'.

McGuinness had a job and a half on his hands as Manchester United was no longer the team they were only a couple of year previously. No longer were they considered among the favourites for the first division title, a good cup run was the most they could expect. Many also thought that Wilf McGuinness tried to run before he could walk, leaving the experience of Bobby Charlton, Bill Foulkes, Shay Brennan and Denis Law on the side lines following a rather humiliating 4-1 home defeat by Southampton, in only the second home fixture of the 1969/70 season. And as the season progressed, it was to become more and more obvious that he was relying on one player alone to carry him through this testing apprenticeship.

George was, by far, the main man in the Manchester United side, the most talented player in the British game. He was also, most probably, the outstanding individual in European football but United were no longer a part of the European scene, so he could only weave his magic in the all too familiar stadiums up and down the country.

He was now a celebrity away from the mudded pitches, gracing the ordinary magazines, not simply those associated with football. His face was known to all, just as familiar as the back of his head was to countless defenders. He was a journalist and a copy writers dream. A player of a thousand headlines.

Following the rather poor start to the 1968/69 campaign, failing to win any of their opening half dozen fixtures, a 3-1 victory against Sunderland at Old Trafford suddenly got the show on the road. 'George is Back at his Best!' the *Manchester Evening News* brought to the attention of their readers. Then seven days later, it was 'Best Transforms United' in the *Daily Telegraph* following George's double at Elland Road against Leeds United. The season was slowly turning into the George Best roadshow.

His name failed to appear in bold letters above the match reports for the 1-0 victory over Liverpool at Old Trafford but four days later, below the Hillsborough floodlights he well and truly captured the show in the 3-1 victory over Sheffield Wednesday.

'Best's Magic Touch Earns the Points', 'Best Lays the Hoodoo of Hillsborough', 'Best Takes the Stage' and 'George takes Wednesday in his Stride' were only a trio of the headlines after George's outstanding, two goal, performance.

In the *Daily Express*, below the latter of the above three headlines, James Lawton wrote: 'Explaining George Best is impossible, like grasping the mysteries of a distant meteor. He simply explodes across the face of a match. Last night he destroyed Wednesday with a raging power and an exquisite timing which brought goals in the 82nd and 83rd minutes of this incredibly transformed game. Who knows when and how his next victims will suffer?'

United took the lead through Brian Kidd in the 12th minute, turning a low corner from George past Springett, who must be faulted for allowing the ball to slip through his grasp and into the net. But true to form, United allowed their opponents back into the game. In the 38th minute, Warboys picked out Ford who moved down the left before sending over an elegantly floated centre directly onto the forehead of Pugh. Stepney was powerless to prevent the goal. The crowd were now looking forward a Wednesday victory.

With the home side preferring something of a kick and rush tactic, United found the going tough but determinedly maintained their poise, for which the reward was later to materialise. It wasn't until the substitution of John Aston for Alan Gowling, eighteen minutes from time that the tide began to turn United's way.

Those who had anticipated a Sheffield Wednesday victory were now looking content to be going home with a point from a 1-1 draw, but with seven minutes remaining that point disappeared and they were treated to something very special.

The substitution of Aston for Gowling, who had partnered George on United's left flank, allowed George to move inside and this was what instigated the swing of the game United's way. Morgan dragged two defenders out of position, leaving a big enough gap for George to latch on to his hard low cross and fire a searing drive past Springett from 12 yards.

One minute later, Charlton a rather subdued figure throughout, indeed in the season as a whole, managed to pick out George in a packed penalty area. Creating space for himself on the edge of the penalty area he then sent yet another unstoppable drive past Springett.

'And still this superb solo performance was not over' wrote David Barnes in the *Daily Mail*. 'Dribbling three times it seemed through an entire defence, Best was within inches of completing an amazing hat-trick.' He added: 'The final whistle brought to an end his short, but devastating display of virtuosity that a courageous Wednesday were totally helpless to stop.'

It was a result that kick-started United's season and the headlines continued in the weeks that followed: 'Best has Final Word', 'Best Spoils it for Arsenal' and 'Best Plays Arsenal Single-handed' following the 2-2 draw at Highbury, then 'Wizard Best Conjures Reds Victory Trick', 'West Ham are left Chasing Best's Shadow' and 'Hammers Shattered by Best' after the 5-2 defeat of West Ham United. The bubble burst against Derby County with a 2-0 defeat but it only a minor blip, as George was to score three goals in the following three games.

Sheffield Wednesday: Springett, Smith, Barton, Young, Ellis, Craig, Irvine, Fantham, Warboys, Ford, Pugh.

Scorer: Pugh

United: Stepney, Fitzpatrick, Dunne, Burns, Ure, Sadler, Morgan, Kidd, Charlton, Gowling, Best. Substitute: Aston for Gowling.

Scorers: Best (2), Kidd.

Attendance: 39,298.

30

Northhampton Town vs United

7 February 1970

The only possibility of any silverware heading Manchester United's way as the sixties gave way to the seventies was in one of the domestic cup competitions, albeit, on the back of one or two favourable draws, as the consistency required to win the first division title was something that even the genius of United's three European Footballers of the Year could not stretch to.

Entry into the Football League Cup had always been compulsory and due to their European escapades, United had only bothered to enter the 1960/61 and the 1966/67 tournaments, much to their eternal embarrassment. Their first venture had seen them paired with Exeter City and it took a replay to dispose of the lower division side, before they were to face humiliation at Bradford City with a 2-1 defeat. In 1966/67 it was little different as they headed to Blackpool on a September evening with the illuminations shining brightly along the promenade. United certainly did not do likewise, losing 5-1.

The 1969/70 competition was to see United last slightly longer than in the past, despite the fact that they were drawn against much tougher opposition than Exeter, Bradford and Blackpool. Exempt from being included in the first round draw, they were paired with Middlesbrough in round two and a David Sadler goal was enough to see them safely through.

Wrexham put up a grim fight in round three, but goals from George and Brian Kidd took them into the giddy heights of Round Four and a Lancashire 'derby' against Burnley, where a much more difficult tie awaited. A goal-less draw at Turf Moor, took the teams to Old Trafford for a replay, where another closely fought ninety minutes unfolded. All that was to separate the two sides at the end of ninety minutes was a penalty scored by George in the eighth minute of the second half. Round five brought another 0-0 draw in the first-leg tie against Derby County at the Baseball Ground and again, just a solitary goal took United through to the semi-finals where neighbours City lay in wait.

In Maine Road first-leg on 3 December United lost 2-1 certainly more favourable than the 4-0 League defeat they had suffered prior to the victory over Derby County, but it was a result that many expected them to turnaround in the second-leg on home turf, more so as it was just a Francis Lee penalty that separated the two sides.

The second-leg was something of a 'classic' encounter and with nine minutes remaining, it looked as though the tie was heading for a reply, with United leading 2-1 thanks to goals from Edwards and Law. But then disaster struck. A foul by Willie Morgan on Bowyer 20 yards from the United goal poised little danger, more so as it was indirect. Strangely Francis Lee blasted the ball towards Stepney, but even more stranger, Stepney attempted to save the shot, but could only parry the ball to the feet of Summerbee who blasted the ball high into the United net. Enough to give his side a 4-3 aggregate victory.

Many however, had been completely unaware of the drama that had unfolded at the end of the Maine Road tie when George had knocked the ball out of referee Jack Taylor's hands as he left the field, most probably aggrieved at the officials awarding of a penalty to City. It was an action that was to prove costly to both player and club as the FA Disciplinary Committee did not simply fine George £100 but suspended him for a month. He was arraigned for conduct 'likely to bring the game into disrepute', or 'ungentlemanly conduct' to define it simpler. Neither did he ask for a personal hearing. A rather severe punishment considering that his list of 'previous convictions' was little more than five bookings over the course of seven seasons along with the sending off in the World Club Championship fixture against Estudiantes at Old Trafford. He had however, been cautioned during the City League Cup tie. He was arraigned for conduct 'likely to bring the game into disrepute, or 'ungentlemanly conduct'. He did not ask for a personal hearing.

In *The Guardian*, Eric Todd summed up the crime and its punishment as such: 'It is a good thing that the disciplinary committee should not differentiate between the exalted and the humble when making their decisions. An offence is an offence be it committed by master or serf. No rational person would deny that the referee was right to report Best for his foolish action. But how many, like me, wonder whether Mr Taylor (the referee) might have been inclined to overlook the incident or even to play it down if the game had not been televised.'

Somewhat surprisingly during George's suspension United went unbeaten in the first division, winning two and drawing two, while their performance in the FA Cup was perhaps more notable. George made his final United appearance prior to suspension against Ipswich Town in the competitions third round, where a Mick O'Neil own-goal took United into Round Four and a home draw against neighbours Manchester City. Even without George, they were able to record a 3-0 victory.

By a strange quirk of fate it was in the FA Cup that George was to make his return to action, in the fifth round at Northampton and typical of the man, he came back with a bang, or perhaps that should be an explosion!

> The operation was performed swiftly and painfully on Northampton. George Best, that master soccer surgeon, provided the early anaesthetic and then the chilling knife to leave Northampton stretched motionless on a muddy field. Out of breath; out of luck; out of the cup. Manchester United were merciless, Best led the massacre with a swashbuckling swagger, scoring six goals and carrying everything before him with supreme skill.

These were the words of Bill Meredith, a famous name in itself from United's past, but this one reported for The *Daily Telegraph*. His match summary however, could well have been ignored by the masses as they were already more than aware of what George had accomplished upon his return to action.

Yes it was a fourth division defence and if the higher paid, more athletic an skilful first division defenders could not cope with George on a normal Saturday afternoon, then what hope had those lesser mortals of Northampton Town?

If there were cobwebs on George's boots then they were soon blown away, although United did endure something of a nervous opening twenty minutes, a period of the game and to be honest, the only one, when the home side stood anything of a chance against United as a team and George as an individual.

'It did not matter how the ball came to Best – at knee, chest or head height. He was the master; a player with an artist's brush in each boot, splashing this cup canvas with generous daubs of brilliant colour' continued Bill Meredith, while Geoffrey Green in the *Sunday Times* penned: 'Only someone with Best's unique gifts could have converted all those offerings. His control, acceleration and change of direction in heavy going were of another dimension.'

Having survived those early twenty minutes United suddenly clicked, upped the ante and George awoke from his six weeks slumber. Almost on the half hour he struck with the first of his half dozen goals. Crerand had robbed McNeil of the ball, slipping it wide to Kidd on the right and from his inviting cross, completely missed by the Northampton 'keeper Kim Book, George headed into the empty goal.

One minute later it was 2-0. A poorly judged ball from Rankmore was easily headed down by Sadler to Crerand on the halfway line. Looking up, he sent an inch perfect pass through to George who left Fairfax stranded before rounding the advancing 'keeper on the edge of the Northampton penalty area and slipping the ball once again into an empty goal.

2-0 at the interval was perhaps little more than Northampton Town had expected but they certainly did not have any idea as to what the second forty-five minutes would entail and within a minute of there-start they were 3-0 down. Charlton passed to Sartori, who in turn released Kidd on the left. His first cross was blocked by Kiernan, but given a second chance, he managed to pick out George more or less in the centre of the goalmouth about 8 yards out. His first effort hit a defender, but collecting the rebound calmly blasted the ball high into the roof of the net.

Northampton then had the opportunity to get back into the game when Edwards brought down McNeil, but from the resulting penalty. Rankmore saw his spot kick palmed onto the post by Stepney, with the United 'keeper then blocking Fairbrother's follow up. It was a miss they were to rue as in the 67th minute, George made it 4-0. Kidd again crossing from the left and George diving forward to head past Book.

Charlton found himself in an ideal position to make it five, but Book in the Northampton goal was equal to the shot, palming the shot over the bar for a corner and from the resulting kick, Kidd scored United's fifth. Charlton was soon to be substituted with an ankle injury, his place taken by Francis Burns who created the sixth, winning the ball midway into his own half before launching the ball forward into George who ran between two defenders before pushing the ball wide of the diving goalkeeper.

Brian Kidd made it 7-0, slotting home the rebound after Best had saved. Northampton gave their supporters something to cheer by pulling a goal back through McNeil, after George had lost the ball in a midfield tussle, but the seven goal advantage was soon to re-appear when Crerand robbed Kiernan, slotting the ball inside to George who slipped past one non-existent tackle on the edge of the area before dipping his shoulder to completely baffle the goalkeeper who dived to his left as George walked past his right before slamming the ball over the line and clutching the post for a brief rest, returning to the half way line with something of an embarrassed look on his face.

Before the end, Large was to head past Stepney to make it 8-2 and bring an end to the scoring on a remarkable afternoon. 'I suppose I treated the game like an FA Cup and European Cup Final rolled into one' said George at the end of the enthralling ninety minutes.

'It was my first game after the suspension and I wanted to give vent to my feelings. Even if I had scored twenty it would not have stopped me feeling that the punishment was harsh. When I went out, I felt really great. Things worked out well, but it could easily have gone the other way. I knew when the second one went in that things were going right for me.'

Scoring those six goals equalled a record shared with Hillsdon of Chelsea (1908), whose effigy once supported the weather vane on the roof of the Stamford Bridge east stand, and Rooke of Fulham (1939) and Atkinson of Tranmere Rovers (1953). Minter of St Albans once claimed seven against Dulwich Hamlet in 1922, but this was in a fourth qualifying round.

As for George, although he was now well accustomed to the adoration of the fans, he showed a distinct nervousness as the game approached its dying minutes, edging ever closer towards the tunnel and was the first player off the pitch as the referee's whistle blew.

Northhampton Town: Book, Fairfax, Brookes, Clarke, Rankmore, Kiernan, Felton, Ross, Large, Fairbrother, McNeil.

Scorers: McNeil, Large.

United: Stepney, Edwards, Dunne, Crerand, Ure, Sadler, Morgan, Sartori, Charlton, Kidd, Best. Substitute: Burns for Charlton.

Scorers: Best (6), Kidd (2).

Attendance: 21,771.

MANCHESTER UNITED YOUTH XI 1963-64

9 / 3 / 66

Above: Manchester United FA Youth Cup winning side of 1963/64.
Back row: Fitzpatrick, McBride, Farrar, Rimmer, Duff, Noble.
Front row: Anderson, George, Sadler, Kinsey, Aston.

Left: Programme for 1965-66 European Cup tie against Benfica in Lisbon. One of his best performances.

Right: Programme for the 1968 European Cup Final against Benfica at Wembley.

Below: The United 1964/65 first division championship winning squad. Back row: Stiles, T. Dunne, Gaskell, P. Dunne, Crerand, Fitzpatrick. Middle: Jack Crompton, Brennan, Sadler, Foulkes, Aston, Cantwell, Matt Busby. Front row: Connelly, Charlton, Herd, Law, George.

EUROPEAN CHAMPION CLUBS' CUP

BENFICA F.C. **MANCHESTER UNITED**

FINAL

ORGANISED BY THE FOOTBALL ASSOCIATION ON BEHALF OF THE
UNION DES ASSOCIATIONS EUROPÉENNES DE FOOTBALL

WEDNESDAY MAY 29th 1968

Kick-off 7·45 p.m.

OFFICIAL PROGRAMME ONE SHILLING

WEMBLEY
EMPIRE STADIUM

MANCHESTER UNITED F.C.   LEAGUE CHAMPIONS 1964-65

Autographs :

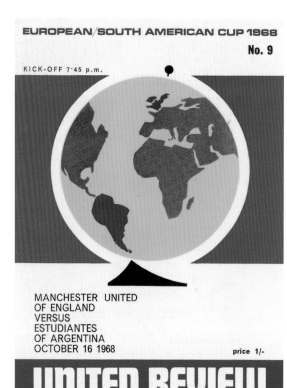

Programme for the World Club Championship tie against Estudiantes at Old Trafford.

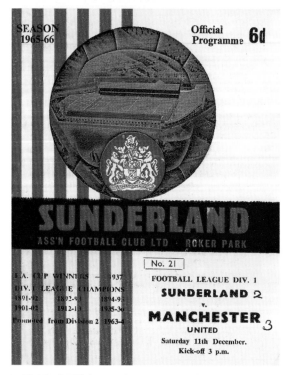

Programme from the 6th Round FA Cup tie against Sunderland at Old Trafford. The first of a trilogy.

The programme for George's last competitive game: Tobermore vs Ballymena.

Programme for the 1967/68 European Cup semi-final first leg against Real Madrid at Old Trafford. Best scored the only goal of the game.

A Vernons Pools advertising leaflet showing George scoring against Sheffield United at Old Trafford in season 1971/72.

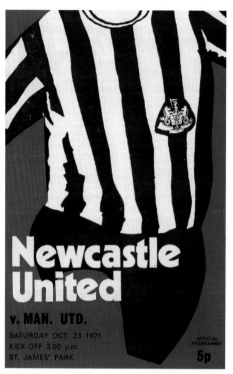

Left: Programme for the 'death threat' match at St James' Park Newcastle in season 1971/72.

Below: George's first ever international appearance. The Northern Ireland Youth team prior to their match with England Youth at Boundary Park Oldham in 1962.

John Napier with George Best. Nr. Ireland Youth Team v England 1962

Above: May 1972 and George hits the headlines for all the wrong reasons.

Right: Programme for United's 8–1 victory over Queens Park Rangers in 1968/69.

The last match of the 1966/67 season when United defeated West Ham United 6–1 to win the first division championship.

United v. Everton — 31st August, 1963
United's first goal scored by Phil Chisnall despite a terrific leap by goalkeeper West.
Photograph by S. J. Hampson, Didsbury

Manchester United vs West Bromwich Albion 14 September 1963. George's first division debut day.

Programme for Chelsea vs
Manchester United season 1966/67.
Another five star performance.

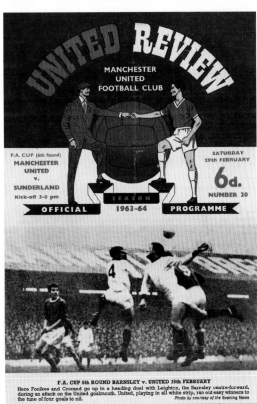

Programme for Sunderland vs
Manchester United season 1965/66.
Two goals in the 3–2 victory.

Above: George scores in the 1968 European Cup Final to put United 2-1 in front.

Below: Manchester United season 1963/64
Back row: Jack Crompton, Foulkes, Sadler, P. Dunne, Brennan, Moore, Crerand, Cantwell, Matt Busby.
Front row: Connelly, Stiles, Charlton, Law, T. Dunne, Herd, George.

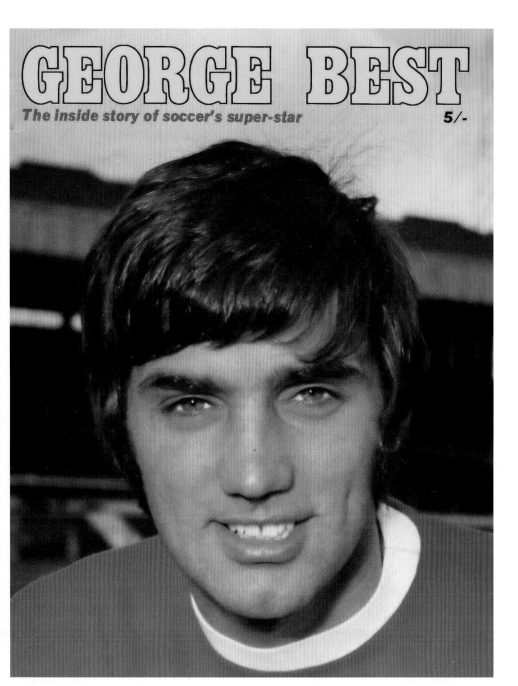

GEORGE BEST

The inside story of soccer's super-star

5/-

Special magazine dedicated to George, published by Jimmy Hill's *Football Weekly*.

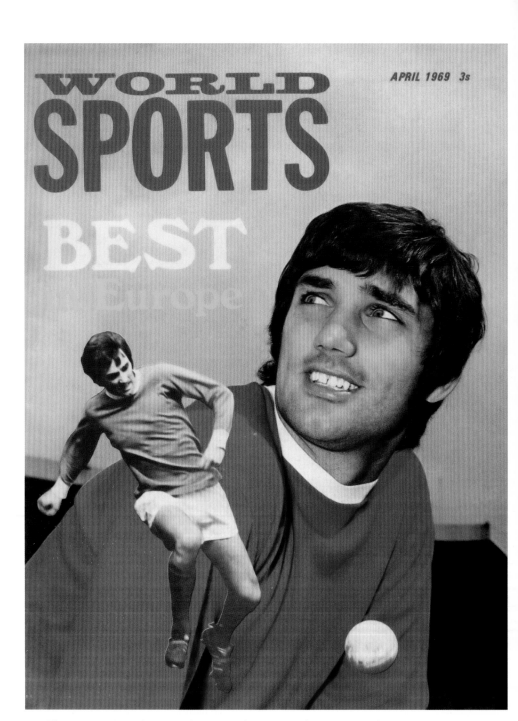

World Sport magazine from April 1969 with George in his prime on the cover.

George Best
1946 – 2005

Cover of the order of service for George's funeral.

United Review

v **West Bromwich Albion** 30.11.05

KICK-OFF 8PM CARLING CUP FOURTH ROUND

THE OFFICIAL
MATCHDAY
PROGRAMME

VOLUME 67 ISSUE 11

£3

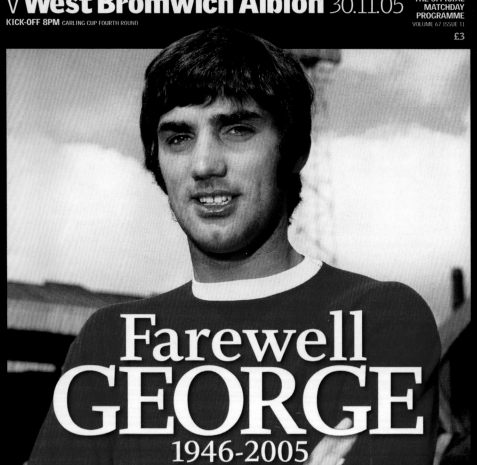

Farewell
GEORGE
1946-2005

31

Northern Ireland vs Scotland
18 April 1970

George won his first full cap for Northern Ireland against Wales on 15 April 1964, a matter of four weeks prior to his eighteenth birthday, playing his part in his sides 3-2 victory. A fortnight later he made his first appearance in the green shirt on home soil, a 3-0 victory against Uruguay.

As it was in club football his name was never far from the headlines, but against Scotland in April 1970, his twentieth cap, it was all for the wrong reasons. 'Belfast Sees the Worst of Best' shouted the *Guardian*, with their correspondent Paul Wilcox writing,

A referee's shirt can be cleaned of its stains. Can George Best's tarnished image? In a match between Northern Ireland and Scotland at Windsor Park Belfast, Best provided a memorably forgettable moment. The memory is of an act of childishness, petulance and idiocy. The memory is of a grown man spraying another with lumps of mud. Best was ordered off the field for the second time in his career and the referee, Eric Jennings, said afterwards: 'Best was sent off for showing dissent, which was spitting and throwing mud.

'But does Best really care?' continued Wilcox. 'Is he bothered that he may be suspended, or about the possibility that he could become the first footballer to be suspended for three months? Does it trouble him that he has let himself down, his international teammates, and Manchester United, or that the consequences of his stupid actions will weaken his club for the beginning of next season while this terms fixtures are still being tidied away?'

The incident in question came in the 65th minute of a game blighted by torrential rain, the pitch resembling a mud bath in places, with water scattered across the surface. George was attempting to reach a ball in the Scottish goalmouth, but was of the opinion that he had had his shirt pulled in an effort to prevent him from making any contact. The referee ignored his claims and George immediately picked up a handful of mud and threw it at the match official, giving him little option but to send him off. Looking at the referee's outstretched arm, pointing towards the dressing rooms, George simply shrugged his shoulders and walk off, conjuring up an image of a pathetic looking figure, sodden green jersey hanging as limply as his dark locks of hair.

It was perhaps little more than an act of frustration as twice in the first half he had clear cut scoring opportunities but on each occasion, as he attempted to shoot, the ball skidded off his boot. But it was a frustration that he should not have allowed to show through in a bit-part performance that not only showed the worst of George, but one that saw him contribute little. A few, inch perfect, long cross-field passes was basically it as he failed to raise his game throughout the dismal afternoon. His mind perhaps elsewhere.

In the dark blue of Scotland, Gilzean of Tottenham and Moncur of Newcastle stood out, while George was overshadowed by Clements and his boyhood travelling companion in Eric

McMordie, but everyone suffered amid the deplorable conditions. On one occasion, Gilzean slipped and slid some 10 yards along the sodden turf.

George had an opportunity to open the scoring when picking up a cross-field pass from Clements, but having evaded Moncur, his shot flew past the wrong side of the post. There was also an early hint as to what lay ahead when he appeared to kick mud at McKinnon as he lay on the ground. The only goal of the game was to come on the hour mark when Gilzean picked out McLean, who in turn lobbed the ball into the Irish goalmouth where O'Hare headed past Jennings.

After the match, Northern Ireland manager Billy Bingham said, 'I have no sympathy with him. If you argue with the referee you must accept the consequences. But I would play him against England on Tuesday. He is still a young man and he has got to learn from these things.'

George did indeed play against England at Wembley, lasting the whole ninety minutes, but he was completely overshadowed by one of his Manchester United teammates, Bobby Charlton, who was representing his country for the 100th time, scoring England's third in their 3-1 victory to round off a memorable evening.

Around the country George was normally welcomed by friend and foe alike, his talents enjoyed, and expected, as part of the admission price. But on this particular evening, following his petulant display at Windsor Park he was roundly booed, cries of disapproval rippling down from stands with every touch of the ball. Even the most delightful of touches and breath catching runs were treated with disdain. He put in an unselfish shift, producing some constructive football and even scoring Ireland's only goal, but still he could do no right in the eyes of the majority of the 100,000 crowd.

In the *Observer*, Hugh McIlvanney wrote, 'Yet, while there is an obvious meanness of spirit about spectators who use their own moral arithmetic in an attempt to subtract from the genius of Best, it is a simple reality that unless he can rid his behaviour of the element of self-indulgent provocation he is going to find more hostility on all sides. The public seem to believe that, as well as losing respect for referees and authority in general, he has lost respect for them, the paying customers.

> Before Tuesday Best had given a long series of disappointing performances on English football grounds. His standards had sunk to an extent that could not be explained even by the tightest marking any player has to face. His equipment is so utterly remarkable – the balance so magical, the athleticism so fierce, the control so fluent and economical – that a prolonged spell of ineffectiveness could never be credited to the opposition.

Northern Ireland: Jennings (Tottenham Hotspur), Craig (Newcastle United), Clements (Coventry City), Todd (Burnley), Neill (Arsenal), Nicholson (Huddersfield Town), Campbell (Dundee), Lutton (Wolverhampton Wanderers), McMordie (Middlesbrough), Best (Manchester United). Substitutes: O'Kane (Nottingham Forest) for Todd, Dickson (Coleraine) for Campbell.

Scotland: Clark (Aberdeen), Hay (Celtic), Dickson (Kilmarnock), McLintock (Arsenal), McKinnon (Rangers), Moncur (Newcastle United), McLean (Kilmarnock), Carr (Coventry City), O'Hare (Derby County), Gilzean (Tottenham Hotspur), Johnston (Rangers). Substitute: Stein (Rangers) for Gilzean.

32

United vs Chelsea
28 October 1970

Whether or not George read the words of Hugh McIlvanney in that *Observer* article is unknown, but in the opening weeks of the 1970/71 season, he seemed to have buckled down, reverting back to being the George Best everyone knew, loved and respected. Obviously, he could not erase his past misdemeanours, the dark side of his character, but his current on-field performances helped shunt them to a distant place in the memory.

Displays by the team in general had been average, some might have said that is simply being polite, but against Everton at Old Trafford in early September, it was 'Everton Have No Answer to Best', turning in a superb display, guiding United back to something of the form expected off them and scoring one of the goals in the 2-0 victory over the Goodison Park side. Then, seven days later albeit, against the minnows of Aldershot in the League Cup, it was 'Best Ghosts in to End Upset Scare' and 'Best Magic puts Paid to Battlers', again finding the net as United drifted into round three on the back of a 3-1 victory. Three days further on, his name was once again well to the fore: 'Coventry Broken by Best', 'Best Rocks Sky Blues' and 'Slick Best Destroys Coventry'. If United were indifferent, then George certainly wasn't.

The victory over Aldershot in the League Cup had earned United yet another comfortable draw in round three against Portsmouth at Old Trafford, but true to their current form, a 4-0 hammering at Portman Road against Ipswich Town, a dreary 1-1 draw against Blackpool at Old Trafford and a 1-0 defeat against Wolverhampton Wanderers at Molineux where the struggle to produce the solitary goal victory was perhaps not unexpected.

Crystal Palace were the next side to take both points of the lacklustre United, but then came a slight upturn in fortune. Bobby Charlton scored his 199th goal to earn a point at Elland Road against Leeds United, followed by a 2-1 victory over West Bromwich Albion. But then, it was back to the League Cup and a much tougher draw than Aldershot and Portsmouth sent current FA Cup holders Chelsea to Old Trafford in round four, a ground they had visited only a few weeks previously and come away with a point from the 0-0 stalemate. But under the Old Trafford floodlights, unknown to the 47,322 as they clicked through the turnstiles, it was going to be a night to remember.

As I have mentioned previously, there are certain games that are part of the George Best folklore. Not necessary complete ninety minutes of never-to-be-forgotten magical brilliance, just games where, perhaps only for a couple of fleeting minutes, George conjures up something really special. This League Cup tie against Chelsea is one of those games and those of you of a certain age, or if you have trawled the internet looking at clips of old games, will already know all about this particular fixture.

As also mentioned previously, United's season to date had been indifferent, but as Eric Todd wrote in the *Guardian*: 'If Manchester United are on their way out, as some people imagine – or hope – they are, then they intend taking their time about it. In any case while there is Best there is hope and so long as he stays at Old Trafford, United can never be written off.'

It was on a rain soaked Old Trafford that the game got underway, with Chelsea putting the United defence under early pressure from Hutchison's trademark long throw in and following a dramatic scramble, Tony Dunne finally managed to clear the danger. At the opposite end, Bonetti did well to hold a shot from Aston, before Hutchison once again caused panic within the home ranks with yet another long throw. On this occasion, the ball was back headed by Osgood before being headed over the bar by Webb.

Charlton forced a fine save from the Chelsea 'keeper after being sent through by Kidd, the same individual and Best then having efforts beaten out by a backtracking Chelsea defence. Rimmer, when called upon dealt comfortably with anything that came his way.

But the deadlock was finally broken in the 27th minute, much to the delight of the home crowd. The Chelsea defence only managed to half clear a Charlton corner kick and the ball was quickly controlled by George and returned it to Charlton who then drove the ball towards Bonetti from all of 20 yards. Such was the power in the shot that the Chelsea 'keeper could not hold it and it flew off his body and high into the net behind him.

It was a lead that was to be short lived however, a mere seven minutes, but it was an equaliser for Chelsea that was perhaps slightly fortunate. Out on the right, Cooke lobbed the ball into the middle where it should have been comfortably dealt with by Fitzpatrick, but the defender failed to control it, allowing Hollins to run in and volley past Rimmer.

United were denied a half-time lead by Bonetti, denying Charlton twice, but then the advantage could have easily have gone Chelsea's way, Hutchison heading a Hollins free-kick past Rimmer, only to be denied by a linesman's flag signalling off-side.

Early in the second half Best put the Chelsea defence under pressure with a pass to Edwards who was clear on the right but with three red shirts awaiting the cross, the full-back sent the ball behind Bonetti's goal. Compared to the opening forty-five minutes, the second half had got off to something of a dull start, but it was to change beyond all recognition in the 70th minute.

Chelsea were beginning to look the more likely side to snatch a winner but suddenly George, just inside the Londoners half, called for the ball from Aston and the winger duly obliged with a perfect pass. Off went George, with three blue shirts in close pursuit. Ron Harris managed to make up ground on him and the Chelsea defender attempted to pull him down from behind but somehow, George managed to evade the swinging boot. Bonetti moved from his line but a neat side step took George clear and despite Hinton attempting to block the route to goal, George calmly placed the ball wide of the Chelsea centre-half and into the net before turning away and sinking to his knees with his arm raised.

'A lot of players would have panicked and had a shot or a chip' said Bonetti later, 'But not George Best. He just kept on coming. One of my defenders came across me at the wrong moment, which didn't help, but I was never in with a chance. It was a great goal.'

In the *Daily Mirror* under the heading: 'A Touch of Genius from You Know Who.' Derek Wallis wrote, 'Every spectator in Old Trafford's 47,000 crowd last night mentally ran every yard, stride for stride with George Best as he devoured ground at first devastatingly and then agonisingly at the crucial moment of this memorable League Cup-tie. If a picture had been taken of every face each United fan would have revealed apprehension and yet expectancy, each Chelsea supporter anxiety.'

Having described the run, Wallis continued, 'You felt he had to score, but how much longer would it be before Bonetti hurled himself at his feet? George Best isn't the man to be hurried in his mood of last night. He rounded Bonetti impudently and scored so coolly that it might have been a beach kick-about in sunny Majorca instead of a match of serious consequences in murky Manchester.'

There were still twenty minutes remaining, but Chelsea were beaten by that one fleeting moment of sheer brilliance, by the only person capable of conjuring up such a moment. 'A Genius and his Creation' was how the *Daily Express* saw it. Their correspondent Alan Thompson writing, 'George Best, long-haired genius whose finely sharpened killer instinct makes Cassius Clay look like one of those peaceful co-exister fellows, scored what I conservatively estimate to be about his tenth Goal of the century last night.'

At the end of the ninety minutes, Chelsea's Peter Osgood walked off the field with one arm around George's shoulder. Carrying him shoulder high would have been a better finale.

The goal ended up as simply one for the archives as despite a 4-2 quarter-final victory over Crystal Palace, United failed to overcome third division Aston Villa over two legs in the semi-final. A result that did Wilf McGuinness little in the way of favours and in the cold light of day most probably got him the sack a short while later.

United: Rimmer, Edwards, Dunne, Fitzpatrick, James, Sadler, Law, Best, Charlton, Kidd, Aston. Substitute: Burns for Law.

Scorers: Charlton, Best.

Chelsea: Bonetti, Mulligan, Harris, Hollins, Hinton, Webb, Weller, Cooke, Osgood, Hutchison, Houseman.

Scorer: Hollins.

Attendance: 47,322.

George was always different both on and off the pitch. Long hair, shirt outside the shorts, flash cars and all the latest fashionable clothes in his wardrobe. He had now gone one step further – a £35,000 house in Bramhall Cheshire. According to a magazine article of the time, it was 'really a flat, three large rooms floating over a double garage and a games room. Probably the most modern bachelor pad in the country.'

Alongside photographs of the rooms, George gave his thoughts on his new residence:

When the house was built, people couldn't understand why all the windows have brown smoked glass. But I can see out – over apple orchards to the Pennines – while outsiders can't see in. Living in my own house means a new way of life. I don't have to keep going out because I've got somewhere to stay in and all the space I need. Nicest thing about the house is the amount of space I've got in the big first floor living room. I can relax here and it never looks untidy or finicky.

I don't entertain many people at once, so the kitchen is small and compact but with everything I need – big refrigerator, split level hot-plate and oven, double sink, built-in storage. The electric kettle switches itself off when it boils and all the saucepans are non-stick.

About the rooms he said,

I've always longed for a sunken bath of my own – and here it is! Not quite big enough for the entire Manchester United team; actually double normal size, and designed by the architect. So far there are only two bedrooms. But the games room holds a full size billiards table, and if I sold the house that space could be converted into two extra bedrooms with their own bathroom.

The house was soon to become nothing like the home he envisaged and before long he would be moving out and returning to his previous abode at Mrs Fullaway's.

George vs United: January 1971

The headlines had always previously been about a special goal or performance, a touch of genius from a player considered by many as the greatest the world, never mind British football, had ever seen. Suddenly those headlines changed. It was now: 'Busby Axes Best', 'Sir Matt's Showdown with Best' and 'George Best on the Verge of Breakdown?'

Underneath the latter, the question was asked if indeed George was heading for a nervous breakdown after having missed training with United on Christmas morning, for which he was fined £50 and then later admitting that he deliberately missed the train for London which was taking the United team south for their match with Chelsea (on 9 January). He said he was tired and fed up and that his problems were entirely football related. He was later to fly south and went into hiding at the home of actress Sinead Cusack.

This was certainly not the first occasion that George had failed to catch a train for an away fixture. On 5 December he had failed to travel with the team to London for their game against Tottenham Hotspur. Then he missed not one but two trains that were taking him to London for a disciplinary hearing, arriving three hours late. At the hearing, he was given a suspended sentence and fined £250.

When the United team arrived in London for the match at Stamford Bridge, Sir Matt Busby, back in charge following the sacking of Wilf McGuinness said, 'George didn't report for training this morning. Naturally I'm unhappy about it. To be frank, the boy has not been doing it for us in recent weeks. I just don't know what's wrong with the lad. Something seems to have upset him. Perhaps his life outside football has got something to do with it. I just don't know.'

This latest episode in George's career was something of a watershed, as it was reported that there was now some resentment among the other players that the club and Sir Matt Busby had been publically humiliated. Suspended for two weeks by the club, Sir Matt Busby said,

> It is not up to us to contact the boy, he must come to us and explain matters. He will be informed of the suspension by letter. Whether he will be allowed to train with the other players during the suspension, or whether he will be allowed to come to the club, will be discussed with him when he makes contact.
>
> I am upset and annoyed by the situation but I am not going looking for George Best. I cannot recall such a suspension before by the club. Once he does come back he will have to play his way back into the first team.

George did make contact with the club and was certainly not late for his meeting with Sir Matt Busby and before the head-to-head he told waiting reporters, 'I am bitterly disappointed with the team's performances in the past month; it was the main reason I staged my protest. I certainly do not want to leave United – I want to see them at the top again.' Surprisingly without George, United won 2-1 at Chelsea, their first victory for eleven games.

Following the half hour meeting George said,

> I am glad it is all over at last. I have apologised to the boss for what I did, and now realise I went about things the wrong way. I was playing well at the beginning of the season but my form has suffered since and I have blamed myself for not being able to help the team out of the doldrums. I have been stupid in trying to make my protest his way. I hope my team-mates don't think

I've been testy – I know some of them have been quite concerned about the way I have been behaving. All I want to do now is get away for some peace and quiet. Then I can put my heart back into this game again.

'We start from scratch again' said Sir Matt Busby. 'All is forgotten. He has had this sort of problem inside him and it has been building up. It is a private matter which we have discussed.'

33

United vs Tottenham Hotspur

6 February 1971

George returned to first team duty against Huddersfield Town at Leeds Road, attracting over 41,000 through the turnstiles, the biggest crowd at the Yorkshire ground for years, giving them a little taste of the familiar magic, playing a key role in both of the United goals in the 2-1 win. In his absence United had defeated Chelsea 2-1 at Stamford Bridge and drawn 1-1 with Burnley at Old Trafford, the victory over Huddersfield extending the unbeaten run to four games. A victory over Tottenham Hotspur would equal the seasons best of five, way back in August/September. They hadn't however, won a home League game for over three months.

A hero's welcome awaited George as he ran out of the Old Trafford tunnel prior to the match with Tottenham. 'That Old Best Magic' proclaimed the *Sunday Mirror* with Peter Shaw writing:

It was as if he had never been away! George Best, I mean of course. On his first appearance at Old Trafford for more than a month, United's prodigal son took just fifteen minutes to make Spurs wish he had stayed away. A spectacular goal then provided United with the impetus to win their seventh pint in the four games since Sir Matt Busby took over the reins again.

Best, in irresponsible mood, went on to hit the post and clip the crossbar and generally irritate Spurs more painfully than a piece of grit in the eye.

Strangely enough, George failed to gain the plaudits as Man of the Match, which went to Alan Gowling, but he could never seize the headlines in the manner in which George did.

Tottenham, from the first whistle, never looked like competing with United and failed to subdue them in defence or midfield, allowing them the freedom to cause havoc. Within the opening twelve minutes, United had won the ball in midfield and surged forward to the Tottenham goal. Gowling shooting wide, with George's effort being deflected for a corner. The visitors luck was soon to run out.

On the quarter hour mark, Crerand's free-kick was palmed backwards by Jennings as Gowling challenged. Collins managed to head the ball away from the goalmouth, but only as far as George, who simply looked up and judged that the only route to goal was over the heads of the five defenders blocking his route to goal. With a perfectly measured lob, the ball floated into the net dipping just under the crossbar.

It was a match bristling with incident and action. Chivers was well policed by Sadler and Edwards, while the often dangerous Neighbour was suppressed by Fitzpatrick as United maintained their momentum. Gowling had a fine effort saved by Jennings before Kidd was brought down by Collins inside the area, the referee having no doubt as to whether or not to award a penalty. Morgan scoring from the spot.

Tottenham equalised in the 28th minute when Charlton blotted his copybook by miss placing a pass intended for George at the feet of Peters after having carried the ball out of the United penalty area. Peters prodded the ball forward and as Stepney rushed from his goal, expecting Chivers to shoot, was beaten more by the Tottenham man failing to make contact than the power in the original shot from Peters.

It was a match bristling with incident and action although play was sometimes a little scrappy and, in reality, United should have won by a much larger margin than one goal. George was back to his old self, sifting through his repertoire of tricks, while inspiring those around him in red shirts. Pat Crerand, recently critical of the United support, did his talking on the field with intelligent anticipation and his usual accurate passing.

George hit the Tottenham post as the game continued to flow from end to end, but thankfully for United the visitors found the going tough and visibly tired in the final quarter of an hour. Their Old Trafford record extending to eighth successive defeat.

'Best back in the side and eager to make amends for his recent indiscretions' was how Alan Dunn in the *Guardian* saw George's performance.

United: Stepney, Fitzpatrick, Burns, Crerand, Edwards, Sadler, Morgan, Kidd, Charlton, Gowing, Best. Substitute: Aston.

Scorers: Best, Morgan (pen).

Tottenham Hotspur: Jennings, Evans, Knowles, Mullery, Collins, Beal, Gilzean, Perryman, Chivers, Peters, Neighbour. Substitute: Pearce.

Scorer: Peters.

Attendance: 48,966

34

Northern Ireland vs Cyprus

21 April 1971

Since his first Northern Ireland full-international cap against Wales in April 1964 George had gone on to represent his country on twenty-four occasions but, unlike his performances for Manchester United goals certainly did not go hand in hand with his appearances; as he had only managed a miserable five out of the thirty-five scored over the course of those two dozen games. A poor average by any standards.

To be fair ten of those twenty-four fixtures had come against either England or Scotland, teams that could be considered superior to and had a much bigger pool of players to select from than Northern Ireland. Other opponents like Holland, Spain and Russia could also be classed at a different level but, there had also been fixtures against Switzerland, Albania, Turkey, Wales and Cyprus so in reality goals should have been more plentiful. All but one of his five goals had come against those latter opponents, having found the net only once against the stronger sides – at Wembley against England on 21 April 1970.

Even at club level, claiming the match ball for a trio of goals during ninety minutes play was something of a rarity. There had been numerous 'doubles' but on only five occasions had he managed to score three or more – one 'A' team, one 'B' team, one friendly, one first division and one FA Cup tie.

On 3 February 1971 George scored one of his countries goals, a penalty in the 3-0 victory, European Nations Cup victory over Cyprus in Nicosia, but it was in the return fixture in Belfast that he finally came to the fore by claiming a rare hat-trick.

Having scored three in Cyprus, who were managed at this time by former Manchester United goalkeeper and Munich survivor Ray Wood, Northern Ireland were fully confident as regards to matching that score on home soil and had the visitors envisaged any hopes of pulling off something of a shock, their dreams were shattered within ninety seconds of the kick-off when Derek Dougan headed a centre from Cork past Herodotos in the Cyprus goal. It should have been 2-0 after six minutes but, Hamilton's drive took a deflection and went the wrong side of the post. Cyprus, despite the early setback, did attempt to reduce the deficit – Stylianov's flick being cleared by Clements.

Hamilton was again denied a goal in the 26th minute but was ruled off-side by a linesman's flag, despite the pressure Ireland had to wait until a minute before the interval before that second goal materialised. George scoring with a 25 yard drive.

Within two minutes of the re-start, George had claimed his second and Ireland's third with a strong cross shot after Craig and Dougan had done the spadework. Cyprus were now down and out, with no answer to the on-fire George or the resourceful Irish side.

George rattled the crossbar with a ferocious left-footed shot in the 50th minute and then six minutes later claimed his hat-trick with a goal of sheer class (or some might say luck), scoring directly from a corner kick.

Despite many being satisfied with four goals, seeing a genius at work rather than an imitation of an adolescent schoolboy of the previous year, they headed for home before the end. However those who stayed were treated to a fifth goal, courtesy of Jimmy Nicholson, five minutes from the end.

George was only to play in a further dozen games for his country and was never to score again. George himself might have debated that last statement and many to this day still do as against England at Windsor Park Belfast on 15 May 1971, with only eleven minutes gone, he flicked the ball away from the visitor's goalkeeper as he threw it into the air before kicking clear. Slipping round the astonished 'keeper, he headed the ball into the vacant net.

To the relief of Banks and the annoyance of the Irish players, never mind George, the referee disallowed the goal for dangerous play. Something it certainly wasn't.

Northern Ireland: Jennings (Tottenham Hotspur), Craig (Newcastle United), Clements (Coventry City), Harvey (Sunderland), Hunter (Blackburn Rovers), Todd (Sheffield Wednesday), Hamilton (Linfield), McMordie (Middlesbrough), Dougan (Wolverhampton Wanderers), Nicholson (Huddersfield Town), Best (Manchester United).

Scorers: Best (3), Dougan, Nicholson.

Cyprus: Herodotos, Kokos, Theodorou, Kavazis, Mihail, Papettas, Koureas, K. Konstantinou, T. Konstantinou, Vasiliou, Papadopoulos, Fokkis, Stylianou.

Attendance: 19,153.

If you had to select one season that epitomises George Best's Manchester United career many would opt for 1967/68 when he played his part in the club lifting the European Cup for the first time, or even 1965/66 when George probably first came to the fore as a world class individual. But for me I think it has to be season 1971/72. Why? Probably due to the fact that there are numerous games from this particular campaign that are worthy of a place in this book and I make no apology for including however many I do manage to squeeze in.

35

Chelsea vs United

8 August 1971

Manchester United were capturing the headlines before season 1971/72 had even got underway and as the weeks and months passed by, little changed. Against Newcastle United, the previous season, a knife was thrown from the Stretford End – an incident that saw the club forced to play the opening two fixtures of the new season on neutral grounds, taking their 'home' matches against Arsenal and West Bromwich Albion to Liverpool's Anfield and Stoke City's Victoria ground respectively. There was a new manager in charge with Frank O'Farrell taking over the reins from a thankful Sir Matt Busby. Not only that, as the season finally got underway there was the shock Watney Cup defeat by Third Division Halifax town at the Shay.

Then there was George.

The first division campaign had kicked-off with the first of the six consecutive away games and a 2-2 draw at Derby County. Four days later United headed for London to face Chelsea at Stamford Bridge and George was on the train heading south with his teammates, but on this occasion it would have been better if he had decided to give Piccadilly Station a miss and headed elsewhere.

For most of the opening stages Chelsea held the upper hand, keeping their visitors on the defensive, but slowly United began to push forward and came close to taking the lead when Denis Law out-jumped Dempsey to a Tony Dunne cross, only for Phillips in the Chelsea goal to punch clear. Law did have the ball in the net in the 25th minute after Phillips failed to hold a shot from George, but the referee had already blown for an infringement. The young 'keeper did well to stop Charlton blockbusters on a couple of occasions.

The game remained goal-less until five minutes before the interval when Tommy Baldwin nodded the ball past Stepney, much to the annoyance of the United players who were of the opinion that Osgood had pushed Alan Gowling as the ball came into the United penalty area. Willie Morgan chased after referee Keith Burtenshaw to protest and was promptly booked for his trouble. George, standing nearby made his way over to the referee and appeared to complain about his teammates booking. Suddenly, with both teams already lined up for the re-start, Burtenshaw pointed towards the tunnel.

George slumped to his knees transfixed, seemingly not believing what had just happened, and it was almost a minute before he began to walk off the pitch accompanied by Tony Dunne and Bobby Charlton. Coach Malcolm Musgrove then took over to lead a tearful George towards the dressing room.

Despite the handicap of being reduced to ten men, United showed tremendous spirit and equalised in the 68th minute when Brian Kidd headed home a Tony Dunne cross before taking the lead from a penalty three minutes later. Kidd raced through as the Chelsea defence appealed for offside, side-stepped the goalkeeper as Phillips attempted to grab his ankles, he stumbled slightly before taking the ball wide, but his shot was to hit the side netting. To the surprise of everyone in the ground, the referee pointed to the penalty spot, having adjudged that the 'keeper had fouled Kidd. Willie Morgan made no mistake from the spot kick.

With eight minutes remaining, Bobby Charlton scored a third for United, a typical effort, bursting through before hitting a shot on the run that left Phillips helpless. Two minutes from the end, Osgood scrambled the ball home, but it was too little too late.

Some had sympathy for George, others didn't. Derek Wallis of the *Daily Mirror* was in the latter camp and, underneath a picture of the astounded United maverick, wrote, 'George Best stands open-mouthed after being ordered off by referee Norman Burtenshaw at Chelsea last night. He may be open-mouthed in amazement at the decision, but he shouldn't be. He's had enough warnings about arguing with referees. It's time he learned to keep that mouth closed ... for his own good, his club's good ... and for the good of football.'

Already under the cloud of a suspended sentence and with a new season 'get-tough' campaign by match officials, George was surprisingly let off for his latest brush with officialdom, thanks mainly to the Secretary of the Professional Footballers Association, Cliff Lloyd. It was stated that George's outburst was not directed at the referee, but at Willie Morgan and the Disciplinary Committee were unable to prove who it was that George called 'a ******* disgrace.'

Following the hearing, George said,

I know finally that there is only one thing that I must do and that is to control my temper. In the past I have said the same thing but I can tell you that this time I really mean it. Now I want to get on with my football and keep out of trouble. It really is a wonderful feeling to have missed being banned. I knew that I was facing a stiff sentence if things went against me, but it has all turned out alright in the end. Now I want to put it all this behind me particularly because the United side are playing so well at the moment.

Chelsea: Phillips, McCreadie, Boyle, Hollins, Dempsey, Harris, Smethurst, Hudson, Osgood, Baldwin, Houseman. Substitute: Cooke.

Scorers: Baldwin, Osgood

United: Stepney, Fitzpatrick, Dunne, Gowling, James, Sadler, Morgan, Kidd, Charlton, Law, Best. Substitute: Aston.

Scorers: Kidd, Morgan (penalty), Charlton.

Attendance: 54,763.

36

United vs West Ham United

18 September 1971

Being released from the threat of a suspension and an unwanted, extended break away from the game was a relief; it could have had a serious mental effect on George. Nudging him away from the game that he once longingly loved and once loved him. But there were no shackles placed round his ankles. No expulsion from the first division or indeed Old Trafford. It was suddenly to look as though a huge weight had been lifted off his shoulders, a release from a long and uneasy sleep, or perhaps it was simply a case of having learned his lesson and finally decided to knuckle down and do what he did best.

Against Arsenal at the rented out Anfield he simply played a bit part in the 3-1 success over the Gunners. However, in the weeks that followed it was not so much Manchester United who enjoyed a run of only one defeat in fourteen League games but the 'George Best Show' that conjured up an enthralling whirlwind mini-tour of England, turning average games into spectacles and draws into victories.

West Bromwich Albion at Stoke City's Victoria Ground brought: 'Wizard Best Baffles Albion' from the *Sun* as George netted twice in the 3-1 victory. Their reporter writing: They say that soccer is a team game, but any Albion man will tell you this morning that they were demoralised and destroyed by one man of astonishing skill – George Best. The little Irishman answered the critics who reckon we have seen the best of him by parading his full repertoire of wizardry to baffle and bemuse Albion's uncompromising defence.' Another reporter purred that George's performance was 'one of those priceless shows that only he can stage. If Sir Stanley Matthews ever reached greater heights of skill on this, his own Victoria Ground, then I for one have still to hear about it.' That victory over West Bromwich Albion took United to the top of the first division, a positon that they were unaccustomed to of late.

Five days later at Molineux George was on the mark again giving United the lead, but one they were to relinquish, in a game that ended all square at 1-1. There was no repeat at Goodison Park in the next fixture, a 1-0 defeat, but a solitary goal from George earned both points against Ipswich Town at Old Trafford: 'Best the Great Blasts Them' as United returned home, while he was the architect of the 3-1 victory over Crystal Palace at Selhurst Park.

Life was good, but it was soon to become better with the visit of West Ham United to Manchester.

Now that Pele has retired – for the last time? – the genius of George Best is unrivalled in world soccer. Two of his three goals at Old Trafford yesterday were indicative of his astonishing control and reflexes. They floored a West Ham team which, for an hour, was marginally the more co-ordinated side. Having given the FA the slip last Monday – on the slenderest technicality – Best now applied himself to West Ham's destruction with a virtuosity which is undiminished.

Wrote David Miller in the *Sunday Telegraph*. Few who witnessed the ninety minutes could disagree with Millar's assessment of George, which continued:

> He continues to amaze and delight the spectator and to confound the most accomplished defenders, even such as Moore. His third goal, the last of the game, was one of pure brilliance. It was supposed the subject of George best had been exhausted, but his miraculous ability with the ball dilutes, even if it does not excuse his occasional clashes with authority. He should now rejoice in his unexpected freedom, as he did yesterday and exploit the refreshing climate of non-violence which made this match, just as it is making others, a pleasure to watch.
>
> It is interesting to speculate on whether Best keeps the ball closer than other legendary dribblers, such as Finney and Matthews. Yet whereas they tended to have to beat only one defender at a time, Best, somehow can beat two or three simultaneously, with several seemingly impossible changes of direction in a few strides.

If George was a thorn in West Ham's side then his namesake Clyde Best was likewise, but without the flare and individualistic brilliance, to the home defence. And it was due to the tall, robust West Ham Number Eight's presence that West Ham enjoyed much of the play. He had the beating of James in the air, while his fellow defender Tony Dunne looked uncomfortable at times against Redknapp and McDowell.

Hurst went close with a half volley, then Law tested Ferguson before George forced the West Ham 'keeper to tip a rising left-footed drive over the bar. From the resulting Charlton corner, the ball flew off Bobby Moore's head towards the back post where George was on hand to nod the ball into the unprotected net to put United in front in the 20th minute. Within four minutes, West Ham were level, McDowell crossing from the far post and Clyde Best rising above the United defence to head past Stepney.

With two minutes remaining before half-time the visitors failed to deal with yet another Bobby Charlton corner and, as the ball fell towards George, some 14 yards from goal, he managed to get clear from a cluster of players before spinning through a full turn before firing the ball through the mass of bodies and past Ferguson in the West Ham goal.

As the second half got underway McDowell was unfortunate not to equalise, his powerful long-range drive slamming against the far post. At the opposite end Ferguson managed to block a shot from George with his legs. A goal could have materialised at either end, such was the flow of the game, but it was West Ham who were to score, equalising with an hour to go, when Brooking moved clear of James and O'Neil before beating Stepney. Their good work however, was undone within minutes as they gifted Charlton United's third goal. Mistakes aside, it was an enthralling game of football, but the best was yet to come.

Ten minutes remained as George, out on the left, beat McDowell not once but twice, drifting into the West Ham penalty area, creating space for himself before firing an unstoppable shot past Ferguson and sending the crowd into raptures.

'It was vintage Best' said *Goal* magazine, while West Ham goalkeeper Bobby Ferguson pointed out: 'We gave them three of the goals and you can't afford to do things like that with George Best around. His first two goals came from purely defensive errors but you have to give him full credit for his third.'

United: Stepney, O'Neill, Dunne, Gowling, James, Sadler, Morgan, Kidd, Charlton, Law, Best. Substitute: Aston.

Scorers: Best (3), Charlton.

West Ham United: Ferguson, McDowell, Lampard, Bonds, Taylor, Moore, Redknapp, C. Best, Hurst, Brooking, Robson.

Scorers: C. Best, Brooking.

Attendance: 53,339.

37

United vs Sheffield United

2 October 1971

United's emphatic 4-2 victory over West Ham United on 18 September took them to second place in the first division league table, two points behind the unlikely, and certainly unfamiliar side, who were sitting above the rest – Sheffield United. The Yorkshire side's advantage was increased to three points seven days later following their solitary goal victory over Chelsea due to United dropping a point with a 2-2 draw at Anfield against Liverpool.

It was still early days with the season still in its infancy, but the meeting between the Division's top two, even if it was only October, certainly caught the imagination with a victory for Sheffield United giving them a distinct advantage at the head of the pack. On the other hand should United triumph then it pushed them to within one point of the leaders, making a clear statement of intent that despite their recent failings, they still had what it takes to be up there challenging for silverware.

All roads led to Old Trafford on that sunny October afternoon. So much so that the red Old Trafford gates were firmly locked forty minutes before kick-off, with an estimated 20,000 outside amid scenes of utter chaos being denied the privilege of watching the country's top two sides in action.

As Brian Glanville pointed out in his match report for The *Sunday Times*:

> Manchester are the proper products of a city once the bastion of laissez faire. They believe in the popular phrase in letting players "do their own thing" and yesterday, as so often in the past, it ultimately paid them. Their parts are always greater than the whole, whereas Sheffield are much more than the sum of their components.
>
> Not that they are without their stars. A couple of seasons ago, seeing them in a cup-tie, one wrote that they looked two years away from being a very good team. They are now an excellent team and in Currie, quite simply, they had the finest player on the field.

Quite a statement, considering the other names gracing the Old Trafford turf and how the game ultimately unfolded.

United were without Denis Law and his absence was noticeable in a game which began nervously for both sides, mistakes littered the opening minutes both in attack and defence, but as things settled down it was the home side who began to gain the upper hand, but only just.

Scullion caused the United defence problem whenever he pushed forward, in one instance forcing Stepney to dash from his goal line to prevent a goal, while his Sheffield teammates rained numerous shots down on Stepney's goal. None however, reached the back of the net. At the opposite end Gowling broke through in the 12th minute, running onto a pass from Kidd, but his final shot went wide of the goal. Ten minutes later it was George who scurried forward but having over-hit the ball Hope, in the Sheffield goal, ran out and collected comfortably.

As the second half got underway it began to look as though United might rue those two missed opportunities as the visitors began to increase their pressure on the home defence. Currie, Woodward and Dearden were all unfortunate not to score. But with all those missed chances, those on the terraces and in the stands began to suspect that they were going to witness a goalless draw.

Asked on their journey to Old Trafford if they would be prepared to settle for a point, the Sheffield United players and supporters would all have answered 'yes', although inwardly hoping that they might be fortunate to snatch a victory. Those hopes and expectations were to be dashed six minutes from time.

When the move which was to lead to that first goal began, wide on the left some 30 yards from goal, there didn't look as if there was any danger to the Sheffield United goal whatsoever. But then again it was George who had the ball at his feet, not just some ordinary individual. With his back to goal, just inside the Sheffield United half, he almost casually brought the ball down under control before turning away from the nearby defenders. Moving to the right, he went past one man, then another before accelerating towards the scoreboard end goal, out stepping a further two defenders before right footing the ball past the advancing Hope. The ball hitting the inside of the far post before going in.

'Best Jinked, Changed Pace, Beat Three Men and Created with Magic One of the Great Goals of Any Lifetime' was the headline in the *Sunday Mirror*, while *The Sun* went with '"Burglar" Best Blows Blades Unbeaten Tag', their reporter Frank Clough wrote:

> When the day comes for George Best to hang up his boots, I'll be tempted to hang up my typewriter alongside them. He'll have his money to warm him and I'll have my memories – and I'm not sure I'd want to swap. Somehow the game won't be the same after the little Irishman has gone – it will be like a crown with the finest gem missing.
>
> So let's thank our lucky stars that there's a good few years mileage still to come from the Belfast boy. And if there are a few more goals in his locker like the one that stunned, savaged and shattered unbeaten Sheffield United, then that's our bonus.
>
> No one else on the field – correction, no one else in England – could have scored it. There were five men between George and goal, but he left them like corn flattened by a storm.

Flattened Sheffield United certainly were unable to lift themselves for a final flourish on Stepney's goal in the hope of grabbing an equaliser that they perhaps considered they were worthy off. George had done the damage. The crowd were still mesmerised from what they had just witnessed, Sheffield United equally stunned, so much so that two minutes later they allowed Alan Gowling to dive unmarked to head home a second United goal from a Kidd cross.

'George hadn't really done anything up to that time' said Sheffield United defender John Flynn. 'But even when we were giving him very little pace I always felt that the moment would come for him to pounce.' His teammate, Stewart Scullion, added, 'How many players can do what George Best did to score? He went past three players didn't he? It was a really sickening feeling when it went in.' Sheffield United goalkeeper John Hope adding: 'How can a player score a goal like that. I still can't believe it has gone in.'

For a Manchester United perspective Bobby Charlton said, 'I thought the Sheffield United defenders had done the right thing by forcing George wide of the goal. But George obviously had something else in mind. I thought it was a terrific goal.'

As for George himself: 'I thought I was never going to score. I had miss-hit a couple and put one over the bar. It was a relief to see the goal go in. If it hadn't Sheffield could have opened up a fairlead at the top of the table.'

United: Stepney, O'Neill, Dunne, Gowling, James, Sadler, Morgan, Kidd, Charlton, Best, Aston. Substitute: Burns for Dunne.

Scorers: Best, Gowling.

Sheffield United: Hope, Badger, Hemsley, Flynn, Colquhoun, Hockey, Woodward, Salmons, Dearden, Currie, Scullion. Substitute: Reece for Hemsley.

Attendance: 51,735.

38

Newcastle United vs United

23 October 1971

To say that George was adored by the Manchester United faithful is something of an understatement. In the eyes of the red and white bedecked followers, he could do no wrong and many of the opposition support had a secret admiration for him despite their vocal taunts of 'Georgie Best superstar, walks like a woman and he wears a bra.'

There were countless other taunts thrown George's way during the course of ninety minutes and beyond, including the odd tongue in cheek death threat, which were simply laughed off as the work of someone with little better to do with their time. However, when another death threat was made against George in the form of a telephone call to a London newspaper this was not laughed off and was certainly not ignored, as it was supposedly made by the IRA. More so due to his sister being shot in leg coming out of a dance in Belfast, it was no random shooting, as she was targeted due to who she was. It wasn't a simple 'you're going to get shot', leaving the actual time and place blank but a more definite threat to his life while in action for United against Newcastle United at the latter's St James Park ground.

In the week prior to the game a woman in Alderley Edge reported that she was accosted by two men asking for George's address and directions how to get there. After they left her house she thought she saw one of them with an object that looked like a gun. On the eve of the game the United team bus was broken into while the team were in a Newcastle hotel. A hotel where George ate his meals in his room accompanied by two detectives, such was the seriousness of the threat received.

On the day of the game, the first division leader's team coach was escorted to the ground with a police escort and upon its arrival, George was bustled into the ground surrounded by detectives.

Newcastle United had suffered four consecutive league defeats, three of those at St James Park, so the odds were immediately stacked against them but the non-footballing matters surrounding the game perhaps gave them a better than normal chance to take something from the ninety minutes of a somewhat out of the ordinary game.

Watched closely by the police off the pitch, George was closely marked by the Newcastle defence on it, although those black and white striped shirts were rather reluctant to get too close to the United number eleven for obvious reasons. The backdrop to the game was perhaps also responsible for the early pace of the game, its speed leading to some untidy play.

Tudor and Hibbitt were too rushed in their attempts at goal, causing Stepney little concern, while at the opposite end Morgan fired directly at McFaul. Charlton tried to slow the pace of the game down to a more relaxed level and George, no matter what was going through his mind, produced his usual box of tricks from solo runs to pin point, cross field, passes.

McFaul did well to palm away a close-range header from Law but it was at the opposite end that the deadlock was almost broken when Tudor headed a Gibb centre against the United crossbar with Stepney beaten.

With the second half only minutes old, the decisive goal of the game was scored. Kidd tried a speculative shot from twenty-five yards out which McFaul fumbled and having escaped his marker, George nipped in to drive the ball high into the roof of the net. It was a goal that Newcastle United defender Ray Ellison claimed should not have been allowed as he said George had shouted 'leave it', a call that made him hesitate when he could have cleared the danger.

It was a goal that knocked Newcastle's confidence and their momentum in front of goal was soon to suffer when Tudor was knocked out by one of his own shots when it rebounded off a defender and hit him in the face. Barrowclough did well as a replacement and alongside MacDonald caused the visitors defence a few moments of anxiety, but when good scoring opportunities did materialise they fell to Gibb rather than a more noted goal scorer.

As the game moved to towards full-time, Charlton had the opportunity to double his sides advantage when George sent him away. Passing to Law, he continued his run and accepted the return pass but his left-footed drive which flashed past McFaul and into the net was ruled out for offside. A strongly contested decision.

In the aftermath of the game George spoke to Hugh McIlvanney saying:

> I knew there were about forty policemen sent into the Newcastle ground because of the threat and I couldn't really get it out of my head that maybe this time the whole thing was real. I was definitely nervous for a while. I never stopped moving on the field. Somehow I felt that I should not stand still. Even when there was someone on the floor injured I kept running around. When I scored the gaol I was hoping I might be taken off. That's how much it had got to me. I kidded the other players that it was the first time I had ever scored a goal without people coming over to congratulate me.

On the way back from Newcastle the Manchester United team bus had an escort of two police cars. They were relieved in relays as county boundaries were crossed. His teammates were just as relieved as George was to get back home. They could slip off unaffected, but for George, Blossoms Lane was guarded by police.

Such was the life and world of an extraordinary footballer.

Newcastle United: McFaul, Ellison, Clark, Guthrie, Burton, Howard, Gibb, Tudor, Macdonald, Nattrass, Hibbitt. Substitute: Barrowclough for Tudor.

United: Stepney, O'Neill, Dunne, Gowling, James, Sadler, Morgan, Kidd, Charlton, Law, Best. Substitute: Aston for Dunne.

Scorer: BEST.

Attendance: 52,411.

George was enjoying his football again. I think everything has improved. Frank O'Farrell must take a lot of the credit for what he has done at United, but I think his assistant Malcolm Musgrove is terrific too.

'My own game has certainly developed because the team is doing well and I have the encouragement I need. I am strictly a front man now. They don't want me going back into my own half. Scoring goals, or at least having a hand in them, is what it has always been about for me so I am going well. I think I am passing better than I ever did before, not more accurately because I thought I always struck the ball pretty well but at the right time. That's some difference.'

In his article for the *Observer* Hugh McIlvanney added,

> One of the joys about talking to George these days is that he has abandoned any attempt to be biased about his feelings for football.
>
> 'You know, I still find a special thrill in playing with goalposts that have nets. When we are training and there are no nets I feel like going in a huff and refusing to play. I still get a special charge when the ball makes that whirring noise as it hits the net.'
>
> Every great game he plays, and most of his performances turn out that way, increases his glamour and his earnings. He is paid about £12,000 a year from Manchester united and makes perhaps three times that from outside sources. The most spectacular of these is the George best Annual. The initial print was 20,000 at £1. It sold out in three days and the sale has climbed to around 120,000. 'I used to joke that my ambition was to be a millionaire. Now it's not so much of a joke. I'll be disappointed if I'm not somewhere near it by the time I'm 30.'

39

United vs Southampton

27 November 1971

Despite a 1-0 home defeat by Leeds United and a 3-3 draw against Manchester City at Maine Road, a 3-1 victory over Tottenham Hotspur followed by a 3-2 triumph over Leicester City, kept United ahead of the pack at the top of the first division with twenty-eight points from their eighteen games, three points ahead of Derby County and Manchester City.

Rather surprisingly with nine goals in the last three fixtures, George's name failed to appear on the score sheet, nudged aside by fellow Irishman Sammy McIlroy, a newcomer to the United first team who scored on his debut against neighbours City at Maine Road. But that lack of goals was more than redeemed on the south coast at the compact ground of Southampton, where some of those inside the Dell were almost overlapping onto the pitch, while others appeared to rather precariously balance on an odd looking structure behind one of the goals.

On this particular Saturday afternoon when the gates were closed a good hour before kick-off and a reported 10,000 locked out, Southampton were no match for United as they were to find George in devastating form. Some felt that the home side were decidedly poor while other considered the visitors to be a cut above their opponents. Either could have been true, but it mattered little as the scoreline said it all.

It took United a mere seven minutes to open the scoring with a goal that clearly highlighted Southampton's shortcomings. Left half Walker, taking control of the ball in his own half, rather foolishly decided upon a one man raid towards the United goal, beating one man, then another before losing possession to Bobby Charlton. The more experienced United man immediately showed the Southampton half-back how he should have used the ball, immediately passing it to George. Keeping the momentum going George in turn passed to Kidd out on the left. Given more than enough space by Gabriel, Kidd centred and up popped George to nod past Martin in the Southampton goal.

The home side, already with problems in a limping Channon following an overly fierce tackle from James, had opportunities to equalise on two occasions. A Paine free-kick on the left of the United area found Davies at the far post, but his firm header went narrowly wide of the post. Then Tommy O'Neil was too casual on the ball, allowing Davies another opportunity in front of goal, but an alert Stepney dived to avert the danger.

Kidd look dangerous whenever he was given the ball and he came close to increasing United's lead with a shot from just outside the box after a cross-field move involving O'Neil, Morgan and George. Martin just getting his hand to the ball and turning it away.

Southampton did, at times, look dangerous and it took tackles from the unlikely defenders in Charlton and George to thwart a couple of promising attacks by Channon and Paine. Another move between Jenkins, Paine and Stokes saw the latter's cross brought under control by Gowling but, as the crowd and the Southampton players screamed 'penalty' for the use of an arm, the referee signalled that it was controlled by the player's chest and waved play on.

Moments later, United were 2-0 in front. McIlroy picked out Morgan with a cross-field pass from left to right and the winger was off and running and when his centre landed in the Southampton goalmouth McIlroy was there to strike the ball past Martin.

Three minutes into the second half a third United goal more or less brought an end to the game as a contest. Charlton crossed from the left, McIlroy dummied, George latched onto the ball, side stepped a defender and scored with a leisurely shot into the right hand corner of Martin's net as the 'keeper squirmed in the mudded goalmouth.

Amid driving rain Southampton pulled a goal back four minutes later, Gabriel jumping to head home Paine's free-kick. But Gabriel's pleasure and providing the goal soon turned to embarrassment when he helped George's header into the net for United's fourth after Martin had failed to hold a shot from McIlroy and the ball spun high into the air. The goal however, was to credited to George.

Determined to make amends for this, Gabriel once again pushed forward and his long high cross from the right was met by the head of Davies who headed across goal. Something of a scramble ensued and as the ball broke loose, Davies moved in to shoot past Stepney.

With nineteen minutes remaining George limped off the pitch with a gashed leg, much to the relief of the Southampton players, but even with the most menacing of opponents off the pitch they failed to keep the score down. As six minutes from time Aston took a corner on the left, Charlton rose above the Southampton defence and as the ball flew over his head, Kidd stepped in to hit the ball high into the net.

'It was the best of Best and the best of United' read one report. 'A demonstration of the oldest motto in soccer – there is no substitute for skill.'

Southampton: Martin, Gabriel, Kirkup, Lovett, McGrath, Walker, Paine, Channon, Davies, Stokes, Jenkins. Substitute: O'Brien for Channon.

Scorers: Gabriel, Davies.

United: Stepney, O'Neil, Burns, Gowling, James, Sadler, Morgan, Kidd, Charlton, McIlroy, Best. Substitute: Aston for Best.

Scorers: Best (3), McIlroy, Kidd.

Attendance: 30,323.

George vs Manchester United: January/April 1972

1972 was far from being a Happy New Year for Manchester United and clubs manager, the soft spoken Irishman Frank O'Farrell. No sooner had the bells rang out, confining 1971 to the history books and heralding the start of 1972 than United were suffering a humiliating 3-0 defeat at the hands of West Ham United in London's east end. The reversal dented United's title aspirations, although they remained two points clear of their two immediate rivals – Leeds United and Manchester City.

Seven days later United were at home to sixth placed Wolverhampton Wanderers and two points from the Old Trafford encounter were expected, rather than hoped for. But during that seven day gap, the club found themselves once again hauled over both the front and back pages of the local and national newspapers without a ball being kicked. George's alter ego had once again reappeared.

There were no hints that there was a problem, nor anything bothering the wayward genius, as he had told his *Daily Express* ghost writer John Roberts that United would be out to bring an end to their recent bad run of results against the Midlands side. But on the morning of the match, it was the front pages of papers, not the back that created an unwanted prelude to the first division encounter at Old Trafford.

'Airport Chase for Soccer Star – Best Flies into Hiding' was the headline in the *Daily Mail*, while the *Daily Express* led with: 'George: I'll Explain All. Fly Away Best'. Both newspapers telling of how George had been absent from training since Monday, with the *Mail* telling of how the club had been told at first that he was in Belfast, then he was ill, but following discreet inquiries it was revealed that he had never moved any further than his house in Bramhall. His housekeeper, Mrs Olga Fullaway, had telephoned the club and asked when he had to report for the Wolves game, only to be told that he didn't and he had to report to the manager on Monday.

Frank O'Farrell had called the team together after training and told them that he had dropped George from his line-up to face Wolves, revealing to the press in a tersely worded statement that he had not trained all week and was therefore not fit to play. A teammate said that the manager appeared 'to be badly let down' by George and had said that the decision to drop George was in the 'best interests of the club'. He added that the players had also felt let down by their teammate and that the last time they saw him was when he got off the train at Wilmslow after the game against West Ham United.

Then on the Friday night George had been spotted at Manchester Airport taking a flight to Heathrow where he was met by a light blue Rolls Royce and whisked away to an unknown destination. He told a *Daily Express* reporter: 'I have an explanation for what has happened. But I just can't say what it is until I've seen the boss. That will probably be Monday.' Speculation was now rife as to George's future with the club. 'Will He Leave United?' asked Derek Potter in the *Express*. 'Dare United sell and who would buy? These are the questions Best has poised with yesterday's new chapter of unease bringing with it public climax for club and player.'

Potter went on to ask what was George's worth on the transfer market was, estimating it to be around £500,000. His fellow *Express* correspondent, Alan Thompson, wrote: 'Just how much George Best will be forgiven this time will depend on the credibility and validity of his reasons for going absent without leave from training for a week.'

Two days later the outcome of George's latest escapade was brought to the fore. Frank O'Farrell described him as 'a lonely boy' and revealed that the player had to leave his luxury home in Bramhall and return to his former digs under the supervision of Mrs Fullaway, that he was fined two weeks wages (estimated to be around £400), ordered to train every afternoon (as well as in the mornings with the junior players) and also forfeit his day off for the next five weeks to make up for the training he missed the previous week.

George simply shrugged his shoulders and went along with it all, saying that he 'deserved it' and was to find himself back in the first team line-up for the FA Cup tie at Southampton. What the other players thought of it all was kept within the walls of the dressing room.

At the Dell George was an inconspicuous figure in the 1-1 draw but came to the fore in the replay at Old Trafford four days later, scoring twice as United triumphed 4-1 after extra time. But just as quick as George had went from one extreme to the other, United's season suddenly crumbled around them.

In the league they lost 1-0 at home to Chelsea, 2-1 at the Hawthorns against West Bromwich Albion, 2-0 at Old Trafford against Newcastle United, 5-1 at Elland Road against Leeds United and 2-0 at White Hart Lane against Tottenham Hotspur. Results that saw them tumble from first division leaders to ninth, ten points behind cross town rivals Manchester City.

There had been a glimmer of hope of success in the FA Cup following the defeat of Southampton, with victories over Preston North End, 2-0 at Deepdale, and a 3-0 success against

Middlesbrough at Ayresome Park, following a 0-0 draw at Old Trafford. A goal from George earned a 1-1 draw against Stoke City at Old Trafford and he was to score again at the Victoria Ground, his 71st minute goal giving United the lead but League Cup winners Stoke equalised three minutes later before forcing home the winner in extra time.

The signing of Ian Storey-Moore (seen as a replacement for George?) brought a change of fortune, if only briefly, with a run of four games unbeaten, which suddenly materialised into four games without a win. George had certainly not been his old self of late, although he had scored against Huddersfield Town, Coventry City and also in the 3-2 victory over Southampton, a result that got United back on winning ways. But six days later, on 21 April, it was reported that the crazy world of George Best and Manchester United was once again thrown into disarray.

Rumours circulated that George had not been in for training all week, while manager Frank O'Farrell was quoted as saying, 'George has had a heavy cold all week and hasn't been feeling well generally. He has been under the doctor's care and that's the reason he has not been doing any training this week. I wouldn't think he will be playing on Saturday (against Nottingham Forest) but that depends on the doctor's report of course.'

O'Farrell also admitted that George's form had dipped dramatically as of late.

However, the daughter-in-law of George's landlady said that she had seen him on Monday and Tuesday and that 'he wasn't showing any signs of a cold then and to me he seemed perfectly all right. He said he had been given a few days off by the club but he didn't say where he was going.'

In his *Daily Express* column George laid out his time table for the close season, mentioning a number of fixtures he was due to take part in, ranging from Germany to Ireland, then Majorca, Israel and Greece. He made it to Germany, but that was it and soon the press were asking the question if George was near to quitting football after failing to join up with the Northern Ireland international side and while sitting beside a pool in Marbella told reporters who had managed to track him down: 'I don't care what people think. What I have to say will be sensational. This time it's the big one.'

While George was in Marbella, his United teammates were just across the Mediterranean in Majorca and all manager Frank O'Farrell had to say to members of the press was: 'If you think I am going to chase George Best all over the Costa del Sol, then you have another think coming. It's Northern Ireland's problem not mine.'

'The big one' that George had spoken about wasn't so much 'big', but gigantic and it saw the *Sunday Mirror* enjoy one of its biggest circulations for many a day by splashing the 'exclusive': 'I Quit, by George Best' across the front page of its 21 May edition.

In the article that followed, George bemoaned his life as a footballer, saying that it had become work instead of something that he once enjoyed and he dreaded getting up in the morning and going into training. Match days had also become something of a nightmare and due to having spent much of the past year drinking, he was now a mental and physical wreck.

Sir Matt Busby, the man who had done so much for George, would not speak about him in the immediate aftermath of the news breaking, but was later to say: 'One thing we have to understand, George Best is a genius. But we are no longer prepared to tolerate his wayward behaviour', while Frank O'Farrell responded to the 'I quit' threat by simply saying: 'We'll live without him.' Adding: 'I am waiting to see George in Tel Aviv on 28 May and if he does not show up then we will take action. In the meantime, I hope George will sort out his problem. I hope he does – because at the moment I have to confess I feel more pity for him than anything else.'

Countless column inches were given offer to this latest escapade in George's career, one that certainly looked now as being at an end. It had even caused a mini fall-out at boardroom level following Sir Matt Busby's comment: 'His re-entry into soccer will be subject to certain reservations. His present behaviour has got to stop.' An angry Chairman Louis Edwards telling

Derek Potter of the *Daily Express*: 'If Sir Matt is laying down conditions it is a lot of tripe and nonsense. We have nothing to say until our next meeting when the George Best position will be discussed.'

Then, as quickly as he had given his 'I Quit' story, George was in print as having had a re-think on his future and had decided to return to Manchester and 'face the music'. 'I've let them down and all I want to do is go back and play football as I can for Manchester United. When I went away, it was to sort things out. But I made the wrong decision.'

Bulgaria vs Northern Ireland

18 October 1972

September 1972 saw George sign a new six year contract, saying: 'I'm with United until I'm thirty-two and that suits me fine. I'm enjoying my football more now than at any time. If four months ago anyone had asked me would I be happy about this situation and me doing well, I would have laughed. But right now, all I want to do is play my part at Old Trafford. It's a new challenge for me.'

Enjoying his football he might have been, but Manchester United were not enjoying the most favourable of starts to their domestic season, with only two wins (ten against Birmingham City and 3-0 against Derby County) from the opening thirteen games. Five of the other eleven fixtures had ended in draws, the rest were defeats. There was the additional worry of having failed to score in seven of those thirteen fixtures. Of the ten goals scored, George was joint top scorer with Ian Storey-Moore on three!

That enjoyment was however soon to be soured, while playing for Northern Ireland in a World Cup qualifier in Sofia against Bulgaria.

Prior to the match, one that George had been looking forward to, he spoke about the game being 'one of the most important matches of my life' as he hoped that it would be third time lucky in his attempt to reach the World Cup Finals and that he would be able to help 'the greatest Irish team I have been with' to the summer Finals in Germany. He went on to add: 'I have the funniest feelings in the back of my mind that I'm going to make it to Munich.'

If he was going to make it to Germany, the road ahead was certainly not a smooth one, with the ninety minutes against Bulgaria as hard as any that he played during any stage of his career.

The Bulgarians were far from being a force in European football, never mind world football, despite being unbeaten at home for sixteen years and were considered to be a team in the middle of a re-building programme, but they were to take the lead in the 18th minute on a heavy pitch due to several days rain and never really looked like losing after that. That opening goal, scored by Bonev, perhaps the home sides most dangerous player, from the penalty spot, did not simply set the home side on their way to victory, but unsettled the Irish due to its controversy and set the tone for the remainder of the match. Such were the feelings among the Irish players regarding the referee's decision to award a spot kick for Hunter's challenge on Kolev, that George and Pat Rice were booked for their protests.

Fifteen minutes into the second half the Irish, now restricted in their attacking moves were 2-0 down and again there was a hint of controversy surrounding the goal. Having awarded the Bulgarians a free-kick, which came to nothing, the West German referee ordered it to be taken again and this time, Kolev blasted the ball home from 20 yards out through an unorganised defensive wall.

Ireland were disappointing, shoddy in defence and lacking any skill or determination further forward. The game itself was notable for its fifty-three free-kicks, seven bookings, very little in the way of genuine football and for its stormy finale.

With the outcome never in any doubt, the Bulgarian captain Bonev moved into the Irish penalty area, where George scythed him down, leaving the referee with little option to send him off. His fourth dismissal of a turbulent career.

'I retaliated ... it's the old story,' George said later. 'They were at me from the start, niggling, jersey-pulling and elbowing. I was kicked twice as I attempted a clearance. I kicked back at their Number Eight but I didn't actually hit him. It's probably lucky we didn't catch each other properly. But I do feel very low about it ... and I don't want to talk about it anymore just now.' He was also quick to add that his new blemish to his career did nothing to make him revive his threat to quit the game.

Bulgaria: Filipov, Zafirov, Stankov, Yonov, Kolev, Penev, Vasilev, Bonev, Denev, Stoyanov, Simov. Substitute: Tsvetkov for Simov.

Scorers: Bonev (2), Kolev.

Northern Ireland: Jennings (Tottenham Hotspur), Nelson (Arsenal), Neill (Hull City), Hunter (Ipswich Town), Clements (Sheffield Wednesday), Hamilton (Ipswich Town), McMordie (Middlesbrough), Dougan (Wolverhampton Wanderers), Hegan (Wolverhampton Wanderers), Best (Manchester United). Substitute: Morgan (Port Vale) for Hamilton.

Attendance: 40,000

George vs United: December 1972

Season 1972/73 had, by the halfway stage, been one to forget for Manchester United Football Club. In fact, in all honesty, you would be hard pushed to find another that had begun so badly. Even the 1933/34 campaign, which almost brought relegation to the third division didn't kick-off in such a mundane and lacklustre fashion.

Back in those distant days of the 1930s, that almost disastrous season produced four wins, two draws and six defeats in the opening dozen games, but in comparison, the 1972–73 season produced one solitary victory, five draws and a haunting six defeats and as you would guess such performances left United propping up the first division table with a paltry seven points, eleven behind leaders Liverpool.

Goals were few and far between, nine in that dozen games, with George leading scorer with three, although there were few outstanding ninety minutes from anyone in the once famous red shirts. George, despite his recent failings, had impressed at times – how could you keep him out of the headlines?

'Best Brightens the Manchester Gloom' and 'George Out of Luck' in the 0-0 draw against Arsenal, 'Best Promptings Fail to Rouse United' from the 1-0 defeat against Coventry City, but an even more startling one hit the back pages a few days prior that Coventry match, when it was announced that George had been given a new six year contract by the club. This for a player who had shouted from the roof tops in the not too distant past that he was quitting the game, turning his back on United for a life in the sunshine.

'I'm with United until I'm thirty-two and that suits me fine' said George. 'I'm enjoying my football more now than at any time. If four months ago anyone had asked me if I would be happy about this situation with United struggling and me doing well, I would have laughed. But right now all I want to do is play my part at Old Trafford. It's a new challenge for me. I realise that for my own sake I have got to cut down on everything and I have done so. My future is with Manchester United.'

A new 'I quit' threat from George was suddenly swirling through the Manchester air as October gave way to November, but it could have been seen as something of a kick in the pants to his teammates as George proclaimed that he would certainly leave Old Trafford if the stadium was to host second division football next season. There was still a long way to go but United were still in a precarious position – second bottom, still level on points with Crystal Palace, although they did possess a slightly better goal average.

Three points from two games: a 2-2 draw against Leicester City at Filbert Street and a moral boosting 2-0 win over leaders Liverpool at Old Trafford lifted United off that bottom spot, but a 3-0 defeat by Manchester City at Maine Road on 18 November saw them crashing back to where they had come. A 2-1 win over Southampton saw them yo-yo back up to fourth bottom, two points above bottom club Leicester City. Seven days later, they had jumped a further two places to seventeenth, but they had beaten Norwich City at Carrow Road with George.

'Absent Best Faces Rap' shouted the *Daily Express* on Wednesday 22 November, following George's failure to turn up for two training sessions and a flu jab. 'I had flu' said George. Then on the eve of the trip to Norwich, it was announced that George was dropped. He was also fined and banned from night clubs, with his private life severely restricted. Oh yes, there was also extra training to make up for what he had missed.

Manager Frank O'Farrell said, 'It is a great tragedy. Inside the club he is perfect. He trains well, he is likeable. All the trouble happened outside. Who is to blame? I suppose everybody. We build super-stars....and then knock them down. Perhaps it's society. I don't know?'

David Meek, the *Manchester Evening News* correspondent who had written about the Old Trafford clubs since the aftermath of the Munich air disaster in 1958, cared little about who was to blame as to George's current predicament. 'Best Must Go' he wrote, saying that United would be far better without him. Almost a week later he penned: 'Call George's Bluff United' going on to add. 'George Best is making a mockery out of Manchester United. Manchester United are the most prestigious club in the country facing a critical period in their distinguished history. Yet here is one of their senior players repeatedly aggravating the club's problems.' David felt that George was simply playing a cat and mouse game with the club in an effort to get a transfer.

David's assumption took a step towards becoming reality on 5 December, when it was announced that George had been put on the transfer list. The player himself receiving the news in hiding somewhere in his favoured London.

At last ... the grand but uneasy alliance is over. The *Daily Express* stated, 'For Manchester United the magnetism and the mischief is over. George Best is on his way ... and last night two questions throbbed through English football. "Who will buy him?" and – perhaps more vitally – "Where will he go?"'.

'Manchester united are selling so much more than a unique football talent' wrote James Lawton. 'They are selling a man who poses serious questions against his own ability to produce again the glorious skills which flowed from his feet. And they are selling a twenty-six year-old man whose personality is clearly disturbed by the trappings of fame.'

Cut, dried and dusted? No chance. This was George Best and a Manchester United barely, no totally, unrecognisable from those famed sides of the '60s, '50s and '60s. Three magnificent teams, one of which George helped make, but he was now making the Old Trafford club the laughing stock of football as within a matter of hours, never mind days, it was 'Best Makes it Up: I Play for United Again.' He was back in training – his first sessions for three weeks, and taken off the transfer list, with chairman Louis Edwards saying, 'I have seen George Best today and discussed recent happenings with him. He only wants to play for Manchester United. I've spoken to directors and to our manager, Mr O'Farrell. Best will start training as soon as possible.'

'Does this mean he is off the transfer list', he was then asked. 'I suppose it does' came the reply.

Stoke City came to Old Trafford on 9 December at returned to the Potteries on the back of a 2-0 victory. United had slipped back down the table to third bottom. A week later they were in London, not looking for George, but looking for two points in what was an early relegation encounter against bottom side Crystal Palace.

At Selhurst Park United, like George on numerous occasions in the past, simply didn't turn up. Even though he wasn't there, he was blamed by more than one reporter for the humiliating 5-0 defeat. Manchester United are very close to the first mutiny in soccer. 'After they had been humiliated by this defeat the players were sick and disheartened' wrote Desmond Hackett in the *Daily Express*. It continued:

> Their tissue-paper defence, their complete loss of heart and ambition was brutally trodden on by every one of the five goals scored by Crystal Palace. Now senior players, men who have given years of service and played out their hearts for one of the most loved teams In Britain are not prepared to take any more from George Best. You cannot blame them when recent events indicate that Best can behave as he does, and then find that there is, apparently one law for him and another for the rest of the players.

Suddenly, the rumour mill was in over-drive with Frank O'Farrell's future coming under deep scrutiny. David Meek believed that the under pressure United manager would neither resign, or indeed be asked to clear his desk. But for once, the *Manchester Evening News* man was wrong, utterly and completely wrong, as not only was Frank O'Farrell sacked following a crisis meeting at Old Trafford on the evening of Tuesday 19 December, George was also banished from the club.

Strangely, or then again perhaps not, the sacking of George received more column inches than that of the manager. The dramatic decision was given the front page on all the newspapers, with Hugh McIlvanney writing in the *Daily Express*:

> The most explosive announcement in the history of British football last night blasted both George Best and Frank O'Farrell, out of the game. Best's removal, according to a solemnly phrased letter declaring that he is finished with football, will be permanent. The board decided unanimously to fire O'Farrell and to tell Best, the Ulsterman who is arguably the most gifted player in Europe, that he will never wear the red shirt of United again. They say that a decision to leave Best on the transfer list and to accept that he would never play another match for the club was taken at a meeting in the morning.

George had written to the board, the letter read out at the hastily called meeting, was as follows:

> I had thought seriously of coming personally and asking for a chance to speak at the board meeting, but once again, I am afraid when it came to saying things face-to-face I might not have been completely honest. I am afraid, from my somewhat unorthodox ways of trying to sort my own problems out. I have caused Manchester United even bigger problems.
>
> I wanted you to read this letter before the board meeting commenced so as to let you know my feelings before any decisions or statements are issued, following the meeting. When I said last summer I was going to quit football, contrary to what many people said or thought, I seriously meant it because I had lost interest in the game for various reasons.
>
> While in Spain I received a lot of letters from both friends and well-wishers – quite a few asking me to reconsider. I did so, and after weeks of thinking it over I decided to give it another

try. It was an even harder decision to make than the original one. I came back hoping my appetite for the game would return and even though in every game I like to think I gave 100 per cent, there was something missing. Even now I am not quite sure what.

Therefore, I have decided not to play football again and this time no one will change my mind. In conclusion, I would like to wish the club the best of luck for the remainder of the season and for the future. Because – even though I, personally, have tarnished the club's name in recent times – to me and to thousands of others, Manchester United still means something special.

While thousands adored George and marvelled at his skills, there were thousands of others who were, by now, completely fed up with his ever frustrating antics. 'Some Good Men Went Down With Best' echoed the *Daily Mirror* with Frank McGhee writing: 'George Best's latest announcement of his retirement from football – and how we must all hope that this time it is final – had a significant difference. This time, some good men went with him.'

A £300,000 price tag was put on George's head by the club and one of the first clubs to show an interest was Bournemouth, although offering slightly below the asking price at £250,000. There was even a hint that Real Madrid were interested in signing him, despite a ten year ban on signing foreign players.

So, it was now George Best ex. Manchester United. Well, for the time being at least.

Following the sacking of Frank O'Farrell, the Manchester United board appointed the Scottish international team manager, Tommy Docherty, as his successor. Results did not improve greatly, indeed it was seven games before the new manager experienced his first victory, a 2-1 home victory over Wolverhampton Wanderers on 10 February. Thankfully an unbeaten run of eight games, between 17 March and 21 April was enough to ward off the evils of relegation and ensure United's first division safety.

Season 1972/73 began indifferently, a 3-0 defeat at Highbury against Arsenal being followed by victories against Stoke City and Queens Park Rangers, which in turn were followed by three consecutive defeats. Goals, like victories, were few and far between with the Old Trafford support stunned into silence as they watched goalkeeper Alex Stepney trot up-field to place a penalty kick past Peter Shilton in the 2-1 defeat by Leicester City.

It was certainly a shock to see Stepney given the role of penalty taker, but it was nothing like the jaw dropping news of the previous week, that with the new season less than a month old, George Best was returning to Old Trafford.

In the *Guardian* following the announcement that George would be returning to M16, Eric Todd wrote:

It appears that Best, footballer extraordinary, who in the past subscribed to no code of discipline unless he made it himself, and no code of loyalty unless it suited him, has decided that he would like once more to play football for Manchester United. So far as I know he is still on the transfer list and, as far as I remember, at least two United officials have said that he would never play for them again. And Best more than once has said that he had finished with football. Now United, warily perhaps, are considering giving him another chance; maybe his third or is it his fourth?

Eric Todd, whose neighbour had moaned about the performances of the current United side and saying he would give a lot to see even half an hour of George Best, rounded off his article by saying:

At a time when the game is sick, and some spectators are making it more so, and when characters and character are becoming fewer, football in general, and Manchester United in particular, could do with the George Best we knew four or five years ago. Not the Best of the nightclubs and the notoriety. As my neighbour inferred, half an hour of George Best would be worth seeing. Ninety minutes could be even better. It is up to him. But if ever he transgresses again, please let there be no more attempts at salvage.

'We want George to come back and start training' said chairman Louis Edwards. 'The question of whether he plays for United again would have to be considered by the board.' From Majorca, where George was in exile, he told reporters: 'I now feel the urge to have another game. A short time ago I could not thought like this. Now I want to get the feel of a football at my feet again. That will tell me what I want to know.' He continued, 'There was a lot of back-biting round the time I left Old Trafford. I suppose it was natural. Results were bad and that brings all sorts of problems.'

George flew back to Manchester and a meeting with manager Tommy Docherty was arranged, the outcome of which saw him make the following announcement:

Manchester United is the only club I have ever played for and I suppose I hope to end up here. I have had nine months to think and get things sorted out. It was always problems outside the game that were the difficulty. I have always missed playing. I think the particular moment when I realised I wanted to come back was in hospital, lying on my back for three weeks after the thrombosis in my leg. I am not coming back because I'm broke. I have always missed the actual playing of matches. The first thing I want to do is get fit. I am not completely unfit. I have not been exactly lying around all this time. I reckon I have to lose about 10 lbs.

Manager Tommy Docherty added, 'The future of George Best is linked with his dedication in training. This I am sure he will show.'

George reckoned that he had a good five more years left as a player and following the 0-0 home draw against Liverpool on 29 September he was given the opportunity to prove it, when the Manchester United board confirmed that they had accepted the recommendation of manager Tommy Docherty 'that Best should return' and they considered it in the best interest of the club.

41

United vs Ajax

3 October 1973

The visit of reigning European champions Ajax to Old Trafford produced a night of high emotion, with a crowd of over 45,000 clicking through the turnstiles in what was meant to be a homage-paying fixture to the 'King' of the Stretford End – Denis Law. His testimonial match however, was hijacked by a bearded individual making a reappearance in front of the supporters who had marvelled at his genius but had also been dismayed by his behaviour. George was back. How many had made their way down to the banks of Ship Canal solely to witness his return in comparison to those who were there to acknowledge the contribution made by Denis Law is undocumented. But the slightly more rounded George was indeed back and what is more than certain, many of those present wondered just how long this latest escapade would last.

Denis Law, as could be expected, received a standing ovation from the United faithful but has the blond-headed Scot left the field on which he had scored so many memorable goals, unable to play due to injury, the spotlight quickly shone on the prodigal son.

It had been ten months since George had trod the hallowed turf and David Meek was to write in his *Manchester Evening News* match report that 'he seemed to me to be shredded with nerves; he nearly fell over the ball the first time it came his way. I am sure he found it an ordeal. But he needs a helping hand along the come-back trail he will find thousands in the Stretford End. They obviously forgive him his slightly podgy look and the fact that his confidence is a long way from returning.'

Early in the game Steve James put his team in trouble with a mistimed back pass but fortunately, as Ajax forward lined up his shot, Brian Greenhoff managed to block the attempt and clear the danger. But despite their exalted role, the visitors did little to impress the crowd, or indeed show that they were worth anything like their guaranteed £18,000 fee.

If George had something of an uncertain start, he soon roused the crowd as he collected a pass from Young before taking the ball past a Dutch defender. From the cross, Morgan's effort was pushed away by Stuy in the Ajax goal. Anderson then beat two players, but his cross towards Macari was too high for his diminutive teammate to reach.

The opening half was somewhat slow with the visitors more than content to play their possession game, content to push the ball around, ignoring the physical side of things. Their defence was breached twice in those opening forty-five minutes but both efforts, from Macari and Kidd, were unfortunately offside.

The clocks were suddenly turned back when George beat three defenders, only to see his shot at goal turned behind for a corner, as United took the game to their visitors, but while not entirely devoid of action, the first forty-five minutes were certainly devoid of goals.

After the interval United pressed forward more regularly, Morgan twice coming close in the space of a matter of minutes adding to the obvious that United were crying out for an out and out goal scorer. A buzz swept around the ground as George found it within himself to beat three defenders, taking the ball up to the goal line, his shot at goal deflected behind for a corner. More was to come mid-way through the half when he pivoted while still some 30 yards from goal, hitting a strong drive towards the Ajax goal and almost catching the 'keeper unawares.

Until the seventy-second minute, there was little more to cheer than George's performance, as it looked odd on that the dull encounter would end goal-less. But an indirect free-kick to United saw the ball rolled into the path of Alex Forsyth who seized the opportunity by blasting the ball beyond the reach of Stuy. Even the Stretford end was caught by surprise as it took a minute or two for them to realise that a goal had actually been scored. The goal seemed to jolt the visitors into life, as they drifted forward in search of an equaliser but it failed to materialise as the game stuttered towards its conclusion. It wasn't about a result though, it was Denis Law's night, or perhaps the return of George, getting ninety minutes under his belt in the long road to fitness.

'What a fabulous feeling it was on Wednesday to come down the tunnel from the Old Trafford changing rooms to hear the roar from 45,000 fans, and above all to be wearing the red shirt of Manchester United again' George told Paul Hince of the *Manchester Evening News*. He continued:

> I have tried to explain before why I decided to come back and all the reasons were capsuled in that one moment when I stepped on to the Old Trafford pitch to take part in Denis Law's testimonial match against Ajax. All the things I had missed so badly in the past year were there. The excitement which the Old Trafford crowd always generate, the thrill of playing against one of the top club sides in the world, and that special satisfaction of pitting your skill against another man. I have read somewhere that Tommy Docherty thinks that with another six games under my belt I will be ready for the first team. I hope he is right.

United: Stepney, Young, M. Buchan, Greenhoff, Sidebottom, James, Morgan, Anderson, Macari, Kidd, Best. Substitute: Rimmer for Stepney, McIlroy for Macari, Forsyth for Young, G. Buchan for Anderson.

Scorer: Forsyth

Ajax: Stuy, Suurbiter, Hulshoff, Blankenburg, Krol, Haan, Neeskens, Muhern, Rep, Mulder, Keizer.

Attendance: 45,156.

As Manchester United crumbled to a 2-1 defeat at Wolverhampton, one correspondent wrote that the 'Red Devils of Old Trafford were now pale pink imitations of the great United sides of the past'. There was a crowd of 7,000, well above the usual attendance, at the Central League fixture against Aston Villa in Manchester.

The extra rotations of the turnstiles were down to one individual: George. Making his first competitive appearance since 25 November 1972. His appearance however, failed to inspire his teammates and the expected victory failed to materialise with Aston Villa wining 2-0, United's reserve eleven's first defeat of the season.

Reserve team coach, and former teammate of George's, Bill Foulkes said after the game:

> He did everything I expected of him and I shall Tommy Docherty he played just great. I didn't give him any special instructions. I just let him play his own game. Aston Villa reserves area strong, experienced side and this was just the sort of training he needs but it could be months

rather than weeks before he is fully match fit. It's not surprising if he lacked pace. I didn't want him to go bursting through the penalty area and get hammered. But he hates to lose and when things are not going right, he has to have a go.

Although wearing the Number Seven shirt George played more of a midfield position, where his lack of speed was not so obvious, nor required. 'It was a great game' said the returning Irishman, 'I enjoyed every minute of it, but I am not 100 per cent fit yet. It will take a few games like that. I sprained my right leg in the second half and felt a bit worried about it for the rest of the game. I'm not worried about the extra weight – I'll soon lose that. I'm not setting any dates on getting back to first class soccer. I'm happy enough to just train and play soccer.'

During the ninety minutes there was the odd flicker of the old George but, it was to no avail. He created two good scoring opportunities for Peter Fletcher but both were shunned, while later in the game he found himself through on goal, but he was to fire over the bar from 15 yards.

His reputation however, was to go before him, as Aston Villa full-back John Gidman kept something of a close watch on him and following one overly hard tackle, George was seen to kick out at the Villa man. Before anything more series could develop, the referee quickly stepped in.

If the expanded attendance for the Central League fixture against Aston Villa was a clear hint as to George's pulling power, then an even greater example was to follow nine days later when United travelled to Dalymount Park Dublin to face Shamrock Rovers in a friendly. Some 20,000 packed into the ground and as the teams appeared, hundreds of youngsters swarmed onto the pitch in an attempt to get George's autograph, delaying the kick-off for five minutes.

With United leading 2-1 and nine minutes remaining the crowd, having already encroached onto the pitch, once again edged closer and closer to the touchline, giving the referee little option but to abandon the game.

42

United vs Birmingham City
20 October 1973

George had played the eighty odd minutes of the friendly against Shamrock Rovers, a further step along the way to regaining full fitness with his training and input during his friendly outings including one in Portugal in a testimonial for Eusebio, that United manager Tommy Docherty felt that he was now ready to return to the first division stage.

He was however, still a little overweight, short of pace and even more obvious, a far cry from the player he once was. 'I am not match fit' he said, 'It is going to take five or six first team games to regain my peak. If I find I am struggling against Birmingham I shall ask to come off. I don't anticipate making a fool of myself.' Tommy Docherty added, 'Don't let anyone expect Besty to be back to what he was in this particular game' referring to his last first division outing. 'My feeling is that, after six games, it's no use giving George another half dozen reserve run-outs. He would still need to gather the first division tempo, whenever he made his comeback. But even a half fit Best is better than most in the first division.'

Manchester United certainly needed George as following the 3-1 victory over West Ham United and the consecutive 0-0 draws against Leeds United (the current leaders) and Liverpool, defeats against Wolverhampton Wanderers (2-1) and Derby County (1-0) saw them drop form a respectable fourteenth to a slightly worrying eighteenth, a mere four points above bottom club West Ham United.

The reappearance of George in a red shirt brought an additional 4,000 odd through the turnstiles, but it was still 5,000 less than had watched the game against Liverpool. Some perhaps might have suspected that there might well be a non-appearance by George and they had little inclination to fork out good money to watch a mundane United performance against a team of little interest to anyone outside the Midlands. It was also 10,000 more than the second highest attendance on the day.

It was not simply a return to first division action for George, but also his 350th League game for United and although a spectacular return was not expected he was given a standing ovation, after the boos of disapproval had died down, following his substitution in the 77th minute.

Conditions were heavy, which were far from ideal for the returning hero who was still around six pounds overweight, but his performance was 'technically sound, liberally laced with slow-motion replays of his old skill, and highly encouraging for a future which could be firmly re-established after another half-dozen games or so'.

The visitors threatened United as early as the second minute when Taylor split open the United defence, only for Graham to deny Burns the scoring opportunity. Then Stepney had to be alert to a Taylor drive which he managed to tip over the bar. But it was full eight minutes before George Graham became the most popular man at Old Trafford when he passed to George to give him his first touch of the ball.

Brian Greenhoff had a shot well saved by Kelly then following a good run by Morgan, Macari did well to reclaim the ball after Buchan had lost it, but his final hot was wide of the mark, as United began to enjoy the upper hand.

George had his first shot on goal in the 36th minute but it lacked power and then just prior to the interval he probed the Birmingham defence with a neat pass to Young, who in turn switched it to Morgan, but his shot was pushed wide by the diving Kelly.

Rather ironically as the game progressed and George became more comfortable, so United improved. At the back Steve James and cult hero Jim Holton were dependable and effective, George Graham was productive in midfield, as Brian Greenhoff did the spade-work, while up front Willie Morgan should hints of George of old and was matched by Macari when it came to selecting a Man of the Match.

But Mike Kelly in the Birmingham City goal was a match for anything that came his way, making three magnificent saves from Macari alone, but that was however, until the 65th minute when faced with his opposite number Alex Stepney from 12 yards out after the ball hit Birmingham left-half Roberts on the elbow, the referee pointing to the penalty spot. Although Kelly dived the correct way, Stepney slotted home his second goal of the season, making him joint top scorer with Brian Kidd, an extraordinary statistic.

Hynd, Pendry and Want were both taunted by George on the edge of the Birmingham area, as he jinked one way and ten another, leaving them floundering before getting another cross into the visitors goalmouth. But the classic example of the player of old came at the start of the second half when, with back to goal, he flicked the ball up and shot overhead, the ball going narrowly over.

Morgan found Kidd who blasted over and then came George's corner that was to produce the only goal of the game. Francis, Hatton, Taylor and Burns all guilty of shunning ideal scoring opportunities. But then again, so should United as George twice created scoring opportunities for his teammates during the second half, but both were allowed to go amiss.

Although tiring, George was disappointed at being taken off.

> I enjoyed every minute. I found myself making a few mistakes, but with match practise I will be challenging for a regular place. I was afraid I would do something wrong, but I always felt we would win. The crowd were tremendous. I didn't want to come off but it is pointless trying to do too much when I am not 100 per cent fit. It will be different after six or seven games. Skill is something I will never lose. I'll have that when I am 100. The question is whether I use it. If I played like I did today every week, I would worry about staying in the team. I'm glad to be back. I'm really determined to knuckle down. I'm trying hard and taking it easy outside the game.

For those who want statistics, George made twenty passes to teammates and four to opposition players. He made one shot on goal and eight times tried to evade an opponent, seven of those were successful. However, on three occasions he attempted to get past a second opponent, but failed at all three attempts.

In the *Daily Mail*, Brian James, under the heading 'Newcomer Best Shows Promise', penned: 'Those who had seen the return of George Best as somehow a sign of light and hope at the end of a grisly week for English football (the national side had failed to secure a victory over Poland at Wembley, therefore missing out on the 1974 World Cup Finals in Germany) must now be reminded most vividly of the close resemblance between a damp straw and a broken reed.

Manchester United were to beat Birmingham ultimately by an eccentric penalty. Best's part in the victory was quite minimal. In truth, his reappearance in this week of all weeks was more painful than otherwise, rather like looking out faded snaps of a loved one immediately following the funeral. Had this been his first game ever, instead of merely his first in the League since last November, the temptation would have been to assemble a phrase of faint praise, something like 'the newcomer Best showed promising touches here and there.'

Strangely, there was no BBC or ITV cameras there to capture George's return but they were banned by manager Tommy Docherty from filming, even for a couple of minutes of newsreel.

United: Stepney, M. Buchan, Young, Greenhoff, Holton, James, Morgan, Macari, Kidd, Graham, Best. Substitute: Martin for Best.

Scorer: Stepney

Birmingham City: Kelly, Clarke, Want, Pendrey, Hynd, Roberts, Campbell, Francis, Burns, Hatton, Taylor. Substitute: Latchford.

Attendance: 48,937.

43

United vs Coventry City
15 December 1973

Burnley were next to benefit from George's return to the footballing stage, his presence for the Turf Moor fixture on 27 October 1973 saw their biggest crowd for five years flock to the town in the hope that they would witness something special, a step back in time to the halcyon days of the sixties. Others were simply curious, wanting to draw their own conclusions between the 'old' and the 'new' George Best.

The verdict at the end of a rather mundane ninety minutes would have been one of disappointment as the game was ground out with a blank score sheet amid the general opinion that George made little impact throughout the ninety minutes. Ronald O'Connor reporting for the *Daily Telegraph* wrote: 'Best rarely tried the close sinuous dribble that is his hallmark but occasionally his long cross field passes opened up a new point of attack with such vision one has not seen from United since Charlton's retirement. From two of those gems, Kidd the post and Buchan forced Stevenson to a fine save, but Best obviously cannot stand the pace of a full match yet.'

At least Tommy Docherty was happy with the result, as it enabled United to remain in sixteenth place in the first division, with the 2-2 draw against Chelsea the following week seeing a further two steps taken in the bid to escape the haunting thought of being stranded in the lower regions of the division.

Many of the 48,000 crowd had done their usual 'ten minutes before time' disappearing act, some having gone long before, after Chelsea had taken a 2-0 lead in the fiftieth minute.

With less than three minutes on the clock United were behind. Houseman, looking suspiciously offside, took a pass from Webb and from his cross, Baldwin shot past Stepney as the United defence waited on the linesman's flag and the referee's whistle.

The visitors defence was only threatened occasionally and United went further behind five minutes after the interval when Houseman again caused their defence problems before his final cross was met firmly by Osgood who out-jumped Griffiths and headed past Stepney.

With United looking down and out many dejected supporters began to make their way home, only to miss Tony Young pull one back with a 25 yard drive with two minutes to go. Then in a dramatic finale Brian Greenhoff slammed home the equaliser. It was a goal that might have been the winner as, with twelve minutes remaining, George had seen his shot from a Macari pass hit the underside of the bar and bounce precariously on the line. Despite protests that it was over, the referee waved play on.

'Great George' saluted the *Sunday Mirror*, while the *Observer* went for 'Best helps to civilise United' as George scored his first competitive goal following his return to the team, against Tottenham Hotspur at White Hart Lane. He had found the back of the net a few weeks earlier against Manchester City in Tony Dunne's testimonial match, but the goal in north London was his first in a 'real' match.

George grabbed the headlines again following the 0-0 draw against Norwich City – 'George Alone Transcends Mediocrity' shouted one, while another kept it simple with 'Best Shines in United Gloom'. The headlines of a fortnight later following the visit of Coventry City to Old Trafford were mainly related to United's dismal performance but, despite this, one or two of the newspapers still gave George top billing with: 'Better Best Back on Target' and 'Best's Fire Sparks Fightback Thrills' appearing.

Against Coventry, United once again found themselves a goal behind when Martin Buchan deflected a Cartwright centre past Stepney just before half-time, but two minutes after the interval, they were all square when George pounced after Glazier failed to hold a Brian Greenhoff shot, slipping the ball wide of the stumbling and scrabbling goalkeeper.

Leslie Duxbury in the *Observer* wrote, 'The second half glittered with incident, including a goal from George Best, whose skills may have declined but they are still far ahead of most of his contemporaries.'

United continued to put pressure on the Coventry defence, Glazier saving a Macari header then a penalty appeal was turned down before the visitors, arguably against the run of play, once again took the lead. Cross easily getting the better of Forsyth and Young before shooting past Stepney in the 64th minute.

Showing great resilience United once again fought back, drawing level once again two minutes later, Macari crossing for Morgan to head home. But with James struggling with a broken rib United were beginning to find it difficult to maintain a grip on the game despite the fine play from George, Macari and McIlroy and it was not surprising to many when Coventry snatched a third, Cross jumping for a centre from a Cartwright centre to head past Stepney. A 3-2 defeat that knocked United back to nineteenth in the table.

Little did those in the 28,589 crowd – United's lowest at home for some eight years – realise, that George's goal would be his last in a United shirt.

United: Stepney, M. Buchan, Forsyth, Greenhoff, James, Griffiths, Morgan, Macari, McIlroy, Young, Best. Substitute: Martin for James.

Scorers: Best, Morgan.

Coventry City: Glazier, Coop, Holmes, Parker, Cartwright, Alderton, Stein, Cross, Hutchison. Substitute: Green.

Scorers: Cross (2), Buchan, own goal.

Attendance: 28,589.

A week later Liverpool inflicted a 2-0 defeat on United making it now only one win in thirteen, far from favourable, it forced George to say,

Last Saturday evening, when most people were building up to the Christmas festivities, I felt down in the dumps after our defeat by Liverpool. It wasn't only that we had lost a game – after all I should be used to that by now. What upset me was the inference people were placing on my performance in that game. To say I played badly would be the understatement of the year. That is hard enough to swallow. But when people start saying that I am up to my tricks again or have no stomach for a fight, that is just about the last straw. Alright, I played badly. Everybody is entitled to a bad game … and that includes me. I know I have made a rod for my own back in the past, but I am trying to live that down – if people will let me.

He continued, 'I can never remember Manchester United players looking so upset after one isolated game. I don't feel ashamed to admit that I was near to tears after the match and I could see that most of the lads felt the same.' Adding: 'I once said I would not play second division soccer – with Manchester United or anyone else. I still don't relish the prospect and I hope to God I never have to make that decision.'

44

United vs Ipswich Town: 29 December 1973 and Queens Park Rangers vs United

1 January 1974

Christmas had been and gone. Santa Claus had bypassed Old Trafford and there was certainly no good will and cheer to anyone connected with Manchester United as a 2-1 Boxing Day defeat at home to Sheffield United saw Tommy Docherty's team slip to twentieth, a mere two points separating them and bottom club Norwich City.

'A lost anonymous soul wandering on the fringes of the game' was how one journalist saw George's performance at Anfield, while reports covering the defeat against Sheffield United making a search for his name a waste of time until you get to the team line-ups.

United's situation was grave, the first half of the season little more than a disaster, with little to give the supporters encouragement for the four months ahead. But if Christmas had been dismal with nothing to celebrate United ensured that 1973 went out with a bang, recording their first victory since 20 October with a 2-0 win against Ipswich Town on 25 December.

Having lost their previous two home games no one took anything for granted, nor indeed expected anything out of the ordinary, so it was to come as something of a shock for those not at the match and at home awaiting the scorers to learn that United had won 2-0.

United began well, but the early stages of the game was blighted by poor passing, particularly in the latter third of the pitch. Brian Greenhoff shot wide from a tight angle in the 24th minute, soon afterwards George Graham headed a Morgan corner wide, while McIlroy caused Hunter countless problems, forcing his fellow Northern Ireland colleague to take drastic measures with numerous fouls for which he was eventually booked. Greenhoff was also cautioned for shirt pulling.

It was with much relief that the first half drew to a close as it had been a dull lifeless affair, but as the second half got underway it was as if, certainly in United's case, different red-shirted players had taken to the field such was the difference.

David Best in the Ipswich goal kept he scoreline blank thanks to a fine acrobatic save from George, while he looked on anxiously as an attempted 30-yard back pass from Viljoen, under pressure from Macari, scrapped his crossbar. McIlroy missed an easy opportunity then stood open mouthed as another effort was headed off the line by Kevin Beattie with David Best a stranded onlooker.

A United goal was sure to materialise at some point, but it was not until the 77th minute that Best in the Ipswich goal was finally beaten. Willie Morgan, forever a threat on the United right wing, scurried down the touchline once again and his cross was headed down by George Graham to Sammy McIlroy who hit a firm low shot past Best from close range. It took only two minutes before a second United goal to materialise and it was Morgan once again the instigator, taking a corner from George, beating Mills with ease before crossing from the right for Macari to head home as the Ipswich defence looked totally immobile.

Morgan however, like George, was a mixture of brilliance and inaccuracy, but there were others who maintained a consistency throughout the ninety minutes. Brian Greenhoff and George Graham controlled mid-field, while up-front Lou Macari showed great determination. In defence, Martin Buchan and the rock that was Jim Holton, stood firm. Alex Stepney in goal was never tested.

While United were well worth their victory, showing a vast improvement on their recent mediocre performances, Ipswich Town were poor. Their manager, Bobby Robson, severely critical of his team said: 'We were awful. This was our worst performance of the season. We got what we deserved – the best team won. We didn't have a shot on goal. I could have played in United's goal myself.'

Three days later United travelled to London to face Queens Park Rangers at Loftus Road, but the good work achieved in their 2-0 success over Ipswich Town was well and truly undone, as it was once again back to the type of dismal, lacklustre performance that had blighted the season.

United's desperation was clearly illustrated right from the start when Tony Young upended Thomas in the opening seconds and had been booked by the third minute. Bowles (twice) and Francis both tested Stepney and by the 20th minute, the home side had taken the lead, former United player Don Givens running through a static defence to beat Stepney.

Ten minutes before the interval, it was 2-0. A Thomas corner from the left was nudged on by Holton towards the waiting Bowles who nodded home with ease. The Queens Park Rangers talented forward completed his hat-trick, his 12th goal of the season, twenty minutes into the second half, getting the better of three United defenders before beating Stepney with a left footed drive. Although well beaten, Stepney did in fact keep the score down to a respectable level with a string of fine saves.

George was described by David Lacey in the *Guardian* as 'heavily bearded and slightly portly, producing half-remembered tricks but all the time lacking the burst of speed that used to take him away from danger once he had beaten his man. Seldom can he have been caught in possession so often, though to his credit he could not be faulted for lack of effort.' Of United he wrote: 'Manchester United found neither the mood nor the method to stop Queens Park Rangers beating them for the first time at Shepherds Bush yesterday and in losing 3-0 took on the haunted look of a side for whom the prospect of relegation will loom large in 1974.'

And so Manchester United's decline continued and none of those who trudged despondently into the gloomy West London night, or had bounced out of Old Trafford those three days previously, realised that, as the red number eleven shirt had disappeared down the tunnel it would be their final sighting of George as a United player.

United: Stepney, Young, Griffiths, Greenhoff, Holton, Buchan, Morgan, Macari, McIlroy, Graham, Best. Substitute: Sidebottom.

Scorers: McIlroy, Macari.

Ipswich Town: Best, Burley, Mills, Morris, Hunter, Beattie, Hamilton, Viljoen, Johnson, Whymark, Lambert. Substitute: Woods for Whymark

Attendance: 36,365.

Queens Park Rangers: Parkes, Clement, Gillard, Venables, Mancini, McLintock, Thomas, Francis, Leach, Bowles, Givens.

Scorer: Bowles (3).

United: Stepney, Young, Houston, Greenhoff, Holton, Buchan, Morgan, Macari, McIlroy, Graham, Best. Substitute: Forsyth.

Attendance: 32,339.

No sooner had the dust settled on the Queens Park Rangers defeat than the rumour mill swung into action, not without undue cause it must be added, when word spread that George had, once again, missed training. Many delved into their record collections and pulled out the Four Tops classic hit 'It's The Same Old Song', but then George came out with the following statement: 'What's all the fuss about? I took a day off work yesterday, for reasons that are very personal to me, and suddenly the whole world wants to know why.'

Manchester United officials certainly wanted to know why when his landlady, Mrs Fullaway, was contacted she said that he had left for training at the usual time. No one had seen him, or received any message as to his whereabouts. 'Obviously I am concerned' said Tommy Docherty, 'but I don't know whether he is ill and will not pre-judge the issue until I know the full facts.' George was eventually seen at his Manchester nightclub, with his manager, Malcolm Wagner saying, 'George is feeling out of sorts and I understand he has contacted the club.'

George himself was later to add:

It's the kind of problem I've always had to live with so I don't suppose I should have been surprised by the reaction when I missed training yesterday. I've explained why I wasn't at the Cliff to my manager Tommy Docherty, and that's as far as I want to go. All the speculation about my absence has been wide of the mark. But with respect to the fans who genuinely take so much interest in my career, I don't want to reveal the real reason publicly. I don't see any necessity to reveal my private life to the world. The only people who need to know are my employers at Manchester United and they have been told. There are no problems as far as my playing career is concerned. People are kicking up a lot of fuss about nothing. The last thing I want is for people to read too much into this. I'm still as interested as ever in helping United to get out of trouble, and I want to play my part tomorrow in beating Plymouth.

George returned to training the following day – thirty minutes early and was included in Tommy Docherty's squad of thirteen players to face Plymouth Argyle at Old Trafford in the third Round of the FA Cup. Docherty's assistant, Pat Crerand, said, 'The team will be decided in the morning. The only doubt is Tony Young, who has a touch of flu', while Docherty himself refused to comment on George's explanation or whether or not he was actually satisfied with it. Only going as far as to say, 'It will be passed on to the directors at the first opportunity and then we will decide collectively what action to take. The information has already been passed on to the chairman. It will be dealt with in the normal way like any other disciplinary matter. The matter is not all that urgent. This incident will be dealt with according to its seriousness. It could be a small fine or it could be a large fine.'

Almost 32,000 people clicked through the Old Trafford turnstiles for the match against third division Plymouth Argyle, all of whom were uncertain as to whether or not to expect to see George in the United line-up. Beneath the main stand, as the minutes to kick-off ticked away, the story becomes rather clouded and to this day is shrouded in mystery due to the number of different versions floating about. George may, or may not have originally been included in the United staring eleven, but what is certain is that he did not play any part in the cup-tie.

One reporter told his readers that Tommy Docherty's opinion before the game was 'that the best side he could choose for the occasion did not include George Best.' In *The Telegraph*, Bob Greaves was to write: 'Two hours before kick-off, Tommy Docherty dropped George Best from United's side. He gave as the reason Best's "loss of form", but to the slightly cynical his curiously late decision seemed not a million miles remote from the little Irishman's unannounced absence from training two days earlier.' Greaves also thought that if the United manager had included George, then the player would have had something to prove and might well have 'had a field day against an Argyle side who rarely looked like living up to their reputation as giant-killers.'

Docherty added, 'If he had been in for training on Thursday he would still not have been playing. I have dropped Sammy McIlroy too, but nobody has asked about him.'

As it was, a headed goal by Lou Macari in the 65th minute was enough to see United overcome a brave Plymouth side.

One week after his pre-Plymouth disappearance, George went AWOL once again. Tommy Docherty was left angry and bewildered by this latest episode in the long running saga, which was beginning to annoy supporters and fellow teammates alike. 'All I can say at the moment is that George Best did not report for training along with the rest of the players today,' said the exasperated United manager. 'One of Best's friends phoned me this morning and said, "George has told me to tell you he won't be coming in today and he is sorry". There was no other explanation. Obviously this is now a serious matter because he has done the same thing twice in the space of a week. His absence from training last Thursday and today will be discussed by the board at their next meeting, which has not yet been arranged. There is nothing else I can say at the moment.'

With no chance of making the United starting line-up to face West Ham United at Upton Park on Saturday 12 January George once again announced that he was quitting football, saving Manchester United the embarrassment of taking disciplinary action. Speaking on television he said, 'I came back because I was missing the game. I thought if I didn't give it another try I might regret it in the future. I got fit enough but that spark, that extra yard of pace, was not there. I felt I was still playing well, but I was not satisfied with myself.'

When asked if there would be yet another United come back he replied, 'I don't think anybody would stand for it again' and as regards as to why he didn't just approach the club and express his feelings with a face to face meeting, his answer was: 'This has always been my big failing. I've tended to run away from things instead of going to the club and telling them what I was doing. I don't know why it should be, because Sir Matt Busby is the easiest person in the world to go and talk to.'

In the *Manchester Evening News* David Meek wrote that Slack Alice (George's Manchester night club) had finally got her man. 'The most talented footballer of this decade clearly now prefers to be a nightclub owner. Once again his night life and job as a professional footballer were on a collision course ... and this time I would say the crash is final.'

In the same newspaper, Paul Hince had an exclusive interview with George. When asked if he had now quit soccer for good and why? The reply was:

Yes, I have decided to retire. It is possible that I may play in one or two exhibition matches abroad from time to time, but I will never play in a League match in this country again.

"The reason is simple. I know now that I have lost for ever that certain 'spark' that set me apart from other players and I also know that I can never get it back. I said when I returned to Manchester United that if I could not recapture my previous form I would call it a day – I am just sticking by that promise.

I began having doubts around Christmas. I had a couple of indifferent games against Liverpool and Queens Park Rangers and when I was dropped for the FA Cup tie against

Plymouth Argyle it brought home to me the fact that I was not the player I once was. I had a long think about my future and decided the following week to quit for good.

It is a blow to your pride when you cannot hold down a place in a struggling team like United – and I don't mean that sarcastically.

Had United's poor League form any bearing on the decision, asked Hince. 'Perhaps it has helped to make the decision easier' came the honest reply. 'But this is not the main reason. I cannot face being just an average first division player.'

So George walked away from a sinking ship, unwilling to add a hand to bailing out, in an effort to see the once proud Manchester United remain in the first division. To say that they went down fighting will bring a nod of the head to those who were there in those distant dismal days and who knows, if the 1973/74 season had been a couple of games longer then United might not have sunk into the depths of the second division. But they had struggled for the past couple of years, a poor team, allowed to disintegrate into mediocracy and relegation was, in all honesty, a blessing in disguise.

George, had he lingered on and knuckled down for the final few months of the season, could well have enjoyed further exalted status at Old Trafford, becoming a saviour and being remembered as the man who kept United in the first division. Instead, he decided that he had had enough. The final curtain had come down. There would be no cries for an encore.

George's life after Manchester United could arguably fill as many pages again, from something relating to regular employment to one-off friendlies, testimonials, or money making appearances across the world.

Following his departure from Old Trafford, his first stop on the magical mystery tour took him to South Africa and the Johannesburg based Jewish Guild. It was far removed from those European Cup nights of old, glittering occasions under the Old Trafford lights or in famous venues across the channel and sadly, even amid opposition of a lesser standard, an unfit George struggled, four games in eight days certainly not helping matters and it was only his bank balance that benefitted.

He was released from his Manchester United contract in November 1975 but, by then, he had played three games for non-league Dunstable Town and countless friendlies and testimonials.

45

Stockport County vs Stoke City: 10 November 1975 and Stockport County vs Swansea City

28 November 1975

It is only a matter of approximately seven miles between Stockport County's Edgeley Park and Manchester United's Old Trafford, but the comparison between the two clubs could easily be a million miles. But strangely United actually contemplated using Stockport's rather Spartan surroundings for home fixtures while Old Trafford was still in a state of disrepair following German air raids during the Second World War. Some thirty-five years later some United supporters would undoubtedly have been among the 8,081 who, with nothing better to do on a Friday night, made their way into unfamiliar territory to see George make his debut in the fourth division.

It was certainly a big drop, no, a huge drop, for someone who had the world at his feet, taking on and beating the best players in the world, on the biggest stages, to playing for a team who were struggling in the lower regions of the football league. Stockport County had nothing to lose. His presence, as long as he turned up, would attract a few more supporters through their rusty turnstiles and on only a short term contract to play home fixtures only, it might earn them a few pounds, as well as a few points. Both urgently required due to their present plight.

His first appearance for Stockport, in his month-long deal, was nothing more than a fundraising game and his presence attracted some 5,000 more than normal. It also presented George with a platform on which to perform, in the hope that he could persuade a club of greater standing to give him a contract. Strangely, county's opponents on the night, Stoke City, were one of the clubs reportedly interested in signing him on a permanent basis.

As a free agent he could negotiate his own terms, with an impressive performance certainly altering the figures on any cheque that would be coming his way. He was however, far from match fit and would certainly struggle at a higher level, so any return from whence he had fallen was a long way off.

George's performance against Stoke was one of non-involvement, something of a bit part player, despite scoring direct from a free-kick. He never exerted himself but every now and again pinged a cross-field pass towards a teammate, attempted to shuffle pass a defender. On one occasion there was even a shot on goal from around 30 yards out and on another, he rattled the crossbar with a left-footed drive.

Moores gave Stoke City the lead fourteen minutes into the second half, but as so often happened in the past, George took only minutes to strike back to earn his new team a perhaps unexpected draw.

After the match George said that he was 'delighted' with his performance but stressed that he was still looking to regain his fitness before thinking further ahead. 'I would be telling lies if I said I was not interested in joining Stoke and if I do join an English club I would prefer it to be Stoke.'

George's return to League football came against Swansea City and once again he paced himself at a level that was as comfortable as it was alien to the once prince of English football. The Stockport footballing public were not used to such high-profile figures strutting their stuff, or at least attempting to, in their own backyard.

But once you have the skills and the know-how, you do not lose them. Like an unused door, the hinges might become a little rusty, but with a little oil and encouragement, it will soon get back to a workable standard. The lack of football had certainly left George rusty, but he slowly blended into the game, creating Stockport's first two goals before scoring their third in the 3-2 win.

With twenty minutes gone three consecutive corners on the left were swung into the Swansea goalmouth by George but only the third one was of any consequence, being turned past his own goalkeeper by Potter. Ten minutes into the second half George burst down the left, astonishingly beat three men before centring towards Bradley to score with ease. Seventeen minutes later George scored with a left footed volley.

Happy days were here again, if only for four games.

Stockport County: Hopkinson, Turner, Buckley, Lawther, Barsdley, Fogarty, Best, Seddon, Hollis, Massey, McNeil.

Scorers: Potter (Own Goal), Bradley, Best.

Swansea City: Potter, W. Evans, Davies, Smith, P. Evans, Harris, Lally, Curtis, James, Gray, Leach.

46

Manchester United 1968 vs Manchester United 1975

26 November 1975

It had been almost two years since George's final appearance at Old Trafford, walking off the pitch that he had graced on countless occasions, unbeknown to both himself and the supporters who lingered on after the final whistle that this was it. The end. There was no wave of the hand, no last look around the terraces and stands, taking in a kingdom that was once his and could well have been for countless years. No one realised that the Belfast Boy had reached the end of his Manchester United career, one that despite the honours and the accolades, was unfulfilled. The tears would come later.

But the opportunity to say goodbye was to materialise when European Cup winning teammate Pat Crerand was awarded a testimonial for his service to the club, a teammate with whom he lodged at one point in the hope that the Glaswegian and his family could perhaps bring some sanity into a lifestyle that was slowly beginning to spiral out of control.

For some, testimonials mean the opportunity to bring some glamour from the continent or a team like Crerand's old club from the east end of Glasgow. Their support was numerous and certainly coffers boosting but Pat made it something of a reunion, an old boys get together, one final hurrah before the legs could not do what the mind wanted them to and before the boots were thrown into the back of the cupboard to gather dust, as he brought together the European Cup winning side of 1968 to face the current United side.

Although the current eleven could boast the likes of Martin Buchan, Steve Coppell, Lou Macari and Gordon Hill, those names were pale in comparison to Alex Stepney, Nobby Stiles, Bobby Charlton, Denis Law, George and of course Pat himself, all of whom could conjure up a collection of silverware that the present team would never get within arm's length of.

Many who would normally have given such an occasion a wide berth, made their way to Old Trafford, not in the hope of rekindling memories as the waist lines were as broad as the years that had passed since that glorious night in north London back in May 1968. Others, too young those seven years previously, but who had been weaned on the tales and exploits of George and his compatriots simply wanted the opportunity to be able to say that they had seen three European Footballers of the Year play together.

George had been keeping himself fit by strutting his stuff here, there and everywhere, but for Denis Law, who walked away from the game when he realised that those ninety minutes out on the pitch were no longer for him, he had put in some serious training to enable him to take part and not embarrass himself or his former teammates. But there was only ever going to be one winner, beside Pat that is, as despite the experience and the medals of the elder statesmen, the current United side were fully fit professionals, playing on a regular basis with a strict diet and training regime and were also determined to be able to say that they once played against such talented individuals and beat them.

The first goal of the night came after only two minutes and it was to leave the beneficiary red faced, as Pat committed the cardinal sin for defenders in passing across the face of his own goal, with his one-time accurate passing letting him down on this night of all nights, the ball rolling straight to the feet of Gordon Hill who beat Alex Stepney with ease. Perhaps Pat forgot his teammates were playing in blue as they did back in 1968.

His embarrassment however, was put at ease ten minutes later when a clearance from Stepney found Charlton, who in turn picked out George with a vintage 30-yard defence splitting pass. The bearded winger then worked his way into the penalty area towards Paddy Roche. To the delight of the crowd George feinted one way and, as the goalkeeper went the same way, he leisurely went the other before slotting the ball home.

The third goal was also one made in Belfast but it was scored by David McCreery who, in the tightest of spaces, latched on to a Stewart Houston cross on the half turn, giving Stepney no chance, as the ball went in off the crossbar.

With five changes at half-time, the 'United 1975' side were completely refreshed and wasted no time in putting the result beyond any doubt. Six minutes into the second half, Coppell beat Stepney for his sides third, the ball going into the net just below the crossbar. McCreery got his name on the score sheet again with a close range effort following a corner making it 4-1. Then in the 64th minute, Nobby Stiles put through his own goal while under pressure from McCreery and Paterson.

Six minutes later Nobby managed to redeem himself, setting up Denis Law for the men of yesteryear's second. But the Man of the Match, David McCreery, completed his hat-trick in the 77th minute before scoring his fourth, and the final goal of the night, with three minutes remaining to make the final score 7-2.

For George it was nice to be return to those familiar surroundings of old for what was to be a final ninety minutes, playing himself back to fitness as he looked to resume a career of sorts at either home or abroad. In the dressing room after the game, as he pushed his boots into his bag, saying to journalist Hugh McIlvanny: 'I wonder where the hell these'll come out next. They've been all over England in the last month,' he was given details of a match in Calcutta. 'Coming back was a lot more appealing when Manchester United gave me a free transfer,' he continued. 'While I was still on their books there was always a terrible rigmarole of clearing it with them if I wanted to play anywhere. Now that's out of the way and obviously if I put myself in shape there's real money about but I'm really attracted at the thought of playing well again. I've come to miss it more because I know in my heart I could still be at the top.'

Manchester United 1968: Stepney, Brennan, Dunne, Crerand, Sadler, Stiles, Best, Kidd, Charlton, Law, Burns. Substitute: Herd.

Scorers: Best, Law.

Manchester United 1975: Roche, Forsyth, Houston, Daly, Nicholl, Buchan, Coppell, McCreery, Lowey, Macari, Hill. Substitute: Mountford for Roche, Albiston for Forsyth, Storey for Daly, Jackson for Lowey, Grimshaw for Macari.

Scorers: McCreery (4), Hill, Stiles (Own Goal), Coppell.

Attendance: 36,546.

It was now a case of 'have boots will travel' and as December 1975 merged into January 1976 George could be found in Ireland, but on the opposite side of the border from his native Belfast.

Despite their flirtation with the League of Ireland league title in season 1973/74, Cork Celtic were arguably one of the 'also ran's' in the Republic of Ireland football attracting small crowds and little media attention. That was until the latter weeks of 1975 when their powers that be decided that they needed to generate some instant income in order to keep their heads above water and asked their captain Bobby Tambling, the former free-scoring Chelsea forward if he knew of anyone who might fit the bill.

Tambling began asking around and word got back to him that George could possibly be available, but only if the price was right. A dilemma for the Cork directors who were wanting to make money, not spend it, but who in the end decided to take the gamble and offer the now nomadic former European Footballer of the Year £1000, if he would grace their Turners Cross venue with his presence.

Having bills to pay in an effort to get his life back on track, as well as the possibility of attracting the attentions of a more distinguished club through putting in some playing time no matter where, George eagerly accepted the offer on the table. Anticipating, and certainly hoping for, a much larger crowd than normal the Cork officials decided to move their forthcoming 28 December fixture against Drogheda United to the much larger and more quaintly named Flower Lodge ground and they were to be proved correct with their decision as an estimated 12,500 were present, bringing in around £6,000 in gate receipts.

Although heralded with a fanfare of trumpets, there was no echoing encores of celebration long into the night as Cork were ultimately beaten 2-0. George's teammates looking somewhat overawed by being in the presence of a genius, even if it was one who had fallen from his pedestal, while the Drogheda player took his appearance on the pitch alongside them as something of a challenge.

'It is difficult playing with a club for the first time. The game was scrappy and disappointing, but has made me feel like wanting to return and play again' a clearly unfit George was to say after the game. Although something of a success, the Cork secretary commented: 'We don't really know how much money we made. It was certainly profitable, and while it is nice to take that sort of money from one game, which will help to keep us going this season, it's annoying to think that had we won we would have been in third place in the league instead of just sixth. We don't know if he is coming back until he phones us during the week.'

Sitting by the telephone like a teenager awaiting a call from the person they had met the previous night the Cork officials were overjoyed to hear from George again and despite missing the 3-0 away victory at Finn Harps, due not being contracted to play away games for the club, he returned to face Bohemians at Turners Cross. On this occasion, there were fleeting glimpses of the player of old as the champions were beaten 1-0, but his appearance, as was that in his next ninety minutes for the Cork side against Shelbourne, little more than a cameo.

Although not contracted to play in away fixtures for Cork, such was his drawing mechanism that Shelbourne offered their visitors a share of the gate money if they could get George to play. Agreeing to appear, some 5,000 came along to witness the one-time Manchester United star in action, but they were to see little of the player of old in Cork's 2-1 defeat. *Irish Times* reporter Derek Jones wrote: 'As far as I am concerned I never want to set eyes on him again. I would prefer just to remember him as he was during his Manchester United days.' Adding that it was 'easy money for a player who showed he simply did not want to be involved'.

This was to be George's last performance for Cork Celtic as the night before the match with Waterford he phoned to say he had flu. Strangely Waterford had just signed a certain Bobby Charlton but he had also withdrawn from the Cork encounter, stressing 'business commitments' as the reason. In his three games for Cork, George was to make more money than the club did during the course of the whole season!

From Ireland, the next stop was the United States of America and the Los Angeles Aztecs in the NASL Pacific Conference Southern Division, where he was to play two dozen games between April and August 1976. Stateside, it was a different ball game, with more than George playing out the twilight years of their careers, earning good money amid the sunshine of America's west coast. Neither was there the pressure-cooker expectation as many were totally unfamiliar with the Best brand and legend.

Playing at outside-left, George regained some of his missing fitness and ended the season on something of a high, missing only one game, scoring fifteen goals and making seven 'assists'.

47

George at Fulham

1976–1977

It was in mid-August 1976 that twenty-nine-year-old George signed for second division Fulham, a fitting destination if ever there was one as this particular area was now as familiar to him as many in his adopted Manchester. It was quite a coup for the Craven Cottage side to capture George's signature, but their location was certainly a huge plus point in his agreeing to pull on their white shirt, while having also added former Manchester City player, Rodney Marsh to their pay role also helped sell the club to him, as did the presence of former England captain Bobby Moore.

At first it was thought that it might take three weeks before George could officially play for Fulham after the move had been first muted, agreeing to a 'pay-as-you-play' deal, but, surprisingly, within days he was lining up for his debut against Bristol Rovers at Craven Cottage, kick-starting a period of his career that is difficult to ignore.

Many missed the crowning moment of this fixture, the only goal of the ninety minutes, due to a larger attendance than normal on the banks of the Thames, some 21,127 compared to the 9,741 average of the previous campaign, keen to witness that initial appearance of not only George but also Rodney Marsh. The latter however, was totally overshadowed as George crowned his appearance with a goal in the opening minute.

On the eve of George's arrival at Craven Cottage, Fulham had drawn 1-1 at Peterborough United in a League Cup Second Round tie and despite having played only three days previously, he was included in the Fulham side for the replay.

What must be remembered that this was not the George of old. He was now a little broader around the waist and a little slower getting up and down the pitch, but he was still capable of producing those memorable moments and against Peterborough he didn't disappoint, scoring a goal still considered as the best ever seen at the London Road ground.

It was a strike best described by Peterborough's record appearance holder Tommy Robson who was to recall, 'I was closing George down and expecting him to pass the ball on as he was about 40 yards from goal. But instead he flicked the ball up with one foot and volleyed into the top corner of the net with the other. The ball whistled past my shoulder and flew past Eric Steele in goal. It was an astonishing goal and not many other players in the world would have even tried it never mind pulled it off.'

From a different viewpoint Jeremy Alexander of *The Guardian* wrote:

Another goal by George Best, unmistakable by its hallmark of impish quality virtuosity, last night helped Fulham through their second round replay in the League Cup at London Road. After forty minutes Best put them out of their uncertainty. Marsh rolled an innocuous pass to him 30 yards out and just to the right of goal. Oakes was sharing the guard with Robson at the time. Best scooped the ball up with his right foot and swerved a volley with the same foot and tantalising perfecting passed Steele's despairing dive.

It was a start that even George could never have imagined. 'I didn't quite know what sort of reaction to my return to expect but everyone, not just at Fulham has been very encouraging' he was to say. 'Scoring in the first two minutes of my debut was no handicap but for Fulham to win those first two matches was the essential thing.

So keen were Fulham to have George within their ranks, they bent their rules to accommodate him. There was no morning training sessions with the rest of the squad, as late nights amid London's bright lights and early rises did not mix, instead he was allowed to train in the afternoon but, while doing so, he certainly put in a shift, possibly going through his paces more enthusiastically than those who had been in a few hours previously.

George was to give the Fulham support and also those at away grounds, immense pleasure, but of all the stand out memories from his spell with the Craven Cottage club there is perhaps one that always springs to mind, coming against Hereford United at home on 25 September 1976.

Having taken a 4-1 lead, and the game moving into its latter stages, George gathered the ball on the half-way line and as he backtracked a couple of yards into his own half, he was surprisingly tackled by Rodney Marsh, not once, but twice, but like numerous defenders over the years, the former City player had little luck in dispossessing his teammate.

While the attempted tackles of Rodney Marsh were friendly, half-hearted affairs, there were others within those second division ranks who, unable to match George for skill despite his best years being behind him, were happy to try and kick lumps out of his legs as he floated past them down the wing. Some of this close attention was tolerated to a certain extent but at Southampton, with things not going his way, he was sent off in front of the *Match of the Day* cameras. Coupled to this, his overall performance had been far from impressive, a Dutch journalist, taking in the game to run the rule over George prior to a Northern Ireland – Holland international considered him to be 'a fallen superstar', no longer able to perform at a high level.

Unaware of the journalist's comments, George was asked for his opinion of the Dutch captain Johan Cruyff and if he considered him to be a better player than he was now, to which he replied, 'You're kidding aren't you? I tell you what I'll do tonight ... I'll nutmeg Cruyff first chance I get.'

Within five minutes of the kick-off, George latched onto the ball wide on the left and instead of his natural instinct taking him in the direction of the Dutch goal, he turned inside, dribbled past three opponents as he made his way towards the unsuspecting Cruyff. Dipping his shoulder a couple of times in that old familiar fashion, he proceeded to push the ball between the Dutchman's legs, running round the bemused player before collection it and running off with his fist raised in the air, as a signal to those in the know in the press box.

George returned to the States and Los Angeles Aztecs for the summer of 1977, returning to London and Fulham in September of that year but played only ten League games, a brief stay, but not without its problems.

Barely had he arrived back in London than he was on a flight bound for Los Angeles without the knowledge of anyone at Craven Cottage, simply telling manager Bobby Campbell that he wanted the morning off to do some business. Then, following an appearance in the 2-0 defeat against Stoke City at the Victoria Ground, Fulham's sixth game without a victory and withdrawal from Northern Ireland's World Cup tie against Belgium, he was not seen at the

London club's training ground for two weeks and was subsequently suspended for a breach of club discipline.

His spell at Craven Cottage was at an end.

America was then George's home until November 1979, playing in the NASL American Conference Western Division for Los Angeles Aztecs between April and June 1978, before moving to Eastern Division side Fort Lauderdale Strikers for the remainder of that season, remaining there for the following summer season.

48

George at Hibernian

1979–1980

Hibs were at the bottom of the Scottish Premier League when they agreed to pay Fulham £60,000 and George somewhere between £1,500 and £2,000 a game, on a pay-as-you-play basis. Good money when you consider that the Easter Road's side top earners were on something like £120. It was a move that saw him echo: 'I shall do my best for Hibs because they are giving me an opportunity, but if I get an approach from England I shall have to consider it.'

As always George was a top draw, with 13,670 turning up for his debut against St Mirren at Love Street, crowning his debut north of the border with a goal late in the game. With little more than sixty seconds remaining, Callaghan pushed a free-kick across the edge of the St Mirren penalty area towards George who almost casually left footed the ball past Thomson before the St Mirren 'keeper had time to react.

An equaliser almost followed in stoppage time when George worked his way past three men on the edge of the St Mirren box before firing the ball goal wards, disappointedly watching as it flashed narrowly wide of Thomson's right-hand post. The standing ovation was well deserved.

Seven days later there were over 20,000 at Easter Road for his home debut against Partick Thistle but arguably his best game in the green and white of the Edinburgh side was his third outing against Rangers at an ice-bound Easter Road on 22 December 1979. On a pitch more akin to an ice rink, it was far from ideal conditions for George at his prime to perform on, never mind the overweight, partially fit 1979 version, but he was the player who stole the show.

The Edinburgh vs Glasgow rivalry was always in evidence during the often ill-tempered confrontation which saw the visitors take the lead in the 37th minute, with their defence keeping a watchful eye on the bearded Hibernian outside-left. In an effort to attempt to put George off his game cans of lager were tossed onto the pitch when he came across to take a corner, but he simply played to the crowd and raised one towards his lips, pretending to drink from it.

Determined to silence the taunts and gain some revenge for the overly physical tackles of the Rangers defenders, he did it in the best way possible, sending a cross-field 40 yard defence splitting pass through towards Ally McLeod, with his cross into the Rangers goalmouth met by the head of Tony Higgins to level the score.

Not content with that he also had a hand in Hibernians winning goal when he took a quick throw-in to Higgins, who crossed for Campbell to head past Young. Despite not scoring himself, he did test Young in the Rangers goal on three occasions.

It was not all good times and glitter at Easter Road, as George, not for the first time in his career was sacked and put up for sale by the Edinburgh side after preferring a Saturday with Scottish rugby fans than resting in preparation for a game against Ayr United in mid-February 1980. But, like in the past, he returned. Although he was unable to help steer

Hibs clear of relegation despite yet another vintage display in a 2-0 defeat of Dundee, scoring a vintage solo goal.

Returning to America and San Jose Earthquakes for the summer of 1980, he was surprisingly to return to Hibs in September of that year, playing four times in Scottish first division and twice in the Bell's League Cup before drifting back Stateside to play in the NASL Indoor League for San Jose Earthquakes.

From March 1981 until August of that same year George turned out for San Jose Earthquakes in the NASL Western Division playing thirty games, scoring thirteen goals, one of which would be up there as one of his best.

Playing against Fort Lauderdale Strikers on 22 July he collected the ball midway into the Lauderdale half and moving forward, he slipped past one man twice as he reached the edge of the penalty area. Faced by another three defenders, he feinted right, moved to the left, before momentarily stopping. Suddenly he went right again, then flicked the ball onto his left foot as he found space between two defenders, proceeding to hammer the ball left-footed past a helpless goalkeeper. It was a goal to savour despite the opposition being far removed from world class. It was a pity it was not at Old Trafford instead of on foreign soil.

His Stateside sojourn ended with San Jose Earthquakes, playing four games for them in the NASL Indoor League during December 1981 and January 1982, having also played four games in October 1981 during their British tour, which took in Hibernian, Linfield, Motherwell and Brentford. The final competitive fixture being for Tobermore United against Ballymena United, a Bass Irish Cup, first round tie, on 9 February 1984.

Between January 1981 and September 1995 he could be found attempting to turn back the years at countless venues around the world. From Tokyo to Torquay, Munich to Newhaven, Bognor to Ballymoney, Dingwall to Devonport and Workington to Welling, making it a case of 'have boots will travel' or perhaps more to the point, most of the time if he was not doing anything and the money was good, then it would be considered.

On 11 August 1991 he made a poignant return to his spiritual home of Old Trafford, albeit for nothing more than a fleeting appearance in a pre-match entertainment veterans United vs City five-a-side kick-about prior to the Sir Matt Busby testimonial match although, a few years previously he had set his eyes on a much longer stroll on the Old Trafford turf.

49

George Best XI vs International XI

8 August 1988

When the idea of a testimonial match was muted, George fancied the idea of holding it at Old Trafford. Despite his somewhat tempestuous relationship with the club in the latter days of his time there it still held special memories and he knew that the many supporters would turn out, forgiving him for his previous misdemeanours. The United board however, were totally against the idea and from day one it was a no-go, in Manchester at least. Even in his native Ireland it looked as though it would never get further than the planning table, with the Irish Football Association turning down request for a testimonial match three times.

The testimonial idea continued to develop and it was finally arranged for Windsor Park Belfast, the second best venue if such a fixture was to take place. 'A year ago I thought my chances of getting a game had gone when the IFA originally refused to sanction it' George was to say prior to the proposed game. 'However, it has all turned out even greater than I expected. I appreciate the support from my native province. I am hoping to play for ninety minutes. I will pace myself, however, and let some of the youngsters so the hard work. It will be a change to play in my own testimonial for I have helped out dozens of fellow professionals.'

But George, now aged forty-one, was also to speak about his life and earlier career, possibly with a little regret having gone from the pinnacle of his profession, through divorce and bankruptcy courts and jousts with alcoholism, saying:

I have thrown away a fortune living life in the fast lane on too much booze and too many easy touches and lots of lovely ladies. But I will hold my head up as the proudest guy in football when I step out for my testimonial in Belfast. Because the fans know I gave them eleven years of sweat and blood as a one club man with the greatest outfit in the game – Manchester United. United were the only ones for me, even though I blew the lot, the sort of money that if it had been invested would have left me comfortably off. Even in those days twenty years ago I was earning fantastic bonus money based on results and pulling the fans in. League titles, the European Cup and crowds regularly over the 50,000 mark meant I was earning £800 to £900 a week.

This testimonial tonight is a bit like being a pension for me and I've been working my butt off to get in the best shape possible for it – I won't let anyone down. I don't deny I still hit bad phases in my life and there are times when depression means I couldn't care less about myself. But my old pride suddenly surfaces again and I bounce back. Right now I feel absolutely terrific.

On a wet Belfast evening around 25,000 supporters turned out to pay homage to a footballing legend, an attendance almost six times that which had watched Northern Ireland's last World Cup game and the city's largest for a football match for twenty years, earning George around

£100,000. Having shed around 24lb in order to give what he was quoted as saying was his 'farewell game' his best shot, he looked in good shape.

Wearing the Number Eleven shirt he took to the field alongside his son Calum surrounded by a posse of photographers and when the action started, his teammates sought to involve him in the action as much as possible. It wasn't however, going to be a vintage display as an early pass, which at one time would have been brought under control with ease was allowed to bounce out of play.

The conditions were far from ideal and prevented the game from being anything like a spectacle although at times, the international XI seemed to adapt better, taking a 2-0 lead with goals from Roy Aitken and Trevor Francis. As the rain continued to pour down the goals continued to flow and by half-time, the score was 4-4, but there were still more to come in the second half.

Everyone wanted George to score, as did the man himself, and as luck would have it the moment soon arrived. George took a pass about 25 yards out, flicked the ball up then took a step forward before sending the ball over the head of McKnight for the goal that everyone wanted to see. George was now warming to the occasion and attempted to beat McKinght once again from a similar position. He did eventually add a second from the penalty spot after being brought down as he closed in on goal, rounding off the scoring for the night: 7-6 to the Best XI.

Best XI: Jennings, Houghton, Breitner, Krol, Watson, Hughes, Henderson, Brady, McAvennie, O'Neill, Best. Substitutes: Dunlop for Jennings, McMurdo for Breitner, McCoy for Henderson.

Scorers: Brady (2), Best (2), McAvennie, Breitner, McCoy.

International XI: McKnight, Coyle, Aitken, Neeskins, McDonald, Ardiles, Francis, O'Boyle, Rep, Clark, McCreery.

Scorers: Aitken, Francis, O'Boyle, Clarke, McMurdo, Ardiles.

Although having said that his testimonial was his final match he did play in numerous other games and was indeed scheduled to appear at Old Trafford on 21 August in a testimonial match for Kevin Moran against Manchester City.

Many in the 25,432 crowd had clicked through the turnstiles simply to see George in action but they were to be disappointed, as he was sitting in a London pub when he should have been in the Old Trafford dressing room.

Apparently he had taken offence to a newspaper article in which United manager Alex Ferguson had said that George would only feature for twenty minutes of the match, as he wanted to use the fixture as part of his pre-season build up and therefore wanted to field his strongest side at some point.

Moran slammed the 'no show' and supporters were also quick to express their disappointment with George's failure to turn up. George continued to participate in testimonials, friendlies and exhibition games up until 1995, but off the field his life was on a downward spiral. Alcohol was an opponent he could not beat.

Alcoholics Anonymous failed, as George said that he 'couldn't do anything anonymous', while Antabuse pellets stitched into his stomach did likewise. In 2002 he was given a liver transplant, amid much controversy, promising to repay the doctors' faith in him, but once again fell by the wayside.

He continued to find his way into the newspapers as the weeks, months and years passed by then on 1 October 2005 he was admitted to the Cromwell Hospital in west London with flu-like infections, only for his condition to deteriorate rapidly as result of a kidney infection at the beginning of the following month. With doctors concerned about his condition, he was moved into intensive care but before being moved he asked for the *News of the World* to come and photograph him as a warning to others on the danger of drink.

On Sunday 20 November George's doctor, Professor Roger Williams announced that the medical team were 'very worried' and that 'the next twenty-four hours would be critical as to whether he is going to survive this infection and all the consequences of it on his body.' In the days that followed, news on George's wellbeing became a priority, as eagerly sought after as any Manchester United result in the pre-digital are when he was in his prime.

Suddenly, the *Manchester Evening News* on the afternoon of Thursday 24 November confirmed the reality of the situation with its hard-hitting front page reading: 'Best on the Brink – Family at Bedside as Fans Told: Prepare for the Worst'. The following morning, newspapers, like the *Independent* confirmed that all was not well, their front page covered by a photograph of George and in the bottom right hand corner the words – 'The End of the Road. George Best Enters his Final Hours'.

Former teammates, Denis Law and Sir Bobby Charlton had visited him the previous day and left the hospital visibly upset and in a statement, Professor Williams said,

> I'm afraid Mr Best is coming to the end of the long road of his ill health. The situation is that, medically, the intensive care team and everybody concerned have managed to cope with pretty well all the complications except the one that's happened again during the night, which you know about, this bleeding … is now affecting the lungs and other parts. There is really no return from that situation. It's just not possible to recover from that episode he had during the night and he is now fading. He is still alive, he is still having standard medical care and treatment, but I have to tell you that his hours are numbered … I can't be precise to a time but it is the final stages of this illness and I am afraid he could die at any time over the next twenty-four hours.

At 12.55 p.m. on Friday 25 November the final whistle blew. Fifty-nine-year-old George passed away surrounded by family and friends.

'Football has lost one of its greats and I have lost a dear friend. He was a marvellous person' said Sir Bobby Charlton while another teammate, Denis Law, said, 'I have lost a great friend. He was one of the greatest players the world has ever seen.'

The newspapers were awash with tributes which took up countless pages, plus supplements. Royalty would not receive much more. In my 'Manchester United Collectors Club' special edition newsletter I wrote:

> Over the past three, four, or more probably five years, everyman and his dog was probably fed up reading the newspaper articles relating to George Best having picked up yet another blonde or spotted staggering from some watering hole or other. They had read it all before. Countless times. Suddenly however, quicker than Bestie ever went past any defender, he was in hospital, seriously ill.
>
> Any mentions within the national dailies were no longer ignored. This wasn't George Best the alcoholic, this was George Best the former Manchester United and Northern Ireland footballing legend. No news was good news, but what was thought as a possible recovery in his London hospital, soon had the fourth official on the touchline with the illuminated board showing how long was left.
>
> George, in typical United fashion, was not going to give up without a fight, but the time added on soon ran out. The final whistle blew and a nation wept. What followed was beyond what anyone, even George's most ardent admirers from way back, could have imagined. The

battle with the booze was forgotten with the death of arguably the greatest footballer to grace the British game.

Even in death, he could command more column inches than any other footballer.

Within a short period of time following the announcement of George's passing, flowers, scarves and jersey's began to appear outside Old Trafford across from the statue of Sir Matt Busby, outside the Best family home in Burren Way Belfast and at Belfast City Hall. Those at Old Trafford would escalate to a density that surpassed those laid outside the stadium following the death of Sir Matt Busby.

As the *Manchester Evening News* wrote:

Many had never seen him play, but it did not matter. Under the watchful gaze of a statue of Sir Matt Busby, the man who gave him his break, football fans came in their thousands to pay tribute to Britain's greatest footballer – George Best. Fans marched sombrely down Sir Matt Busby Way on their way to leave their personal mementos, ranging from football shirts to poems and pictures. Best may have last kicked a ball at Old Trafford decades before some were born, but that proved no obstacle for many of those who came to mourn him as one superlative-filled description followed another.

Prior to United's match against West Ham United at Upton Park on Saturday 26 November, a photograph of George appeared on the big screen as the players and supporters of both teams applauded for a minute, as did those at Parkhead and Molineux, while at Highbury you could have heard a pin drop as a minutes silence was observed prior to their match with Blackburn Rovers. At Eastlands, prior to Manchester City's match with Liverpool, the planned minutes silence didn't last long as the home support responded to shouts from the travelling support.

United vs West Bromwich Albion

30 November 2005

A more poignant tribute was to follow four days later as United had a home Carling Cup tie, by a strange quirk of fate, against West Bromwich Albion, the team George had made his first team debut against.

A poster of George was given out to each supporter as they passed through the turnstile and as the two teams emerged from the tunnel, those posters were held aloft to form a huge sea of George Best faces, while around the perimeter of the pitch, the electronic advertising hoardings proclaimed, 'George Best – Manchester United 1963–1974. 470 appearances, 179 goals, 1 genius.'

Onto the pitch strode not simply the two teams for the Carling cup fixture, but George's son Calum, members of United's 1968 European Cup winning side, United officials and members of the West Bromwich Albion side from his debut back in September 1963, including the man who marked him on that occasion – Graham Williams. Don Fardon's song 'Belfast Boy' echoed out over the tannoy as the managers of United and West Bromwich Albion, Sir Alex Ferguson and Bryan Robson, walked to the centre circle carrying wreaths.

Master of ceremonies for the evening, David Meek, who had covered United for the *Manchester Evening News* during George's career introduced Sir Bobby Charlton who said: 'On behalf of the Manchester United family here in this stadium and all the Manchester United fans around the world, I would just like to say a big thank you to George Best. You'll never be forgotten.'

The rustle of the 40,000 odd posters was the only noise to be heard as a minutes silence was observed. As for the match itself, with a place in the quarter finals of the Carling Cup at stake, there was every possibility that it would become something of a non-event, but United were determined to mark the occasion with a victory. Sir Alex Ferguson even went to the extreme of putting out something resembling a full strength side, instead of the reserve looking eleven's that the competition usually merited.

United dominated the opening period and went two goals in front within seventeen minutes. Saha had the ball in the West Bromwich net after only six minutes, turning in a Rossi cross, but the French striker saw his strike rightly ruled out for offside. Five minutes later United were in front. Kamara tripping Ronaldo just inside the area, the united forward licking himself up to score from the spot.

Having been denied his first United goal since January and not having started a game since April, Saha broke his duck within five minutes of Ronaldo's penalty. Rossi slipping the ball through and he ran unchallenged to the edge of the penalty area before shooting past Hoult. Two goals in front and in no danger of losing the tie, the match dropped down a gear and the air continued to be filled with 'George Best' chants.

Ronaldo, supplied by the clearly rejuvenated Saha, had the ball in the net but was denied the goal by a linesman's flag. Rossi hit the post following a Saha/Ronaldo move and then at the opposite end Horsfield hit the ball wide of Tim Howard's goal when in a good scoring position. Eleven minutes into the second half United's went three in front, O'Shea playing a neat one-two with Saha before beating Hoult. Ellington scored a consolation goal for the visitors in the 76th minute, but the contest was over long before that.

United were through to the quarter finals. The tributes had been paid to George. Everyone went home happy, reliving the night and the memories of the boy from Belfast.

But the tributes were not over and there were more tears still to shed.

George's funeral was held in Belfast on Saturday 5 December and it was to turn into something you would expect for royalty. The service was held in the Great Hall of the Northern Ireland Parliament building at Stormont and as the hearse made its way there from the family home in Burren Way an estimated 500,000 lined the route, many of those were clad in the red of Manchester United or the green of Northern Ireland. Some had chosen their vantage point the previous night. But only 30,000 were allowed through the gates of Stormont, while the funeral service itself was limited to 300 family, friends and dignitaries.

Once the hearse had completed its journey, the coffin was carried up the steps of the building by Denis Law, Billy Bingham, Harry Gregg, Pat Jennings, Gerry Armstrong and Derek Dougan before being passed on to family members who carried it into the Great Hall.

After the service, the hearse took George on his final journey to Roselawn Cemetery, where he was laid to rest alongside his mother.

Thanks for the memories, George.